AMERICA'S STATE QUARTERS

THE DEFINITIVE GUIDEBOOK TO
COLLECTING STATE QUARTERS

DAVID L. GANZ

RANDOM HOUSE REFERENCE

NEW YORK   TORONTO   LONDON   SYDNEY   AUCKLAND

This is a revised and updated edition of a work that was originally published as *The Official Guidebook to America's State Quarters,* published by House of Collectibles, an imprint of the Random House Information Group, a division of Random House, Inc., New York, in 2000.

This book is available at special discounts for bulk purchases for sales promotions or premiums. Special editions, including personalized covers, excerpts of existing books, and corporate imprints, can be created in large quantities for special needs. For more information, write to Special Markets/Premium Sales, 1745 Broadway, MD 6–2, New York, NY 10019 or e-mail *specialmarkets@randomhouse.com.*

Please address inquiries about electronic licensing of any products for use on a network, in software, or on CD-ROM to the Subsidiary Rights Department, Random House Information Group, fax 212–572–6003.

Visit the House of Collectibles Web site: *www.houseofcollectibles.com*

Library of Congress Cataloging-in-Publication Data

Ganz, David L. (1951–)
The official guidebook to America's state quarters / by David L. Ganz.
Includes index.
1. Quarter-dollar—Collectors and collecting—Handbooks, manuals, etc.   2. Coins, American—Collectors and collecting—Handbooks, manuals, etc.   3. Commemorative coins—United States—Collectors and collecting—Handbooks, manuals, etc.
4. Emblems, State— United States—Miscellanea.   I. Title.
CJ1840.S73 G36 2000
737.4973'075—dc21
00–061318

Printed in the United States of America

ISBN: 978-0-375-72259-2

10   9   8   7   6   5   4   3   2   1

Second Edition

To Michael Castle, John Lopez, and Philip N. Diehl, without whom there never would have been an America's State Quarters program; to the members of the Citizens Commemorative Coin Advisory Committee, who became true believers before it became reality; and for my wife, Kathy, who was present at the creation.

And to 500 remarkable men and women who volunteered their time to serve on various state advisory committees that assisted in picking and choosing state quarter designs.

The idea of a circulating commemorative has been around the hobby for decades, but frankly, good ideas are a dime a dozen. Far more rare is the ability to move an idea to reality, especially in the rough and tumble environment of Washington, D.C. From my vantage point, the lion's share of the credit for making the 50 States program a reality goes to David Ganz, for his persistence as an advocate, and Congressman Michael Castle for championing the proposal through Congress. David gradually persuaded me of the merits of the proposal, and we at the Mint, in turn, convinced Treasury and the Hill that it was doable. There are other claimants, to be sure, but the hobby owes a debt of gratitude to Congressman Castle and Mr. Ganz.

—Philip N. Diehl, Former Director of the United States Mint,
Washington, D.C., (December 11, 1998)

Reprinted by permission of Numismatic News
(Krause Publications, Iola, Wisconsin; David Harper, Editor)

Mint medal struck by the U.S. Mint for
Philip N. Diehl, director, United States Mint.

CONTENTS

ACKNOWLEDGMENTS

No book is written without a context. This one began 15 years ago when, as president of the American Numismatic Association, I was called by Philip N. Diehl, then director of the U.S. Mint, and invited to become a member of the Citizens Commemorative Coin Advisory Committee (CCCAC) under an appointment by Treasury Secretary Lloyd Bentsen. As Diehl wrote some years later, in December 1998, the start of the statehood quarters program came from that committee. I will always be grateful that Diehl gave me the opportunity to make the case for circulating commemorative coinage, and that he permitted himself to be persuaded that it was in the best interest of the Mint, and the nation, to proceed.

The next person who should be thanked, profusely, is my agent, Scott Travers, an accomplished author in his own right, a well-known numismatic personality, and a highly respected professional numismatist (rare coin dealer). He made the introduction to Dotty Harris of Random House, which brought out the original edition, and it was his persuasiveness that caused a revised edition, and finally this second edition as the series nears completion. He reminded me of deadlines and encouraged me to meet them.

In the earlier edition, I acknowledged the assistance of many who lent time, talent, energy, and data. Their assistance forms the basis of this book, without which it would not have been possible: the Professional Coin Grading Service, Fred Weinberg, Alan Herbert, Ed Reiter, Sue Kohler, Charles Atherton, Andrew Fishburn, John Mitchell, Arnetta Cain, Ken Rubin, Jean Gentry, Andrew Cosgarea, David Pickens, Steven Grossman, Bob Leuver, Steve Markoff, David Sundman, the staff of David's Cookies (formerly at 79th Street and 3rd Ave., New York City), Josie Harrington, Julie Abrams, Mark Salzberg, Numismatic Guaranty Corp., Dennis Baker and NumisMedia, Randy Campbell, ANACS, Teletrade, Ian Russell, CCCAC members Charles Atherton (nonvoting member), Elvira (Lisa) Clain-Stefanelli, Reed Hawn, Daniel Hoffman, Elsie Sterling Howard, and Thomas Shockley III, John Lopez, Jim Miller, David Harper, Chet Krause, Clifford Mishler, Burnett Anderson, Barbara Gregory, Steve Babbitt, Lynn Chen, Kathy Gotsch (now Kathy Ganz, my wife), Beth Deisher, Alan Stahl, Leslie Elam, Bob Korver, Steve Markoff, Jeri Hollinger, Teri Towe, Chuck Asay, Milt Priggee, Rep. Michael Castle, Elroy Young, Jason Russell, Wayne Pearson, LaVaugn Scott, Andrew Aslinger, Edward Ficht, Richard Lakatos, Kris Liaugminas, Michael White, James Ruffin, Office of Public Affairs, United States Mint HQ, Jon Turner of the Washington Mint (for State Quarter products), Randy Campbell, ANACS, Signe Wilkinson (editorial cartoonist for the Philadelphia Daily News),and the late Diane Wolf, who died too young.

Sue Kohler of the federal Commission of Fine Arts was helpful beyond words, both in the first edition, and this major revision. She was my eyes and ears—spurred by an ongoing Freedom of Information Act request—and her clips of the Fine Arts Committee actions make their work come alive. In the earlier edition, Sue's colleague, and my friend, commission secretary Charles Atherton, was of immense help. I served with Charles for four years on the Citizens Commemorative Coin Advisory Committee (1993–96), of which Charles was a nonvoting member. Only his untimely death in a pedestrian–motor vehicle accident prevented him from helping on this edition.

Sue culled through the archives of the Fine Arts Commission and pulled out relevant minutes relating to the State Quarters program; she also permitted copies to be made of designs that did not see the light of day—which have made this book the richer.

David Sundman of Littleton Coin Co., Littleton, New Hampshire, was kind enough to provide me with his deluxe custom coin album, which I have used to hold circulation examples of the series as they have come to my attention. His office helped on illustrations in the second edition. So did Dennis Tucker of Whitman Publishing, a leading hobby purveyor.

Philip Diehl, director of the Mint, has my profound thanks. Through his sponsorship, I was appointed to the Citizens Commemorative Coin Advisory Committee and, in that capacity, determined that a circulating coin was an issue. Despite what he himself called a "Johnny One Note" approach to the subject by me, he did not stifle the discussion (and he could have), but first encouraged a formal report, and gradually turned around his own views on the subject. After my tenure was complete, he invited me, and my wife Kathy, to many of the first-strike events for the coin program (and permitted me to start one of the presses for the Delaware coin issue). We have certainly worked together on many other issues, but on this, he took an idea, made it better, adopted it as his own, acknowledged the source, and created a growth industry in and of itself.

The Numismatic Guaranty Corporation of America, now of Sarasota, Florida, and its president, Mark Salzberg—and Professional Coin Grading Service and its head, Michael Haynes—are specifically thanked for providing up-to-date population reports on encapsulated coins that enable valuable points of comparison to be made, allowing readers to draw their own conclusions as to the relative scarcity of some items. I said that several years ago, and with six-figures' worth now slabbed, the data is even more valuable.

Dennis Baker of NumisMedia (www.numismedia.com) is a good friend and a true "gem uncirculated" guy. I chided him in the first edition that his price guide, available in print and online, did not carry information about the State Quarters—despite which he did yeoman service when I asked for fair market values. He searched them out and reliably reported them so that they could be reprinted in this book. Originally, this was exclusive to the Official Guide; I hoped that it would spread to his periodical and online version so that collectors everywhere can see the tremendous march of progress of this series for upper-grade coins. It did, and while the pricing here is no longer unique, it is very, very accurate. He now uses them in NumisMedia's *Wholesale Market Dealer's Price Guide.*

Dennis provided current fair market values for coins of Philadelphia (P or plain) and Denver (D mint marks) in superior grades (MS-65 and higher). Valuations are as of May 30, 2007, and are provided exclusively to the *Official Guidebook to America's State Quarters.* Fair market value prices listed are for certified coins only (usually PCGS, NGC, or ANACS). Raw coins may bring substantially less. Prices may fluctuate considerably as new issues are brought on the market and certified. As populations increase in a particular grade, coins may be easier to obtain and prices may fall. Where an asterisk appears for a grade, NumisMedia has not seen enough trading activity to establish a price at this time. Valuations ©2008 by NumisMedia, Inc. All rights reserved. Used by permission. A comprehensive listing of Fair Market Values of American coins is found on the NumisMedia Web site (www.numismedia.com). My thanks as well to my Random House editor, Helena Santini, who made this a more commercial project and well-edited book.

I said last time that I would surely be remiss if I did not extend a personal and formal acknowledgment to my wife, Kathy, in addition to the much more informal thanks that I have given her. Not only is she a good "first" editor, reader, and compiler, but she has the knack of asking critical questions that have made this book more focused and readable—especially since she is a noncollector. Many times, she has accompanied me to the events that are discussed, and photos taken by her are included in the book. She devoted "our" time to talking shop about this book, and I want to repeat and reiterate—Kathy, I owe you a "really expensive gift." The red Chrysler Sebring convertible is on me. I also thank you for all of your support in the very early days of the proposal to issue circulating commemorative coins, when I felt like the voice in the wilderness. In more ways than one, you made a dream come true. Thanks also for being photo editor. I could not have done this without you. Your expert editing of the state drawings makes this a better book.

David Harper, editor of *Numismatic News* (Krause Publications), is another good friend whose assistance in this book was of invaluable assistance. His suggestions for columns for my long-running "Under the Glass" (which first appeared in *Numismatic News* in 1969) have been incorporated into this book several-fold. Many years ago, from 1969–73, I was the Washington correspondent for *Numismatic News Weekly* (as it was then called), and eventually became an assistant editor, living and working in Iola, about 60 miles west of Green Bay and Appleton in central Wisconsin. Chet Krause (the founder, and then the publisher) and Clifford Mishler (then the executive editor, and later president of the company) taught me a great deal about the true issues facing the coin hobby, and through the use of Clifford's raw materials on the American Revolution Bicentennial Commission's Coins & Medals Advisory Panel, I first learned of the need for circulating commemoratives—and the fight that the government would put up to prevent that singularly important action from taking place. Later, Burnett Anderson, a veteran news reporter, became Washington bureau chief for Krause Publications, and he was privy to many of the discussions about the circulating commemorative coin proposal, some of which he wrote about. His final illness and untimely death allowed me the brief respite of stepping back in time for several months to once again become KP's Washington correspondent, even as I had long-since changed careers and become mayor of my own municipality in Fair Lawn, New Jersey—later an elected county supervisor, or freeholder, and a practicing lawyer in New York City. It also afforded me the opportunity to "cover" many of the events leading up to the successful conclusion of the legislative initiative, thanks to Dave Harper's confidence. Krause Publications has been supportive in the publication of my columns and articles over the last 35 years, and in providing photos of some of the commemorative pieces illustrated in this book. I appreciate its commitment to the coin hobby, and its assistance with this book.

I am deeply indebted to Steve Ivy and Jim Halperin of Heritage for their continued willingness to provide illustrations for my many writing ventures. More than just throwing their Web site (www.HA.com) open, they have been true friends and collaborators in making a book like this possible.

In this edition, there are a few otherwise anonymous researchers who responded to queries initially directed to their state governors. I want to specifically thank Jan Wolfley, assistant librarian, Research Library Legislative Counsel Bureau, Carson City, Nevada; Sarah Elliott, Montana Quarter Design Selection Commission; Joe Horton, SLS Reference Kentucky Department for Libraries and Archives; Assemblyman (NJ) Robert Gordon and his chief of staff Mauro Raguseo, for locating in archives the report of the New Jersey coinage design committee; Melanie Hardy Mohney, reference services, Maine State Library; David Snead, Missouri state archives, and his boss Patsy Leubbert; Missouri Secretary of State Robin Carnahan; Claire Ennis, director of Community & Citizen Services, Office of the Governor, North Carolina; Michael McCormick, director of Reference Services, Maryland State Archives; Governor of New Hampshire appointeeVan McLeod of the N.H. Department of Cultural affairs, David Sundman; Arthur Friedberg; Dennis Tucker (Whitman); Charles Anderson, Whitman Publishing; Gwenda Bond, who was a communications specialist in Kentucky's Paul Patton administration and a member of the Kentucky Quarter Project Committee; Michael Haynes, PCGS; and Mark Salzburg, NGC. Also Ashwin Pai and his Lansend IT team, who made my computers work despite themselves; John Darkow and Missouri's *Columbia Daily Tribune* for generously allowing a reprint of three biting editorial cartoons concerning the Paul Jackson design debacle; Jennifer Rachaner, my indefatigable campaigner and freeholder aide, for scanning the cartoon of Chuck Asay's coin of her native Arkansas. Thanks, too, to Cynthia Carter for last-minute put-together in my law office.

I am certain that I have left out of these acknowledgments individuals who were of immeasurable help and assistance. Some of them are mentioned by name elsewhere in the book, but all who helped have my thanks and gratitude.

New York, N.Y., March 2008

INTRODUCTION
TO THE STATE QUARTERS PROGRAM

Three shifts a day, seven days a week, the United States mints at Philadelphia and Denver churn out America's quarters, coins destined to honor each of the 50 states. The last state quarter, Hawaii, was issued in August 2008. By the end of 2009, the program will include America's five insular territories—Guam, Puerto Rico, the Virgin Islands, American Samoa, the Northern Marianas—and the District of Columbia.

Meanwhile, at a convenience store in New York City, a customer receives a new Massachusetts quarter, looks at the front with the Minuteman sentinel, and casually flips the coin over from the 12 o'clock position to the 6 o'clock position only to find that George Washington is upside down. The coin is a mint error, a rotated die worth up to $500! The result is the great chase to examine America's change, with nearly half the nation's population participating in the process.

Welcome to the New Age of American coin collecting, where every ten weeks, for the past ten years, a quarter with a new design has left the Mint for its rendezvous with destiny. Most of the quarters will not be errors (some of them will be, and that is why they are scarce and valuable) but each of them is part of an extraordinary series that began in 1999 and will collectively circulate for as long as there is American money.

These coins are legal tender (there are other collector coins that are never intended to reach circulation) and each has a face value of 25 cents, one-fourth of a dollar. You can use them to feed a parking meter, to make a down payment on a vending-machine purchase, or in a hundred other ways where the design on the coin matters not a whit. But the excitement of these coins goes well beyond a 25-cent face value, for even as the Mint sells these items by the $1,000 bagful, a secondary market has developed whereby even new issues are selling for double their face value or more as collector's items.

In the past, when the number of collectors was two or three million, or even eight million—depending on what estimate you use—this didn't matter very much. There was always a sufficient supply to meet even high demand. Today, however, Mint statistics and marketing studies suggest persuasively that more than 140 million Americans—more than 60 percent of the U.S. population—are actively collecting the 50-states quarters, and more than 85 percent of the country is aware that the coins are being produced in this manner.

How Successful Is the State Quarters Program?

Without question, this is the most ambitious and aggressive program that the U.S. Mint has ever undertaken—and its sole (but considerable) profit comes from the seigniorage, or difference between actual cost to manufacture and face value. This is nothing to sneeze at: the government will make profits well into the hundreds of millions of dollars each year. Then–Deputy Mint Director John Mitchell disclosed to the House Banking subcommittee handling coinage matters on March 28, 2000, that U.S. Mint profits in 1999—largely fueled by the State Quarters program—exceeded $1 billion. As of March, 2008, the number has increased to a staggering $5.8 billion.

The success of the State Quarters program knows almost no bounds. Consequently, it has a thousand fathers and mothers, each of whom qualifiedly, but unabashedly, claims credit for the idea and the huge profits that the Mint is racking up. The program is so successful that the "50 State Quarters" name has been trademarked by the Mint, and the marketplace simply adores the coins for the various ways that they can be sold and appreciate in value.

This is a program that goes beyond traditional coin collectors. *Parade* magazine, stuffer advertising, daily newspaper ads for a 50-state map that holds the coins, patents, copyrights, and trademarks, all are part of the subsequent history of the 50 State Quarters program.

Why Collect State Quarters?

Collecting state quarters is a fun hobby, and a profitable one. It represents the opportunity that comes but once in a generation—to get in on the ground floor of a smart investment, with little more than face value at risk. The 1999–2008 state quarter series has valuable error coins that you can find in pocket change, lower-mintage coin dates and mintmarks, rarefied prices (for a modern issue), and a great story to tell.

Coins are a form of living history and state quarters are no exception. The 50 state quarters represent a mirror of what the citizens and governing body of a state think a snapshot of themselves ought to depict. They reminds us of history, economics, politics, religion, our nation's sociology, and its intellect. These all come together with coin designs that vary state by state, unified with a common obverse featuring our nation's first president, George Washington.

State Quarter Design Elements

Each of the coins in the series has a template. The obverse is identical on every coin, the reverse an ever-changing canvas whose top and bottom frame a different portrait each time. Significantly, all of the design elements, front and back (obverse and reverse), appear in a space of under 25 millimeters (24.6 millimeters, to be precise) utilizing a denomination whose history of service to its country dates back to 1796, a mere four years after the Mint was authorized by Congress on April 2, 1792.

Just what the coins contain is actually set down by law; for only the Congress has the power to coin money and regulate the value thereof. And here, Congress was required to authorize the design twice. First, it set forth general parameters; then when it found that these did not work, it allowed alterations: some elements previously required on the obverse were moved to the reverse, and vice versa.

Whereas the denomination usually appears on the reverse (or back) of a coin, it has been moved to the obverse (or front), beneath the bust of Washington, which is modeled after a sculpture by the great classical French sculptor, Jean-Antoine Houdon. Also moved from front to back was the "United States of America" inscription of national origin. The reverse template set up by the Mint requires that the name of the state and the date of its entry into the Union appear above the central design, while the lower quadrant displays the date of issue and the motto "E Pluribus Unum" ("Out of many, one"). Dates usually go on the obverse of a coin. The motto has been given a much cleaner look than before.

The Treasury Department also issued guidelines for the designs. Guideline #1: each state must "maintain a dignity befitting the Nation's coinage." Thus, Alabama could choose Helen Keller in a studio pose, Kentucky a quarter horse, Iowa an image from a Grant Wood painting, Maine a lighthouse, and Illinois a mood-inspiration of Lincoln, and all would be in compliance with a standard of dignity.

Another guideline stated that "Designs shall have broad appeal to the citizens of the state and avoid controversial subjects or symbols that are likely to offend. Suitable subject matter for designs include state landmarks (natural and man-made), landscapes, historically significant buildings, symbols of state resources or industries, official state flora and fauna, state icons (e.g., Texas Lone Star, Wyoming bronco, etc.), and outlines of the state." This resulted in designs showing icons of the state: New York showing the Statue of Liberty and the Erie Canal, Minnesota its lakes, West Virginia its natural wonders, Colorado its mountain majesty above a fruited plain.

Though some would disagree, the Treasury was adamant that "State flags and state seals are not considered suitable for designs." So there are none.

To help develop a new generation of coin collectors, the Treasury's guidelines provide that "Consistent with the authorizing legislation, the states are encouraged to submit designs that promote the diffusion of knowledge among the youth of the United States about the state, its history and geography, and the rich diversity of our national heritage."

They then go on to provide that "Priority consideration will be given to designs that are enduring representations of the state. Coins have a commercial life span of at least 30 years and are collected for generations."

That is an important example of why people collect quarters: a coin lasts and lasts, retains its intrinsic value, oftentimes maintains a face value, and still can be pulled from circulation, the way bicentennial quarters with the colonial drummer boy still are more than 30 years later.

NEARLY TWO GENERATIONS AFTER IT WAS ISSUED, THIS
BICENTENNIAL QUARTER IS STILL FOUND IN CIRCULATION.

What types of designs should be avoided? The Treasury states that "Inappropriate design concepts include, but are not limited to logos or depictions of specific commercial, private, educational, civic, religious, sports, or other organizations whose membership or ownership is not universal." The Wyoming rodeo rider on horseback is a calculated exception.

Many of the states have chosen colonial themes for their coin designs. New Jersey and Virginia used those themes successfully: the attack by Washington on the Hessians during the Christmas holiday of 1776 and the discovery vessel that celebrated Virginia's quadricentennial (with noncirculating commemorative coinage) in 2007 respectively.

What You'll Find in This Book

This book traces the story of America's 50 State Quarters program from its earliest origins through its authorization by Congress, the manufacturing process of the coins, the errors that have resulted (and their values) and a cornucopia of other information.

There is nothing available elsewhere that comes close to the information that is collected in this volume. For example, here you'll find information taken from the minutes of the Commission of Fine Arts, which had a final say on all design elements. You also will find personal insights from the Citizens Commemorative Coin Advisory Committee, on which the author served from 1993 to 1996, and from which the entire State Quarters program emanated.

Both the Citizens Commemorative Coin Advisory Committee (now called the Citizens Coin Advisory Committee) and the federal Commission of Fine Arts had important input on the design elements contained on each of the coins. The legislation surrounding America's State Quarters requires that the Fine Arts Commission review the designs, and there is almost always a modification suggested to make the designs artistically more pleasing. The Citizens Commemorative Coin Advisory Committee has likewise made its mark on the reverse designs of the state commemoratives with modifications that have given them a more thematic approach.

Sometimes, it was a technical suggestion, such as the matte finish on the map that is shown on the Massachusetts coin; other times, as in the case of the Delaware coin, it can be removing or altering lettering. Regardless, and overall, the contributions of each have made for a more artistically pleasing program—and that is important from a visual standpoint, which in turn enhances collectibility.

For your convenience, the profile of each state quarter in this book contains the same common elements: a picture of the coin, a description of the reverse design, what mints have struck the coins, what quantity was minted in regular quality, what number in proof, and what number quantity in the silver version that is marketed to collectors. Quite naturally, each entry begins with some basic information about the states, since this is after all a program about them and their history. The profiles also include a history of the design concept and commentary on positions taken by the Commission of Fine Arts and the Citizens Commemorative Coin Advisory Committee.

An important section shows the current encapsulated coin population—the number of coins from Numismatic Guaranty Corporation and Professional Coin Grading Service which have been "slabbed," or authenticated and graded, and placed in a tamper-proof plastic holder—which gives some sense of the number of coins available in better-grade condition. An analysis of investment possibilities is also included for each coin.

In addition to profiles of the 50 State Quarters, this book includes the legal and legislative history of America's State Quarters program, along with a bibliographic essay to give the reader appropriate information and sources to consult for more information. It also includes pertinent info on grading, investing, and storing your collection.

It is the intention of the author and the publisher for this to remain

SOME OF THE STATE QUARTER DESIGNS, ALL UNCIRCULATED.

a work in progress; this is its third revision over the ten-year life of the program, and we have continued to add information about designs, mintage figures, and price updates, making this the most up-to-date guidebook on the subject.

Mostly, this book is a labor of love about a program that seems destined to change the face of coin collecting and in the process provide an indelible, handheld record of American history that will stand for all time.

1

THE HISTORY AND LEGISLATION BEHIND THE STATE QUARTERS PROGRAM

The state quarter coinage produced by the Mint for each of the 50 states is a long way from what was originally contemplated, and even proposed, by the Citizens Commemorative Coin Advisory Committee. The CCCAC began a drumbeat in 1993 that reached a crescendo at a Congressional Coin hearing in the summer of 1995.

What eventually emerged from a modest proposal to promote "our national ideals . . . and our esteem as a nation" grew into a proposal that was described as "the most tangible way to touch the lives of every American."

The story of the subsequent legislative history—how the Mint was required to first study the matter, then report back to Congress, and how three separate Congressional laws were required before it became reality—is repeated here.

John F. Kennedy once said that "Victory has a thousand fathers, but defeat is an orphan." So, too, America's State Quarters program has a growing paternity with an ever-larger list of individuals who claim to have originated the idea, and to have single-handedly brought it to fruition. What actually happened is far more subtle, and there is more than enough credit to spread around.

Purpose of Commemoratives

American commemorative coinage began its long history in 1892 as part of the Columbian Exposition in Chicago. The coins were sold at a premium over their face value and intended primarily for collectors of memorabilia, not coin collectors, since there were millions of them made and hardly more than a handful of true coin collectors in the United States at the time.

From 1892 until 1954, the U.S. Mint produced 144 different commemorative coins in silver (when you count all of the dates, mint-marks, and designs) in three denominations: one 25-cent coin, a silver dollar, and the rest 50-cent pieces. There were also nearly a dozen gold coins of various sizes and denominations.

Commemorative coins abused the purpose of coinage, but served a salutary purpose: commemoration and raising of funds for various groups and endeavors. That proved its undoing, and by 1930, President Herbert Hoover vetoed a commemorative coin bill passed by Congress. That set the stage for vetoes by all succeeding presidents through Dwight D. Eisenhower, though some measures made their way through.

The commemorative coinage system of the 1930s and 1940s became so abused that it was shut down in 1954. The Treasury Department was so opposed that a generation later, when it should have been obvious that America's Bicentennial should be commemorated with circulating commemorative coins, the Treasury Department actively opposed the measure—though it allowed that noncirculating coins might be acceptable. (The story of how this happened is told in a book I authored entitled *The Story of How the United States got its Bicentennial Coinage*.) It's fascinating how one person, Mint Director Mary T. Brooks, turned around a government department to sponsor noncirculating coin legislation, and how another person, John Jay Pittman, then president of the American Numismatic Association, persuaded Congress that a circulating quarter dollar that became the Colonial drummer boy coin, belonged in the mix.

The State Quarters program of 1999–2008 comes directly from the lessons learned from the earlier commemorative efforts as well as the Bicentennial program of 1975–76. I can say this authoritatively, because when I drafted my recommendations to the Citizens Commemorative Coin Advisory Committee and to the House coinage subcommittee, the facts from those days were never far from my mind.

Lessons Learned to Be Applied to State Quarters

Lessons learned from Bicentennial coin sales have become part of the legislative process, and at least six key lessons were derived from the Bicentennial circulating coin program and the numismatic products that it spawned:

- First, it was a mistake to produce a fixed number of coins (45 million silver pieces, split among three denominations), rather than establish a maximum and produce only as many as there was demand for. This was particularly painful, because hundreds of thousands of silver proofs and silver uncirculated Bicentennial coin issues sat in mildewed bags. Many eventually had to be melted because they had suffered damage and were unsalable.

- Second, the Mint learned the marketing ratio that is preferred by collectors: proofs, overwhelmingly, over the identical uncirculated coins.

- Third, it witnessed the usefulness of a copper-nickel clad commemorative coin that circulated. Jack Ahr's Colonial drummer boy, more than 30 years after the last coin was placed into circulation, still can be found as a permanent reminder of the Bicentennial.

- Fourth, without special interests benefitting from the merchandising of the program, it could nonetheless be a highly successful endeavor—and there could be considerable involvement of the community at large in the program.

- Fifth, a wide-open design competition, however interesting, produces only a small percentage of useful designs—and a high percentage of those entering did so for a variety of reasons that had little to do with artistic ability.

- Finally, the lesson that should have been learned either hasn't been, or has been ignored: absent some assistance to the marketplace, the price of the commemoratives cannot be sustained once interest in the program moves on.

In the 1980s, as commemorative coin programs once again grew in popularity, more groups wanted their own coins. It became almost impossible to deal with, something that I predicted back in July 1987, writing as a contributing editor to *Coinage Magazine*.

I wrote:

What really remains as a problem, however, is deciding what new Coin issues ought to be produced by the Mint—in other words, making the initial recommendation as to which events are to be commemorated, and which more properly should be ignored, or subject to national medals.

National medals, once the be all, and end all (from 1954 to 1980, they were the only real chance that most groups had) have now fallen into eclipse. One benefit that they did have, though, was that they were a good catch-all for ideas, and offered a large size for attractive designs.

Determining what commemorative Coin programs ought to be created should not be left in the hands of Chief Justice Burger, however well intentioned (or even correct) his assertion that the Bill of Rights is America's legacy to the world.

Nor should it be left in the hands of Congressman [Frank] Annunzio, whose efforts have in fact revitalized the coinage program of the U.S. Mint and made it world-class in terms of competing with other country's commemorative programs.

Toward an Advisory Committee

The creation of a citizens advisory panel to make formal recommendations to the Mint and the Treasury Department, and to coordinate efforts with the Fine Arts Commission seemed to be the answer.

Eventually, this became a legislative reality. *Coin World*'s editor, Beth

Deisher, shares her observations of the 1992 law signed by President George H.W. Bush:

> If you check the record and with Rep. Esteban E. Torres, D-Calif., you will find that the Bush Administration had little or nothing to do with the creation of the CCCAC. True, President Bush did sign the legislation into law. However, Torres was sponsor of the reform legislation. His staff (Roddey Young) drafted the language from his notes of a session that included Torres, Young, and me. I had requested a meeting with Torres for the purpose of an interview (story published in *Coin World*) about the proliferation of commemorative proposals before his committee (he was the new chairman of the subcommittee). He and Young had obviously done their homework and commented specifically on an editorial I had written that suggested a commission or committee similar to what the Postal Service has for stamps. After the interview was complete, the three of us spent more than an hour talking exclusively about the scope of such a committee, the types of background and experience its members should have, terms of service, etc. I presumed the topic would be the subject of a public hearing at some later date. A couple of months later, when the reform legislation had been put together as an omnibus bill, Roddey called and had a couple of points he wanted to clarify. He was referring to the notes from our meeting. It was at that time I learned they had drafted a separate title and were creating the CCCAC within legislation they felt sure would pass.

The point here is not to get personal credit, but rather to point out that a Democratic chairman of the subcommittee, Esteban E. Torres, initiated the CCCAC. Had it not been for Torres, I do not believe the CCCAC would have been formed.

Congress Acts Even Before the Advisory Committee Meets

Even as the Citizens Commemorative Coin Advisory Committee was slated to meet in mid-December 1993, seemingly chartered by Congress to limit noncirculating commemorative coin issues, Congress passed five new commemorative coin programs to be issued in 1994. Coins honoring Thomas Jefferson, the U.S. Capitol, and various military matters created ten new coins (in proof and uncirculated qualities) to go alongside the existing six World Soccer Cup commemorative coin issues.

Waiting in the wings were still more commemoratives, namely those already authorized in 1992 to commemorate the Civil War battlefields, together with the Olympic issues scheduled for 1995–6. Altogether, before the Citizens Advisory Committee had even met, there were eight different commemorative coins struck and sold by the Mint in two different conditions in 1994. This would then be closely followed by three different designs for Civil War battlefields in 1995, sold together with eight Olympic Coin designs also struck in proof and uncirculated. For 1996, eight more Olympic Coin designs were authorized.

Although the new programs had relatively modest mintages, the primary purchasers of the coins still were the nation's coin collectors, who had been the principal purchasers in the past of every major coin program except that honoring the centennial of the Statue of Liberty.

All told, in 1994, 1995, and 1996, if a collector at the time had wanted to buy all of the available current-year proof and uncirculated commemorative coin issues, that would have come to a total of 27 different designs (and 54 total coins), or about a third of all the 144 silver pieces produced from 1892 to 1954 in all dates, mintmarks, and varieties.

Though the Citizens Advisory Committee had been created on his watch, then–Mint Director David Ryder had stalled on implementing it, using "austerity" in government as a rationale. As a result, he was frozen out of the process while a career civil servant, Eugene Essner, ran the Mint on a day-to-day basis as deputy director. A political appointee, Philip N. Diehl (formerly chief of staff to Senator and then–Secretary of the Treasury Lloyd Bentsen) became executive deputy director, superseding Essner. Diehl would ultimately make the suggested appointments to the Citizens Advisory Committee, and Bentsen would approve the nominations.

In early December 1993, Philip Diehl started making telephone calls to individuals he thought would make good members of the Citizens Advisory Committee. One of those calls was to me. At the time, I was in my 12th year as a member of the board of directors of the Industry Council for Tangible Assets, and my eighth year as a member of the Board of Governors of the American Numismatic Association (the first of a two-year term as president of the not-for-profit organization chartered by Congress back in 1912 for the purpose of advancing the science of numismatics). I accepted with alacrity.

I cannot, of course, speak for the other members of the Advisory Committee. They read their agenda books prepared by the Mint, and they applied the knowledge that they had about coinage (or what they learned). My approach was different, and perhaps that is because I had a different agenda.

As a writer in the field for more than 30 years, and as president of the largest national association of coin collectors in the world, my view was (and had been for some time) that contemporary commemorative coinage could avoid the abuses of the past only if there were no surcharges imposed on the sales, or no beneficiaries for the largesse of the program involved—and if there were circulating coins. It was my feeling that it was absolutely essential to "grow" the Mint's market by introducing circulating commemorative coinage so that it would appeal to those on limited income (mainly young adults and seniors) as well as children.

Even though I had reported on, and was familiar with, the legislative history of the Citizens Advisory Committee, the general mantra was that the Advisory Committee was supposed to deal only with the problem of noncirculating legal-tender commemorative coins. My view was different, however, and to get there, I fell back on my training as a practicing lawyer to look at the text of the statute authorizing the Advisory Committee, to see precisely what Congress specified, and then to see if the envelope could be stretched to support a different meaning.

The applicable section of law is found in Title 31 of the U.S. Code (Money and Finance) in Section 5135, which (in edited part) says:

Sec. 5135. Citizens Commemorative Coin Advisory Committee (a) Establishment Required. (1) The Secretary of the Treasury shall establish a Citizens Commemorative Coin Advisory Committee to advise the Secretary on the selection of subjects and designs for commemorative coins. (2) The Advisory Committee shall be subject to the direction of the Secretary of the Treasury. (3) Advisory Committee shall consist of 7 members appointed by the Secretary of the Treasury, 3 of whom shall be appointed from among individuals specially qualified to serve on the committee by reason of their education, training, or experience in art, art history, museum or numismatic collection curation, or numismatics; 1 of whom shall be appointed from among officers or employees of the United States Mint who will represent the interests of the Mint; and 3 of whom shall be appointed from among individuals who will represent the interest of the general public. A member of the Commission of Fine Arts may participate in the proceedings of the Advisory Committee as a nonvoting member. Members of the Advisory Committee shall serve without pay.

Duties. The Advisory Committee shall designate annually the events, persons, or places that the Advisory Committee recommends be commemorated by the issuance of commemorative Coins in each of the 5 calendar years succeeding the year in which such designation is made; make recommendations with respect to the mintage level for any commemorative Coin recommended and submit a report to the Congress containing a description of the events, persons, or places which the Committee recommends be commemorated by a Coin, the mintage level recommended for any such commemorative Coin, and the committee's reasons for such recommendations.

From my reading of the law, there were several areas that could be utilized—if there was an effective advocate—to advance a slightly different cause. The first was in a subparagraph that required a designation of the event to be commemorated. If the event was not related to a "funding" mission, then it might be possible to remove one of the key objections. The second related to another subparagraph to make recommendations as to the mintage level for any commemorative coin recommended (from the earlier paragraph). This became the no-brainer: pick a topic, and then set the mintage at 350, 500, or 750 million pieces—enough to make sure that the coin would truly circulate, just as the Bicentennial coins did a generation earlier.

To be certain that the recommendations were not received perfunctorily, the statute required that the theme be conveyed in a report to Congress together with the mintage level and, most importantly, "the committee's reasons for such recommendations."

A briefing book for the meeting, prepared by the Mint staff, arrived a week or so before and I had pored over its contents, which consisted of about an inch full of papers in nine separate tabs that had been placed in a white spiral binder.

Inside the binder, I covered my top page with just two notes of reminder to me: the first says "Don't forget camera," to be sure that there would be a photo record of the event, and "circulating comm. cn.," for circulating commemorative coin, which I intended from the first meeting to bring to the committee's attention.

Also inside the binder was a proposed "Charter for the Citizens Commemorative Coin Advisory Committee," which had a different view of the job responsibilities of the group, except that it specified in broad language that the committee was to comment on "any commemorative" that it recommended, a mandate I took very broadly.

The Citizens Advisory Committee Participates

I was honored to be appointed as one of the first members on that new Citizens Commemorative Coin Advisory Committee. Each of us introduced ourselves at that first meeting, and I used that opportunity, as I did with each successive meeting over the next couple of days to make a formal recommendation that the committee take its mandate from Congress seriously, explore the idea of circulating commemorative coins, and make an affirmative recommendation in its annual report to Congress favoring such a proposal. It was a drumbeat that I did not stop during the four years that I served on the committee.

Initial response to the proposal was less than lukewarm. It was downright chilly. My notes from that first meeting held at the Mint headquarters in Washington reflected significant opposition from Philip Diehl, then executive deputy director of the Mint (who had been announced, but not yet confirmed, as director). "It's not within our mandate," was the substance of what he said at that first meeting. This appeared to me to be based on advice from longtime Mint staffers who still recalled 50 years of opposition within the Treasury Department to commemorative coins.

As its primary (and initially only) advocate, the discussion was always my initiative. The next in-person meeting of the Advisory Committee was slated for February 22, 1994, in Washington, but there were two interim telephone meetings. My notes aren't specific, but somewhere along the line Philip Diehl got so tired of hearing about circulating commemorative coins that he suggested that if I felt strongly about it, a report could be presented to the committee at its next meeting.

At the February meeting, several presentations were slated for the afternoon. First was the Mint's outreach program, with a dynamite educational video program. Then came an invitation that I had tendered, as president of the American Numismatic Association, to have the first public outreach—a CCCAC meeting at the ANA convention in Detroit that summer.

Dan Hoffman then was to present a discussion on a young collector's views on commemorative coin themes, while at 3 P.M., my presentation was slated for "concepts and options for a circulating commemorative coin."

During the month of January, I worked on a report that covered commemorative coinage in several different contexts, the most important of which was how circulating commemoratives took their place beside noncirculating legal-tender coins.

By January 27, a 5,000-word report was completed and shipped off to the Mint for inclusion in the binder going to each of the committee members. There were 42 separately numbered footnotes in the report and some illustrations that were thought to be helpful for those who were not experienced in the history of commemorative coinage.

The opportunity to make a report and oral presentation to the committee was what really excited me, because that made it plain that the idea would be the subject of debate, discussion, and possibly action. Years of attending hearings at the Senate and House banking committees as a witness testifying, as well as in the capacity of a reporter, taught me that a written report should be complete, but that an oral presentation should be quick, precise, and to the point. My goal was to be able to make the presentation in five minutes or less.

"At our last meeting, I reiterated the importance in my view of making a fundamental change in the way that commemorative coins are thought of, and are issued. I brought this point home several times because I believe, sincerely, that if we are to meet our mandate, it is essential that we consider not only themes for coin designs, but also how those coins will be marketed," my remarks began.

" . . . I want to tell you why it is essential that our report at the end of 1999 advise the Secretary [of the Treasury], and the Congress, that it is our view as a committee that circulating commemorative coinage (with collector versions as a bonus) is essential if the next dozen years are to be as fruitful as the past dozen have for coin issues.

"If we suggested that 1.5 billion quarters . . . be produced commemorating some subject or the other, it would be obvious enough that the only way that this could be absorbed in the marketplace would be by making the coin a circulating one.

"So whether we proceed directly or indirectly, it is my view that we must ultimately cross that Rubicon and systematically back circulating coins as a means of saving commemorative coins from themselves."

A couple of minutes later, I wound toward my conclusion by mentioning Canada's ten-province and two-territory program, which had been a significant success. "The circulating counterpart did not detract from the sale of the collector coins," I said. "It heightened the interest. The bottom line to this is profit to the Mint, and more new coins to the general public."

I concluded by saying: "It would be naive of me to suggest that only commemoratives worthy of circulating in pocket change ought to be produced by the United States Mint, or indeed, any world minting authority. However, as the evidence shows, there is a strong history in many countries outside the United States that utilizes coinage as a medium of expression to the population as a whole for certain commemorative themes that are deemed worthy (by the issuing authorities) of seeking popular support.

"I suggest to you as a guidepost that the Citizens Commemorative

Coin Advisory Committee adopt as a recommendation for a resolution providing that at least one coin issue each year be produced as a circulating commemorative coin issue; that a sufficient quantity be produced to effectively circulate the coin; that a special collector version (in precious metal, as a proof issue; or in base metal, as a proof issue; or both) be produced; and that any design or theme chosen be of a character of sufficient importance as an event to warrant its introduction into commerce as a circulating commemorative coin."

At each meeting of the Citizens Commemorative Coin Advisory Committee that was held that year—and there were five or six more—the topic of circulating commemorative coinage came from me with repetitive regularity. For a time, it was like a traveling salesmen's convention where jokes are identified by number, to save time. I simply had to ask for the floor and say "circulating commemorative coin" to hear the groan.

Philip Diehl, reflecting on this in an interview by Kari Stone, editor of *Coinage*, called me "Johnny One-Note" on that subject.

Near the end of the government's fiscal year, as the committee met to consider its annual report to Congress, I drafted a proposed chapter that was faxed to each member strongly advocating that we propose a circulating commemorative coin.

Sent September 18, 1994, my fax to each committee member suggested that we state that "In making this report to Congress, the Committee does so with the recommendation that at least one commemorative Coin, every two years, be produced in substantial quantity, and utilized in circulation, as well as being offered to collectors."

As the year moved on, the idea finally began to catch on for all the right reasons. It was economically beneficial to the Mint and the country and, more importantly, worked to support the Mint's other programs.

Annual Report to Congress

The next real fight was the test of the Annual Report, the first that the committee was charged with developing for Congress. It was drafted for us by the Mint's helpful professional staff after listening to our discussions and views. The committee had agreed that we would formally recommend to Congress the creation of circulating commemorative coinage, but the Mint staff simply omitted it, perhaps unintentionally, perhaps because members of the staff opposed it.

Fortunately for me, Philip Diehl had become a convert, even if his staff had not, and ordered a rewrite. I volunteered to do a draft, and initially worked up 500 words or so as to why it was worthwhile, and why it would work. I ultimately edited this to 250 words and presented it to our group.

My draft began:

The Committee strongly endorses issuance by the Mint of a circulating commemorative Coin. Coinage is the most tangible way to touch the lives of every American. Circulating coinage promotes our national ideals, builds pride in being an American and our esteem as a nation, and also reaches millions of visitors whose lives each Coin touch.

A circulating commemorative Coin is a regular, legal-tender Coin issued with a distinctive design, but without surcharge. It is used in circulation. All profits from the sale of the Coins go to the Treasury as an off-budget item.

Congress directed by the Act of Mar. 4, 1931, Ch. 505, 46 Stat. 1523, that the Bicentennial of George Washington's birth be remembered with a circulating commemorative Coin, and the quarter dollar designed for that remains in circulation to this day.

In 1973, Congress enacted Pub. L. 93–127, 87 Stat. 456 (Oct. 18, 1973) which caused a commemorative quarter, half-dollar, and dollar reverse to be issued by the Mints, which replaced, for 18 months, the familiar design on the back of the Washington quarter, the Kennedy half and Eisenhower dollars.

Canada, in 1993, successfully issued a series of 12 circulating commemorative quarters (one for each province), that stimulated demand; attracted new collectors to acquire the Coins (and, subsequently, other mint products); and generally called attention to the national coinage to the population of the nation as a whole.

The Committee believes that the U.S. Mint should do no less, picking at least one Coin every two years that is intended to circulate in the coinage system, but bears a commemorative theme. The seigniorage on the Coin (the profit between its metal cost and all Mint overhead, and nominal face value) would accrue strictly to the Treasury, as now, as an off-budget item.

Three coins could lend themselves to such a program: the quarter, half-dollar, or dollar Coin. To accomplish this within the scope of any programs already authorized would require a new legislative initiative, approved by Congress, since the Act of September 26, 1890, otherwise precludes design changes more frequently than once in 25 years.

If it were to be implemented for a Coin not yet authorized, then the Committee recommends that Congress give strong consideration to choosing either the quarter, or a new small-sized dollar Coin.

If the quarter is chosen, instead of typical annual production of about 1.5 billion coins, the Mint would probably have to manufacture about two billion coins to accommodate demand. The seigniorage on this would also be about $100 million more than at present from existing quarter production. (Mint seigniorage on *all* coins presently totals about $700 million annually, all "off budget" items.)

If a small-sized dollar were chosen, it would be introduced as a new denomination, since the Susan B. Anthony dollar last circulated a dozen years ago. It is reasonable to conclude that between 500 million and 750 million of such Coins would be required in the first eight months of production. Seigniorage or profit to the government on this would be a minimum of $400 million, and could be as high as $650 million.

Several committee members wanted to work on the edit, and the final version—four paragraphs in the First Annual Report (pages 10 and 11)—truly incorporated all of our views, even if many of the surviving words were originally mine:

Finally, the CCCAC endorses issuance by the Mint of a circulating commemorative Coin. Coinage is a tangible way to touch the lives of every American. Circulating coinage promotes our national ideals, builds awareness and pride in our history, and informs millions of foreign visits who use U.S. coins.

A circulating commemorative Coin is a regular legal-tender Coin issued with a distinctive design but without a surcharge. American taxpayers would be the only financial beneficiaries of the issuance of the Coin.... Two modern precedents ... are the George Washington quarter authorized in 1931 (still in circulation today) and the Bicentennial [coins]....

The CCCAC recommends that Congress authorize the Secretary of the Treasury to issue a circulating commemorative Coin ... the Coin would continue to circulate as a medium of exchange but would also become a collector item.

Diehl's subsequent espousal of that position made all the difference. Ultimately, all of the members came around, and by the time that the CCCAC filed its first report to Congress in December 1994, there was a sincere consensus that circulating, legal-tender commemoratives should become part of the U.S. coinage scene.

From the time that the Citizens Commemorative Coin Advisory Committee threw down the gauntlet in its December 1994 report, the idea of a circulating commemorative coin was no longer a voice in the wilderness, but rather something that was moving toward the mainstream.

Hearings Before the House Coinage Subcommittee

After the CCCAC's report to Congress, there remained opposition to the concept within the Treasury Department itself—though increasingly, Mint staff members who opposed the change of position either retired, or decided it was in their best interest to change their views to accommodate a majority position. By the summer of 1995, it was clear enough that there were other problems with the overall commemorative coinage program—in particular the gold and silver noncirculating legal-tender programs—that had caused mintages to drop precipitously and had made virtually every program a hard sell.

Hearings were scheduled before the House coinage subcommittee.

The scope of the hearings was to reform the noncirculating commemorative coins. For those who have never testified before a congressional committee, it can be a heady experience—one that is at once humbling and a bit mysterious. I took the same approach that I did before the Citizens Advisory Committee—the bulk of my focus, my testimony, and the exhibits all had to do with the need for a circulating commemorative coin.

The testimony of the other witnesses took a different approach. *Coin World* Editor Beth Deisher called for elimination of surcharges, but acknowledged that, "it would be unrealistic to expect the U.S. Mint to sell modern commemoratives at face value. . . ." (Hearing transcript, p. 64). Dr. Alan Stahl, then a curator at the American Numismatic Society, focused his prepared remarks on the need to have beautiful designs and the importance of involving outside artists in design competitions. Harvey Stack, a coin dealer from New York City representing the Professional Numismatists Guild, used his prepared remarks to rail against unconscionable pricing by the Mint and the authorization of too many coins by Congress. Mint Director Diehl's prepared testimony covered a panoply of issues—though not a circulating commemorative coin.

First mention at the hearing on the topic of circulating commemorative coins came from Stahl, a true historian (with a PhD in history from the University of Pennsylvania) and excellent lecturer who was able to put commemorative coinage into a historic context. He closed his oral presentation "with a few thoughts on the relation of commemorative coinage to circulating coinage." He observed that "to many Americans, the only true commemorative coin issued in their lifetimes is the Bicentennial quarter, as it was the only one which circulated."

Next came Harvey Stack, the New York dealer, whose oral remarks made a small but important mention: "I, as the others, have advocated a circulating commemorative which would cost nothing to the people, but would project history."

My opportunity came to speak after a brief committee recess. My remarks focused almost exclusively on the need for circulating commemorative coinage available at face value. Not only was the entire

5,000-word report to the Citizens Advisory Committee included as an attachment, but I summarized the Advisory Committee's position, reciting that the CCCAC not only wanted to see lower mintages for noncirculating legal-tender coins but "made a unanimous recommendation signed by all voting members of the Committee that Congress give serious consideration to the issuance of a circulating, legal-tender commemorative coin—a coin without surcharge—which would have its designs regularly changed to exemplify contemporary commemorative themes. The purpose of this would be to stimulate the general public to look at their coins, and their pocket change. . . . There is no better means of . . . promot[ing] public awareness of coin collecting . . . than with a new circulating commemorative coin, emblematic of the very values that has made our country great."

On page 40 of the hearing's printed transcript, at the end of a rambling monologue on commemorative coinage history, Harvey Stack stumbled onto a proposal he had made to the Citizens Advisory Committee earlier in the year: "We could do the first 13 states and issue new commemorative coins every year or two that would commemorate the other states as they came into the Union, and then cover at least the first 50 states."

Chairman Mike Castle, who represents Delaware (the first state to ratify the U.S. Constitution), called it "a brilliant idea," adding "Delaware was the first state."

By the end of 1995, the Citizens Advisory Committee had another annual report to make to Congress. It clarified that "The CCCAC unanimously endorses the issuance of a circulating legal-tender commemorative Coin"—a face-value commemorative. Since the director of the Mint is a statutory member of the committee, that completed the cycle and brought it full circle—to have support from within the Mint.

Legislation Begins

Legislation to accomplish a 50-state commemorative coin program that would have production spread over 10 years would not become reality until late 1997. There are those who will claim that they merely mentioned the idea and it became reality, but the parties carrying the real load were Philip Diehl at the Mint, John Lopez at a staff level on Capitol Hill, and Mike Castle (R-Del.), the chairman of the House Banking subcommittee that dealt with coinage matters.

Congressman Castle wrote the proposal, H.R. 3793, directing the Mint to strike 50 different coin designs—one for each state over the next 10 years—that was introduced July 11, 1996. (A silver version of each coin would also be produced for collectors.)

The bill began with legislative findings. Among them: a circulating commemorative coin could produce earnings of $110 million and produce indirect earnings to the Treasury of $3.4 billion.

It went on to state, "It is appropriate to launch a commemorative circulating Coin program that encourages young people and their families to collect memorable tokens of all the States for the face value of the Coins."

The week following Labor Day, 1996, was slated to mark the occasion of the House passing historic legislation that would create a 10-year-long continuity program of circulating 25-cent commemorative coins. A House vote was scheduled for September 4. Circulating commemorative coinage honoring all 50 states inched toward reality as the Senate and House of Representatives in early October 1996, directed the Secretary of the Treasury to study its implementation.

On September 30, 1996, President Bill Clinton signed into law the commemorative reform legislation limiting new noncirculating commemorative coin issues to two per year, maximum. Of course, since Congress made the law, it could change it at any time, a fact not lost on the sponsors. On October 3, Senator Alphonse D'Amato (R-N.Y.), chair of the Senate Banking Committee, rammed through legislation that authorized seven new commemorative coin issues and directed study of the 50-state circulating coin proposal that had already passed the House unanimously.

The Senate version called for the Treasury Secretary to study and report by June 1, 1997, on the feasibility of a 50-state circulating commemorative coinage program. Specifically, "The study shall assess likely public acceptance of and consumer demand for different coins that might be issued in connection with such a program (taking into consideration the pace of issuance of Coins and the length of such a program)."

Also ordered: "A comparison of the costs of producing coins issued under the program and the revenue that the program would generate, the impact on coin distribution systems, the advantages and disadvantages of different approaches to selecting designs for coins in such a program," and other factors.

There were differences between the houses of Congress. Normally, that is cause for a conference for the two bodies to work out their differences. The House chose compromise, and the Senate version of the bill prevailed.

As finally agreed upon, the bill gave a clear mandate to the Secretary of the Treasury: report to Congress by August 1, 1997, as to the viability of a circulating commemorative coin program using 50 different coins—one for each state. One key issue: the United States Mint was already slated to produce 19 billion coins in 1999 before considering the commemorative proposal. If the final determination was a positive one, the program would start up on January 1, 1999—unless the Secretary of the Treasury, Robert Rubin, postponed that date of commencement. But if he did, he would still have to decide when production would begin—the first date to appear on the coins .

The task was a daunting one—particularly since a circulating commemorative coinage program of this magnitude had never been undertaken before. The easy part would be the designs, because Congress directed that they relate to the states of the union in their order of entry. The difficult part would be the production. The Mint staff began to have attacks of apoplexy, recognizing that a circulating commemorative coin might add 700 million production units to an already heavy workload, and that five new coins per year could add upwards of three to four billion new pieces. On that basis, the Mint prevailed upon the sponsors to suggest a study of the problem first, in order to make sure that the result could in fact be achieved.

That the Mint would balk at creating new circulating commemorative coins was not especially surprising to most close observers. I predicted that the bureaucrats were going to report the same tired facts, slanted against circulating commemorative coins, cloaked in production arguments. I wrote: "They'll cite coinage demand studies and projections that show that the Mint won't be able to keep up with the demand for circulating coinage. (The record, to the contrary, shows that the Mint and the Fed don't have a good track record in forecasting long-term coinage needs.)

"It's likely that they'll also claim that there will be a problem of hoarding of new circulating commemorative Coins, and that millions will be withdrawn from circulation—unspent—by the nation's Coin collectors.

"There is a partial truth to that, but all manufacturers should be this lucky, to produce a widget at a cost of three cents that has a wholesale (and retail) value of more than eight times cost, or 25 cents.

"The more that the Mint produces, the more profit that they make. That's pretty simple. The more profit (even off budget), the greater the economic benefit."

That the U.S. Mint is capable of producing large quantities of coins is beyond cavil. Its production facilities at Philadelphia, Denver, San Francisco, and West Point, whose physical plants are designed to produce 13 to 15 billion pieces a year, can turn out 17 to 19 billion pieces with a bit of hard work. The issue was whether other coinage demand had slacked off sufficiently in order to permit the Mint to produce three or four billion coins beyond the cent, nickel, dime, and half-dollar that were already planned.

Fortunately, by the late spring–early summer of 1997, the Mint concluded that it could accomplish producing the program that Congress mandated—with one coin for each of the 50 states, producing five coins a year for a total of ten years. No quarter dollars would be produced with the Washington design of 1932, and the heraldic eagle on the reverse; the concept would be five circulating legal-tender coin designs, one from each state, which would be rotated approximately every two-and-a-half months.

The Mint was committed to a circulating commemorative coin program, just as it was committed to expanding its physical plant to permit it to strike needed coinage of the realm together with the commemoratives. The plan was also to "assist the Citizens Commemorative Coin Advisory Committee and Congressional banking committees in designing a circulating commemorative coin program compatible with our circulating coin production mission."

An important public study of the utility of circulating commemorative coins, undertaken on behalf of the Treasury Department by the "big eight" accounting firm of Coopers & Lybrand, was then released by the Treasury and sent to Capitol Hill on June 10. Its key findings, based on a statistically sound survey of more than 2,000 individuals interviewed by telephone, were announced 10 days later than the statute which ordered the examination had requested. The delay was worthwhile, because the startling results showed that only 11 percent of those surveyed opposed a 50-state commemorative coin program. More significant was that 75 percent of those polled declared that they would be "almost certain" to start collecting the series, or minimally that there was a "good possibility" that they would do so.

Each coin that is collected and removed from circulation represents a 22-cent profit for the government, meaning that hundreds of millions of dollars in seigniorage profit were likely to accrue in any lengthy program stretching over ten years' time.

"I am very pleased about the study, and hope that this positive report means the Treasury will 'green-light' my proposal to give the quarter a new look," Castle said. "This proposal has many benefits. By placing a symbol of each state on one side of the quarter, we are paying tribute to our country as a whole and commemorating each of our 50 very different states." Significantly, Castle said, we also would be "saving the taxpayer money we otherwise would be paying on the U.S. debt and making the process of getting change more educational and a lot more fun."

The task then facing Treasury Secretary Robert Rubin, who was required by August 1, 1997, to make the decision whether or not to go ahead, was therefore a daunting one—particularly since a circulating commemorative coinage program of this magnitude had never been undertaken before. With the outcome of the proposal hanging in the balance, the consensus of observers, including some knowledgeable staff members on Capitol Hill, was that the administration's decision would have little to do with the merits of the proposal—which was nearly universally acknowledged to have merit—but on raw intra-party politics.

Secretary of the Treasury Takes Action

Robert Rubin finally did give his mandate for change. Your pocket change, that is. He gave the program a thumbs-up.

What finally moved the program from conceptual idea to reality was the push given by Congressman Castle's office in the face of opposition by the Treasury Department. As little as a week before the final decision was made, oddsmakers said the decision could go either way.

With the decision hanging in the balance, Castle sprang into action, soliciting a letter that went from the speaker of the House, Newt Gingrich, to the majority leader, Dick Armey, to the majority whip, Tom DeLay, to the chairman of the House Banking Committee, James A.S. Leach, to Castle himself, to Rubin asking for the change in our change.

Rubin's July 31 response followed. His approval was tepid, and appeared to require congressional reapproval, which was all but certain to succeed. In a July 31, 1997, "Dear Mike" letter, signed "Bob," Rubin stated:

[I have] reviewed the proposal for a fifty-state circulating commem-orative quarter program and the study that the Treasury Depart-ment commissioned from Coopers & Lybrand. The study, through extensive polling and market research, concluded that while there is a substantial degree of interest in the program, there is a also a large percentage of people who are indifferent to the program or are unfavorably disposed toward it. I am concerned that this pro-gram could affect the public's perception of our coinage." He there-fore asked for legislation to assure that "our Money includes elements symbolic of the basic principles of our nation ... for the full consideration of these and related issues by requiring design review by the Citizens Commemorative Coin Advisory Committee and the Fine Arts Commission," plus the Treasury chief, to "ensure that no frivolous or inappropriate designs are implemented.

The CCCAC advocated the program as a billion-dollar budget maker. In the text of the law, Congress concurred with this, stating that the circulating commemoratives "could produce earnings of $110 million from the sale of silver proof Coins and sets over the 10-year period of issuance, and would produce indirect earnings of an estimated $2.6 billion to $5.1 billion to the United States Treasury."

Determining the Design

One of the first editorial cartoonists to take on the State Quarters program was the *Cincinnati Enquirer's* Jim Borgman. Reprinted by permission.

To help prepare for the program, the Mint was allowed to produce coins with the existing Washington quarter design by John Flanagan, issued originally in 1932 as part of a one-year circulating commemorative for the bicentennial of George Washington's birth, throughout calendar year 1999, even though they might bear the 1998 date.

A comparable freeze in designs was permitted when the Mint produced hundreds of millions of Bicentennial quarters in the 1975–76 period. It was explained then, as now, as a means of preventing a shortage of coins.

Just what would appear on the coins remained subject initially to pervasive speculation, though Congress imposed certain restrictions and limitations to be certain that the coins wouldn't become the tools for commercial endorsements or political statements.

Design selection involves the Secretary of the Treasury consulting with the governor of the state being commemorated, or "such other State officials or group as the State may designate for such purpose." Also required to be consulted: the Federal Commission of Fine Arts.

Each design must be reviewed by the Citizens Commemorative Coin Advisory Committee, but neither it nor the Fine Arts Commission—or even the state itself—has veto power over a coin's design.

It is interesting to note that from 1999–2008, the states submitted concepts and the Mint engravers prepared their renditions of them. Then, for a brief period in 2004, the states began to submit finished artwork which the Mint followed, making no changes in the designs. For coins dated 2005 and beyond, the Mint went back to accepting only written concepts, which they did for the six coin program enlargement for 2009 (see chapter 7).

When Rubin first came out in favor of the 50-state commemorative proposal in the summer of 1997, he wrote to Castle that he hoped that the designs would not include some of the proposals that had already been raised, such as Michael Jordan for Illinois.

The legislation responded to that concern by declaring that, "Because it is important that the Nation's coinage and currency bear dignified designs of which the citizens of the United States can be proud, the Secretary shall not select any frivolous or inappropriate design for any quarter dollar minted."

To that end, the law also was changed to require scenic or pictorial depictions, rather than individuals that a state might choose to honor. That is accomplished by the clause requiring that "No head and shoulders portrait or bust of any person, living or dead, and no portrait of a living person may be included in the design of any quarter dollar."

The nation's editorial cartoonists have had a field day in designing pseudo-coins. One, by Jim Borgman, in the *Cincinnati Enquirer*, depicts an Arkansas coin with the motto "We Aren't All Crooked." Another coin showcases the "Free Republic of Leaveusthehellalone Montana." One of my favorites is the well-researched editorial cartoon of Chuck Asay in the *Colorado Springs Gazette-Telegraph*. He drew "The Clinton Commemorative Coin" in which the president's face appeared to be doubled; the new national motto read "In Rhetoric We Trust," while in the lower right-hand corner, a suited lawyer who resembled me in physical appearance exclaims "Hey! That's a double-die coin. It's worth a lot of money!" only to have someone else exclaim "No: They're ALL like this!"

Signe Wilkinson, editorial cartoonist in the *Philadelphia Daily News*, referring to the police arrest of some Amish people for drug possession,

CHUCK ASAY'S TAKE ON THE STATE QUARTER WITH THE AUTHOR'S CARICATURE IN THE RIGHT-HAND CORNER.

offered the inscription: "Pennsylvania—where even the Amish know how to party." Like Milt Priggee in the *Seattle Times*, she also allowed for a "write-in" to reflect readers' votes.

In humor we find the success of the State Quarters program. The designs have become mainstream, and the finished designs struck by the Mint have become a permanent part of our society.

2

THE COINING PROCESS: HOW AMERICA'S STATE QUARTERS ARE MADE

Coins themselves have been produced since the time of the Lydians, around 750 B.C., when crude lumps of electrum were stamped with equally crude dies. By the time of the ancient Greeks, the manufacture of coins, and indeed the minting process, had been elevated to fine art. Kimon, among the earliest of the sculptors of the Greek city-states, hand-cut his dies and created magnificently stylized art in metal. Originally, dies were all done in intaglio, which is to say that the design was prepared in reverse in the metallic die. When the die was pressed into a blank planchet (the metal approximately the size of the coin), the design flowed into the contours of the die, in reverse. This method is still used in the year 2008, and indeed, every coin in America's state coinage series is made from intaglio dies.

The earliest coins evolved from nuggets of electrum, or white gold (an alloy of gold and silver which occurs naturally). Inevitably, these early coins are one-sided only. The reverse invariably has a punch mark left by the tool that was used to force a lump of annealed metal into an obverse die which itself was fixed into an anvil.

By the time of the Greeks, there was a more sophisticated technique that allowed for two-sided coin designs. The lower die, inevitably containing the obverse, was embedded into the anvil. A hammer was utilized by taking the upper, or reverse, die and placing it upon the planchet (underneath which was the obverse). Several sharp blows into the annealed surface then impressed the design. Inevitably, the reverse which bore the blow wore rapidly and was relatively short-lived.

The basic principle of coin die design from the Lydians and the ancient Greeks survives to the present day, though machinery now does the work once done by hand. Depending upon the skill of the craftsman, the designs could appear sophisticated and constitute exquisite works of art, or could appear to be quite crude. For example, the coins produced in Judea during the Jewish revolt that started in 132 A.D. reveal what one scholar referred to as the product of "die cutters working for the rebel mint, [which] were by no means masters in the tradition of Greek glyptic art. They did not reach even the average level of engraving practice of Hadrianic times, though their typical work is no worse than many contemporary products of the provincial Roman mints.... Simple Jewish craftsmen, unskilled in the art of engraving, were therefore entrusted with the cutting of the coin dies. They carried out this specialized task with more or less aptitude."

Ancient coins normally have a high relief on thick and relatively heavy flans, or planchets. By medieval times, the Western planchets were inevitably thin and in low relief. The basic methodology involved the hand-cutting of dies, the cutting of a blank planchet, and the use of a hammer. This continued right up through the Renaissance. The art of the Greeks and the Romans was lost by the time of the fall of Constantinople, and hence Byzantine coinage is often perceived as far more crude. Nonetheless, the techniques utilized to produce the coins were identical.

The Renaissance brought a new coining invention, created by none other than the multitalented Leonardo da Vinci. Da Vinci invented a coin stamp which cut out the blank and thereafter stamped the impression. Whether or not this was ever used cannot be proven, but a century later that point was rendered moot with the invention of the screw press.

The screw press utilizes an elementary principle of physics—the lever. A stationary die, impressed in a blank metal planchet, is forced into the metal by means of a weight and counterbalance, whose pressure is maintained downward, by turning the bar which holds them down a threaded hole that resembles a wood screw. As the pole rotates down the screw, the die sinks into the metal, and after a turn or two of the press, a coin is created.

By the time that the U.S. Mint was authorized in 1792, coinage techniques worldwide had matured to a more sophisticated level. Still, by contemporary standards, they were primitive at best. Precious metal was annealed (the treatment of a planchet through a heating and cooling process that softens it and readies it for striking), and washed. The ingots were then brought to a rolling room which produced strips for small coins, initially at the rate of 7,500 ounces of metal each day. The rolling mill was run by a team of horses that tramped around a stationary pole which revolved and turned the mill. A drawing machine equalized the crudeness of the strips.

Eventually, a planchet cutting press and a milling machine were utilized before the screw coining press did the actual stamping. In 1793, Adam Eckfeldt invented a device for automatically feeding and ejecting the planchets after striking. It consisted of "a very powerful upright screw, on the top of which was affixed a heavy and strong lever worked with great apparent ease by one man at each end, and by which the screw is made to make about one-fourth of a revolution before returning to its former position. At the lower end of the screw, a die is affixed which gives the impression of the obverse, while beneath is the die containing the impression of the reverse."

Well into the 19th century, dies for coinage were still being individually cut by hand into steel which was then hardened by fire. Although master engravers skilled in their craft copied designs faithfully, there are minute but distinct differences in every single die (even of seemingly identical coins) because each version was separately cut into the master model.

Many of these die varieties are widely collected. Others are so insignificant as to not even be generally noted among collectors. Mint records, however, disclose that hundreds of dies were used each year during this period of time—not surprising given that each die was good for only thousands of impressions, rather than millions of them.

Tens of thousands of dies are used by the Mint even today; the Denver Mint alone produces more than 140,000 coin dies each year, but with a critical difference from the earlier times: technology has evolved such that nearly every die is alike. Standardization of coin design into truly imperceptible differences between dies was impossible until the invention of the pantograph, epitomized by the Janvier reduction-engraving model.

The technique for this traces back to the writing machine invented by Thomas Jefferson which copied his correspondence. That machine utilized a device that connected two pens to each other some distance apart. As one pen moved, so did the other, thus copying the movement (and the writing) onto paper. The reduction copying machine is not dissimilar, at least in theory. An engraving tool is positioned on a die while the other end is a fine-tuned tracing device that slowly goes over the surface of a model identical in design to the desired end product. As each portion of the design is gone over, it traces itself in reverse, etching into the metal of the die. The Janvier machine, through a series of

JANVIER REDUCING MACHINES MAKE COIN ENGRAVING A CINCH. *Taken at the Philadelphia Mint by the author.*

levers, cog wheels that turn the rounded dies at different rates of speed, and other mechanical devices, is capable of actually reducing at an identical ratio any of the master designs which are created on a copper piece (or sometimes an epoxy piece), called a galvano.

Although this was done in the middle of the 19th century, it is still being done this way as America's State Quarters program is being rolled out. Even with this technique, master engravers are still required to make fine-line engravings into the die's surface, usually for lettering and other minute details.

There are, altogether, about a dozen different steps that transform an image in the mind's eye of the designer into a coin that can be acquired. The first is a drawing of the design, which is typically (in the case of America's State Quarters) initiated at the state level and shipped to the Mint, where the "concepts" are converted by skilled designers and engravers at the Mint into a coinable design.

From the approved design, a plastileneor modeling clay version set on a plaster basin is made. This is a "positive" model that appears to be a larger version of a coin, with fully contoured surfaces. Once the artist or engraver finishes with this, a negative plastilene version is made by pouring plaster over the plastilene.

The resulting model itself becomes a mold so that a plaster positive can be made; this in turn becomes a mold from which a negative plaster is made. The negative plaster model is electroplated, and once that is done, solid backing is added and the model becomes a galvano. The galvano is taken to a reducing machine, usually a Janvier engraving-reducing machine, or a reducing pantograph (portrait lathe) from which a master hub is produced.

A long, straight bar runs along the front of the lathe and is hinged to a fulcrum. A short distance from the fulcrum is a stile, or cutting tool, which (as the device turns to allow the stiles to trace over the design) cuts into the metal that will become the hub. After several times, a final version is prepared. The master hub is then used to produce two master dies. The master dies produce the working hub, a positive, that produces the working die, a negative. Working dies are then made, and these working dies produce coins.

In the 20th century, a variety of new minting machines were

invented, including hydraulic coining presses, and even completely automated minting facilities where technicians supervise anywhere from four to a dozen coining presses while overhead conveyor belts effortlessly, silently, and without human assistance move heat-treated blanks from burnishing mills to the coining press. Thereafter, robots remove the products from the coining press to be counted, bagged, and shipped into circulation.

Hydraulic coining press at the Philadelphia Mint, striking a Delaware quarter, December 1998.

The typical coining press today—including the kind producing America's State Quarters—produces at a capacity of about 600 coins per minute and perhaps operates more typically at a bit less than a third of that level. Proof coins are produced on hydraulic presses operating at much slower rates, and that allows for the coins to be struck with two blows from the die, rather than the single blow that is typical of circulation strikes.

3

GRADING

Circulated Quarters

Most of America's state quarters have gone directly into the circulation pool. The coining presses churn out hundreds of coins a minute per press, thousands of coins per hour and in the aggregate, more than a hundred million coins each week during the production cycle of about two-and-a-half months (ten weeks) per coin, at both the Philadelphia and Denver mints.

Once the coin is struck, it is ejected into a bucket attached to each coining press, and the bucket fills until it is dumped onto a conveyor belt that takes it to the coin counting machines.

Throughout this process, the coins come in contact with other coins, and tiny contact marks, or chinks in the metal are found to occur. The coin counting machine is gentle, but it is nonetheless metal against metal, allowing for more minute abrasion. Sometimes these marks go into the "field"—the un-designed, flat surface on each coin. A nick or a scratch there, or perhaps on a high point of the design, is bound to happen.

That's why the Delaware quarter is in such poor condition. It has a lot of exposed surfaces and as a result, the field between the rider, the horse, and the edge of the coins dinged or damaged frequently. There are many more uncirculated coins in MS-65 or MS-66 than there are MS-67, in contrast to many other state quarter designs.

A small percentage of the coins that go through this process receive no metal damage, or perhaps pick up a nick or a scratch that is simultaneous with a curl on Washington's hair lock, so it simply does not show. Perhaps another has simply had the chink of the metal hit at a rate that is less damaging. Regardless, those who examine the state quarters in depth are aware that a high percentage of these coins have minor marks, abrasions, metallic chinks, or other minor surface damage on each coin. The number of specimens that are truly unimpaired and visually pleasing, even under a 5- or 10-power magnifying glass, is few.

In January 1999, when America's State Quarters program was in its infancy, *Numismatic News* Editor David Harper and I performed an admittedly unscientific experiment at the Florida United Numismatists (FUN) show, held each year in January in Orlando, Florida. We looked at hundreds of Delaware coins to try to assemble four or five coins from circulation that could be photographed in order to show the new design. After several hundred specimens were examined, we were astonished to find that only about five pieces merited photography, and that even here there was typically one side that was better than the other, with none reaching that ethereal perfection that many collectors crave.

Of course, this is anecdotal rather than scientific research, but the near universal anecdotal experience with the 50 State Quarters program is that the rim has been lowered and the basin for the coin design upon which the features appear has been raised. The consequence of these technical details is that the coins get banged up rather easily and their designs are marred.

This is not to say that the coins are still not uncirculated, for they are; uncirculated is an art, and a defined term, rather than a scientific or precise meaning of "not in circulation," which by definition a coin obtained in change cannot be.

Collectors grade coins as a means of describing their surface and overall appearance and, ultimately, to determine the price they are

1999-P
DE 25C
PCGS MS66
Delaware
Series: 39
Coin: 148
5944.66/71767820
LIBERTY
QUARTER DOLLAR
DE
PCGS

Delaware quarter in PCGS holder.

going to pay. It is important for the beginning collector—or the person who hopes to acquire America's state quarters from pocket change—to realize how grading affects price and value.

Verbal descriptions of "uncirculated" and other conditions were utilized first by collectors, but a numerical method of grading has been in use for more than a half century—and, in the last 15 or 20 years, this has come to predominate as the method of describing coins' conditions, and ultimately their value.

If you are not a collector, you would probably assume that coins were graded on the same numerical scale that all of us were used to from the time we were in grammar school: 1 to 100. That might make a lot of sense, and coins certainly could be graded that way, but the coins that form the basis for numerical grading are old U.S. large cents and half cents, and the grading of these was not so much descriptive, initially, but was a set of numbers reflecting basal value. A scale of 1 to 70 was utilized. A coin in poor condition, with a basal value of 1, would cost 1/60th of the amount of the same coin in uncirculated condition (Mint State-60). A coin in uncirculated condition but of a better grade

(Gem or Mint State-65) according to this theory should have had a price of about 5% more than an MS-60 example of the same coin.

The inventor of the system, Dr. William Sheldon, was a Yale professor and mathematical genius who was also famous for advancing a theory that by studying bare anatomy, it was possible to predict intelligence. Like the concept of mathematical pricing through grading, the physiological photographs are part of a discredited theory.

Even though the theory is long since gone, numerical grading is here to stay using a 1 to 70 scale, and all coins are graded and described using these numbers. Because the value of all of America's state quarters depends so much on their grade or condition, it is important to understand coin grading in its historical context—for that format serves as the underlying basis for grading all coins today. Put differently, if you understand the concept of how a coin is graded, it does not matter whether you are grading state quarters or a rare old silver dollar. The principles are identical.

Coin collecting is sometimes termed a precise and exacting science, but coin grading is an imprecise form of it at best. This is because coin grading offers a succinct definition or interpretation of the state of preservation, and the relative condition, of one or more coins.

This is done through an examination of the surfaces of the metal, the strength of the strike, the luster or sheen that time has given the piece, and the rendering of an opinion of these factors coupled with eye appeal. This is as true for America's state quarters as it is for an Indian Head cent made prior to the start of the 20th century.

Having said that in the abstract, the lack of a definite, fixed standard has a great deal to do with the comparative nature of grading—the examination of one coin, and the inevitable mental image or physical comparison of that coin to another specimen. To that extent, grading is personal, and not unlike comparing great wines, where adjectives—or even numbers alone—cannot adequately convey a subjective impression.

Many times, a grader will examine a coin and conclude that it is "the best" example that is known. Comparisons of lesser specimens are automatically drawn to that coin. If, at a later time, a different and better specimen becomes known to a grader or cataloger, so inevitably does the point of comparison.

In one case where the Federal Trade Commission was bringing claim against the grading practices of a dealer who sold rare and other coins, its experts (renowned coin dealers) were asked to grade the identical set of coins, piece by piece. The supervising federal District Court judge was astonished to find that they disagreed as to the grades of nearly half of them, and in several instances by more than one grading description or numerical point.

That coin grading is imprecise in the abstract does not mean that a dealer, whose livelihood depends on the grade—or a trained collector—cannot uniformly apply a personal standard. They do, every day. In a world of subjectivity, where each element is inherently non-objective, amid the imprecision and lack of consistent, objective standards or means of interpretation, it is nonetheless important to collectors and coin buyers to have in some concrete form the fundamental basis under which a system of comparative evaluation can operate. Dozens of articles, and a number of books, have attempted to do this with respect to the grading of numismatic items. Some existed prior to the 20th century, others are far more current.

The lowest common denominator is that in describing the condition of a coin or grading, it continues to be what it always has been—a highly subjective opinion that offers an interpretation of the particular state of preservation of a coin.

Rudiments of coin-grading standards or methodologies were quite limited even as recent as three decades ago. They can best be summarized by stating that except for early American copper coins, adjectival descriptions were widely utilized by collectors and dealers alike in a very general way. Coins were principally termed Good, Very Good, Fine, Very Fine, Extremely Fine, About Uncirculated, or Uncirculated, or defined as being struck as a proof or specimen coin intended for collectors. Uncirculated coins may be broken down into typical uncirculated, choice uncirculated, and gem uncirculated.

The original Sheldon parameters of 1 to 70 are widely followed, as originally stated in *Penny Whimsy* in 1948: good condition starts at 3;

fine is 12; extremely fine is 40; about uncirculated starts at 50; uncirculated is between 60 and 70. However, wide differences have developed among mint state coins, where specimens are now being graded on a single-digit basis between 60 and 70.

Most experienced collectors and dealers can differentiate between a typical uncirculated coin and a choice uncirculated specimen. Most can also distinguish between a technically graded MS-65 and an MS-63 coin. There are those who believe they can identify, time after time, without error, intermediate grades such as MS-61, MS-62, and MS-64 (without confusing an MS-64 with an MS-63 or an MS-65, for example). This is unlikely, however, for even the best graders and the catalogers frequently will admit that they may view a point differently in the morning than they will at the end of a tired day, and that the perception of whether or not a coin is MS-63 or MS-64 (representing a significant price difference in the marketplace) often will depend on demand in the market—which means that grading is market-driven.

Q. David Bowers, a respected expert in the coin industry, states in *Adventures With Rare Coins* (1979) that "often five different sellers will assign different grades to the same coin, perhaps differing just slightly but still differing, often with important financial consequences. . . ." For example, although the difference between an MS-65 and an MS-67 is only two points, the difference in the monetary value of coins in these two grades can be great, even for America's state quarters, which are so new. For some of the state quarters, an MS-68 may have a value of several hundred dollars, while an MS-65 may be worth just 10 times face value.

Unlike other objets d'art, a coin cannot be repaired or added to. Its condition can worsen with time, in which case its grade will also worsen. On the flip side, there are a number of examples where coins submitted to grading services actually have "improved" in subsequent submissions by receiving higher grades. What all this goes to show is that even the experts have difficulty consistently identifying condition and that in grading, there are no absolutes.

The *American Numismatic Association Grading Guide* discusses numerous factors to take into account when judging coins. For example, the book recommends that a magnifying glass of 4- to 8-power should be used. A 10-power glass is likely to be too powerful and will show marks and imperfections on even the finest coin. In some instances the features on a coin may appear "weak" as a result of imperfections in the die used to strike the coin or because the die was worn at the time the coin was struck. Under the *ANA Grading Guide*, such characteristics do not lower the grade of the coin since they do not affect the coin's level of preservation. They are, however, to be noted separately along with the grade—for example, "MS-65, weakly struck."

In addition, the *ANA Grading Guide* discusses how to account for "toning," or the changes in a coin's natural color that take place naturally over time. It then states that "The presence or absence of light toning does not affect an Uncirculated coin's grade." As true as that may be, coloration or toning anecdotally affects price.

The ANA book also comments that the quality of "luster" on the coin, or "mint bloom," is an important factor in grading the coin and determining its value. Unattractive luster, such as when the coin is dull, spotty, or discolored, will normally lower the grade. Clearly, this adversely impacts price, though in some cases it can be artificially improved by a professional cleaning of the surface. "Slabs," or encapsulated grading, was a natural progression from a photo certificate used by the American Numismatic Association. The slab protects the coin and, once sealed, assures the integrity of the product.

To help you learn how to judge the grade of a state quarter yourself, visualize a ruler a foot long. At the "1" end of the ruler is a coin in poor condition; at the "11," uncirculated starts and each of the minor lines of an eighth or sixteenth of an inch constitutes a different uncirculated grade (uncirculated 60, uncirculated 61, uncirculated 62, and so forth).

For purposes of the 50 State Quarters program, it is perhaps more useful to focus on *how* a coin is graded, and *why* a coin might be classified as MS-62, MS-63, MS-64 or MS-65, since these are the coins that are most likely to be encountered.

Grading is a form of shorthand, with a numerical or adjectival term that is intended to describe the overall appearance and condition of a coin. It takes into account luster, the condition of the planchet, distractions on the surface such as scratches or minor chinks in the metal, signs of surface wear, the natural sheen that the coin exudes, and its overall visual appearance contrasted with other coins. As a coin enters commerce, it quite naturally comes in contact not only with other coins, but also with machinery that counts it, bags it, rolls it, and separates it, together with the hands of consumers that rub it, jingle it, and otherwise handle it. All of this creates a minor residue of metal that is removed from the surface, altering the "perfect" state of preservation that a coin typically starts with when it is produced by the United States Mint.

The minting process is a harsh one; strips of metal about 3 inches in width and many feet in length are fed into a blanking press which punches out a planchet that is blank on both sides. The metal at this point is too hard to be struck into a coin, so it has be annealed, or heat-treated, in ovens that reach temperatures of thousands of degrees. The heat-treated metal is then cleaned in a soapy solution and tumbled with ball bearings to clean off the surfaces. This already impregnates the surfaces with imperfections—but the next step in the process, which transforms the blank into a coin, both beautifies it and entombs the imperfections for eternity.

Blanks are placed in a hopper and fed into a coining press that applies several hundred tons of pressure to a planchet (or coin blank) where an obverse or front die meets a reverse die. The metal blank in the middle, when struck under pressure, flows outward to a collar. The edge is then reeded, if applicable, the design struck up, and the coin ejected. Assuming that there is not an error on the planchet, at this point in time the coin is pristine, but each ker-plink or ker-chunk that involves one coin coming into contact with another creates a flaw, and the minor flaws gradually, but cumulatively, start to detract from its overall condition.

As they enter the circulation pool, the vast majority of the uncirculated coins would be called somewhere between MS-60 and MS-63, fewer yet MS-65, and even fewer MS-67 or above. Of course, some fit grades that are in between, and some coins actually seem to be struck "uncirculated" with discernable wear, or with marks all over the planchet that bring down its overall condition. As coins remain in circulation, the metal begins to wear more subtly on the surface. For example, on the Delaware quarter, the head of Caesar Rodney or his knee, both high points in the design, may begin to flatten out, and other fine details may become obliterated. The curls on George Washington's wig or his chin may begin to show signs of blurring in the metal. All of these elements conspire to reduce the grade (and ultimately the value) of the coin.

There are certain common elements of the obverse design (the constant in the series) where wear is likely to be seen. The same is true for each of the other coins, though they must be described separately because their designs are different. On the reverse (the "state" side of the quarter), the date and E Pluribus Unum (Latin for "out of many, one") always appear at the 6 o'clock position of the coin, while the name of the state appears at the top, or 12 o'clock position, together with the date the state ratified the U.S. Constitution or joined the Union. The obverse with Washington's portrait is the constant in the series, and its signs of wear will be evident in the field opposite Washington's nose and above the national motto "In God we trust."

Regardless of which side of the coin is involved, there are certain general principles that are nearly universal. It is inevitably the high point of the coin design that will first show signs of wear, and will pick up the nicks and scrapes and minute metal particle alterations that change the condition of the coin. There is an easy way to visualize what takes place. Image that you have taken an 8½-by-11 sheet of paper and drawn a circle on it along with a design of George Washington. This is a "pure" MS-70 Coin. Take an 8½-by-11 sheet of tracing paper and put it over Washington's face, then take a light No. 2 pencil and shade a portion of his jaw and a portion of his curls. This is designed to simulate minor portions of wear. Next, take another sheet of tracing paper and put five or six dots in the left field opposite Washington's eyes. This is designed to simulate metal fatigue where the design has been damaged lightly by contact marks. Looking at the coin overall, it is not especially displeasing; this is probably the equivalent of uncirculated condition. If you remove the tracing paper with the shading on the chin and ear, it is now somewhere between MS-63 and MS-65, since there is no wear on the coin but some design damage of an infinitesimal degree.

The grading of America's state quarters is important, and ultimately, in future years, will have a substantial impact on their value. Indeed, it already has a significant impact. For example, the Delaware quarter that remains in change is probably in extremely fine condition at this point in time. It has little more value than its nominal legal-tender worth. Meanwhile a typical uncirculated coin (MS-62) is selling seven years after issue at $4 per coin. Examples in MS-68 are in a $2,000 price range, and the MS-70 is over $7,500.

Proof Quarters

Quite unlike the process of examining circulated coins for minor defects, proof coinage is made differently, looks very different, and in at least one respect is much easier to grade. Proof coins are struck on specially selected planchets that were previously cleaned in a cream of tartar solution that leaves them with a mirror-like sheen. They are produced on a hydraulic press that can strike several coins a minute at a maximum, contrasted with hundreds of coins a minute on a regular production press. Regular coins are struck just once, while proof coins are struck twice (or more) to bring up the design while simultaneously maintaining a mirror-like finish in the fields. Sometimes the design elements are struck in a mirror-like manner; other times they have a "matte" finish because of a production technique that has no effect on condition.

In the 21st century, virtually all proof coins, off the press and into the packet, will have a grade of at least Proof-65, and some will go higher quite easily. At an earlier time, even in the 20th century, mint production, storage, and coin interaction many times lowered the grade into the Proof-62 or Proof-63 range. It is always useful to remember that when it comes to the grades Proof-68, Proof-69, and Proof-70, there really aren't a lot of coins that merit these descriptions. Hence, even though the Mint might offer a proof set at $32.50 complete with the 50 State Quarters, a single state quarter 18 months out of production in Proof-68 condition typically had a $30 price tag, which means a five-fold return on the investment if all coins in the set were of the same grade and condition.

In Chapter 6, grading hints have been supplied for each coin that is in uncirculated condition. Generally, this section focuses on the high points of the coins, and shows how they wear. Even with this good information comes an important caveat: when coins are in circulation or come in contact with people or other coins, the mars, nicks, scratches, digs, and contact marks can show up in the darndest places. The third edge of a coin is its rim; it should always be examined for contact marks, although to be candid, a small "ding" on the rim has far less effect on the value of a coin than one on the facial element, in the field opposite the face, or in the large reverse field.

Traditionally, collectors have emphasized the condition of the obverse over the condition of the reverse. Thus, if a coin was MS-65 on the obverse and not quite as nice on the reverse, it probably would get a higher designation of MS-65. On the other hand, historically, if the reverse was MS-65 and the obverse was MS-63 or MS-64, it would *never* achieve an MS-65 grade.

As the program enters its 10th year, it is apparent because of the heavy focus on the 50 States portion of the program, that collectors will give far more emphasis to the reverse side of the series than to the obverse. The little "scratch" or the little "ding" or contact mark on the reverse will more likely have a greater substantive effect on condition than before.

4

MINT ERRORS

State quarter mint errors that you find in pocket change are like hitting the lottery. Find a state quarter mistakenly struck on a nickel planchet and you could be $1,500 richer. Find a state quarter with an orange color that signifies that the cladding was improperly applied at the Mint and your wallet could be $350 the better. Other errors are valued at less, and more, depending on type and availability.

Manufactured unintentionally for the most part at the U.S. Mint under tight security, mint errors have a long history dating back to the 1790s. Defects in the production process cause a mint error. It happens many times each day as it does in any factory, but most are caught by mint employees, and the coins are melted down before they ever leave the minting facility.

The difference between other factories and this one is that its mistakes are avidly sought after by collectors. There are massive quantities of quarters produced at the United States mints at Philadelphia, Denver, San Francisco and West Point (mintmarks P, D, S, and W). Instead of producing a quantity of 500,000 coins (the entire production of quarters from 1796 to 1814) in a long period of time, the Mint is making more than three million coins per eight-hour shift—six million quarters in a single day—which is what it takes to produce 420 million quarters in a ten-week period.

There's a fault ratio—so many errors per thousand coins produced—that is anticipated in any manufacturing operation, whether we're talking about widgets or coins. When produced by the Mint in such prodigious quantities with such frequency, the ratio doesn't change—but what does change is the quantity of Mint errors overall, and the chance that some will be discovered. With quarter designs changing every ten weeks, five times annually, instead of just once each January, the possibility for mistakes has quintupled.

Lincoln Memorial cents have been produced for about a half century (1959), Jefferson nickels since 1938, and Roosevelt dimes since 1946. The statehood quarter's duration is a mere ten weeks for each design. Thus, for the first time in recent memory, mint engravers have made leaves on fauna (plants) different—high, low, and "normal"—with two for the Wisconsin statehood quarter.

WISCONSIN QUARTER. THE ARROW POINTS TO THE LEAF THAT WAS ENGRAVED HIGH AND LOW IN ERROR.

Maybe they added a tree to the crowded design and missed it in the review phase for the Minnesota statehood design. Other times coins are struck on the wrong planchet—a Florida or Pennsylvania quarter design struck on the copper-nickel stock of a five-cent coin. Look at it quickly, and it looks normal. Examine it more closely and view a 21.2mm diameter planchet (nickel-sized) versus a 24.3mm quarter-sized planchet. The difference is 3.1mm—or about 0.1168 inches. That silly millimeter longer represents a $1,500 price difference.

While there is no reliable count on their number, error dealer and specialist Fred Weinberg has spotted and sold wrong-planchet state-hood quarters from Delaware (the most common), Pennsylvania (only about six are known), New Jersey, Georgia, and Connecticut—all in the first year of production. More errors followed in 2000 and 2001. In 2003, Illinois had five state quarters struck on a nickel planchet and Maine had one. The following year, only Florida had an off-planchet design; only about six—all struck on nickel planchets—are known.

The granddaddy of all state quarter errors is the $1.25 coin—a state quarter married to a Sacagawea dollar coin. (Some would call this a dollar coin error, but the coin is demonstrably part of the statehood quarter series by virtue of its design). With a state quarter obverse (undated) and a Sacagawea die reverse (also no date), there's no way of telling exactly when it was produced, but the price is well known: $56,300 in a May 2001 Heritage coin auction.

The catalogued sale of the most valuable statehood quarter mint error is a Philadelphia Mint–manufactured 2000-P $1 Sacagawea dollar muled with a state quarter dollar of unknown date. "Mules" or "muling errors" of rare patterns and restrikes were produced intentionally during the 19th century and have long been known to exist. Heritage's view as cataloger and auctioneer is that "A mule that combines the obverse and reverse of two different denominations would seem to be the most unusual mistake that can be made in the Mint."

A $1.25 FACE VALUE STATE QUARTER; THIS "MULE" WITH THE STATE QUARTER OBVERSE AND SACAGAWEA DOLLAR REVERSE HAS SOLD FOR OVER $55,000.

Struck on a dollar planchet in the Philadelphia Mint, the mule (and its owner, Jeff Allen who bought it on eBay for $41,295) were featured on the Discovery Channel's "The Best Kept Secrets of Money," broadcast on March 15, 2001. A muling error on a circulating American coin was unknown until this piece was discovered and, as such, it represents a numismatic discovery of the greatest importance.

Despite some initial speculation that the mule may have been intentionally produced by a Mint employee, on June 19, 2001, the U.S. Mint issued a press release acknowledging the Sacagawea dollar–Washington quarter mule as a legitimate error. Apparently, it was produced when an obverse Sacagawea die cracked, and was accidentally replaced by a quarter obverse die. Upon discovery by Mint employees, several thousand mules were apparently retrieved and destroyed.

Another error on the quarter is the overstrike (worth $3,200). Heritage sold one in 2006, also from the Philadelphia Mint: a 2000-P $1 Sacagawea Dollar—a double denomination on a struck Maryland quarter. That coin was described as a lustrous "superb gem," beautifully preserved and toned in lovely steel-blue and chestnut colors. Although well struck, traces of the Maryland quarter undertype remain visible. The 2000 date from the undertype is visible beneath the Sacagawea mintmark, and a tree branch from the Maryland design is seen on her shoulder beneath the slumbering baby.

Yet another error is the Sacagawea dollar struck on a state quarter blank planchet—a $2,760 item at a Heritage May 2007 auction that again came from the Philadelphia Mint: a 2000-P $1 Sacagawea Dollar struck on a 25-cent planchet. The confirming factor is the weight of 5.7 grams, making this an off-metal error that was both well struck and fully lustrous, with a hint of gold toning to the pristine surfaces. The rims are broad and have a stretched appearance, where metal struggled to reach the collar.

The commonality of the Philadelphia Mint soon caught the attention of authorities. It was discovered that between December 1998 and March 2000, U.S. Mint press operator David J. D'Angelo was making and then stealing pennies, nickels, dimes, and other coins that were accidentally minted incorrectly—"error coins" that bring high prices from coin collectors. Assistant U.S. Attorney Maryanne T. Donaghy said

"D'Angelo made about $80,000 selling the stolen coins to collectors and Internet auctioneers before he was caught." He pleaded guilty and was sentenced to six months imprisonment, two years supervised probation and an $80,000 fine.

The timing of the arrest cast doubt on some legitimate errors that have crept out of the Mint in the last several months and even cast doubt on blanks that have made it through the process without the design being imprinted.

Let's look at some hypothetical questions. In producing a proof set, the engraving staff of the Mint overlooks something tiny—a mintmark—and creates a low mintage rarity. It goes out in the mail but is discovered, and a furious recall takes place. Can it be legally held? Probably yes.

When does the quarter stop being property of the U.S. government? Through the years, the Mint has given conflicting answers to the question, as have United States attorneys in various districts, when the cases involving them have been prosecuted.

Where the government has the least difficulty, it seems, is when they actually release an item directly—even with an error. When they attempt a recall, they can stop it even if it has been placed in the mail. Once the coin is out, however, the Mint will generally support the right of collectors to own it, provided the coin made it out of the Mint legally.

According to error and die variety expert Alan Herbert, who has been writing about Mint errors for more than a quarter century, "I can make the general statement that any of the 460-plus classes of minting varieties that have previously been found on the [non-state] clad quarters will . . . [eventually] be found on the state quarters." Bill Fivaz, another maven in the error field who served with me on the board of governors of the American Numismatic Association, and also devotes considerable energy to the field of errors and varieties, agrees with Herbert that there will be new error coins to collect, though he disagrees on the terminology.

"I, along with 99 percent of the other error/variety collectors/dealers, have a real problem with Alan's use of 'variety' for everything in the P-D-S system. We feel 'variety' is confined to die aberrations, while 'error' is associated with planchet and striking abnormalities."

Regardless of the terminology utilized, the reason why many of these errors (or varieties, if you will) can occur is that mint personnel are used to looking at designs on four or five circulating coins that don't vary in design from year to year. Reverse designs that change every 10 weeks, by contrast, are something new to look at—and to figure out. Consequently, it is problematical in the first element of quality control: visual review of the product.

There are a number of different types of general errors that affect all coins, including the state quarters, though the one that brought state quarters to page one of the daily press turned out to be a rotated die (180-degree rotation) that was erroneously valued at $500 or more.

Common Mint Errors

Errors can occur at almost any time during the production process, though there are far fewer today than in the past. Die errors, lettering mistakes, doubled dies, and even one date cut over another, are all errors from the past unlikely to occur in the State Quarters program.

What is more likely are striking mistakes, where a coin blank moves off-center and is improperly struck, or is struck twice before it is ejected from the coining press, and these have become the truly interesting coins that many collectors seek.

What's exciting about errors and die varieties is that they are scarce, even rare—and hence valuable—but they are also available by searching your change, or searching through bags of the new state quarters that can be acquired (at face value) from many banks.

Here's a listing of general classifications of mint errors known to have appeared on state quarters, with a brief explanation of how the error was created and (where there are known prices) a general sense of the value of the mistake.

Alan Herbert devised a planchet (P), die (D), and striking (S) method of cataloguing errors, which is easy for serious collectors to remember because it mimics the three main mints and their mint marks: Philadelphia, Denver, and San Francisco. He starts with planchet varieties such as **improper alloy mixtures (1)**, meaning that the copper-nickel mixture is off from the standard. This can be measured chemically, but more often is seen visually and confirmed by weighing the coin (the weight will differ depending on alloyed composition). Typically, this increases the value of a coin like the state quarter 20 to 50 times face value. Die variety specialist Bill Fivaz reports, "I have two Georgia quarters that have improper metal mixture in the clad layers—specific gravity is way off, and they look very dark—so it has occurred on the state quarters."

Another type is the **damaged or defective planchet (2)**, which is the blank upon which the coin is impressed. Variations on this include planchets whose cladding simply isn't properly produced, metal flaws including gas bubbles trapped in the metal, planchets rolled too thin, and even an undersized planchet or one that is elliptical. These have not been widely seen, but an elliptical Massachusetts 2000-P in choice brilliant uncirculated condition recently carried a $400 price tag.

Clipped planchets (3) are yet another type. Clips come in all sizes and shapes and price ranges. A 1999-D Delaware quarter, 4-percent clip (i.e., 96 percent of the design remains with a small thumbnail size portion clipped away) carried a $75 price tag in a recent price list. A Delaware double clip (7 percent total) saw a $125 asking price. A 20-percent corner clip on a New Jersey quarter (1999-D) had a $600 price tag. A 15-percent double clip New Jersey runs $15; a 9-percent double clip from Georgia is listed at $110, while a triple clip ($125) from Georgia is a $140 coin. A Connecticut double clip (12 percent) sells for $115. A double-clipped Massachusetts (22 percent) carries a $325 price tag. And so on.

A DOUBLE-CLIPPED NEW JERSEY QUARTER.

Lamination flaws or split and broken planchets (4) are yet another major type of error. Foreign substances become trapped in a bad alloy mixture. This includes clad coinage with missing clad layer (fairly scarce) and can be on one side or both. (Bill Fivaz, the error expert, notes, "I don't recall ever seeing both clad layers split off . . . it's usually one or the other.") A Minnesota 2005 obverse clad layer missing was recently available at $475; with the reverse missing, it's a $750 coin.

Next is a **wrong stock planchet (5),** for example a state quarter struck on planchet of a nickel. Just three millimeters in size difference makes this a tough one to spot visually since it's less than one-sixth of an inch in diameter. Delaware is the most common (it is still a scarce item), but in general, anything post-2004 is very scarce.

The way it most likely happens is that a nickel blank gets mixed into the state quarter bin accidently, or a blank is picked up off the floor and pitched into the coining bin. These are neat coins when you compare

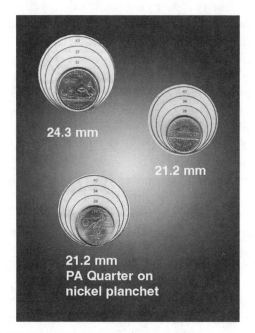

THE PENNSYLVANIA NICKEL. STATE QUARTER STRUCK ON 5¢ NICKEL STOCK.

them side-by-side with a regular state quarter. No two are alike in terms of what is shown; it's the luck of the draw. **Extra metal on the planchet ("cud") (6)** is yet another possibility and occurs on approximately one-fifth of all state quarters; Bill Fivaz defines this as "a piece of the die breaking away, leaving a void, causing the planchet metal to ooze into the cavity, creating an unstruck blob on the coin." In the summer of 2007, a Kentucky 2001 with a cudmark was quoted (uncertified) at $40.

Yet another choice is a **blank (7),** which for the state quarters is indistinguishable from any other clad quarter coin. A **near blank (8)** is a 98-percent off-center strike.

Within the production process, there are more types of die varieties than can be easily imagined. Die varieties generally do not produce a unique coin; they produce errors into the hundreds of thousands of pieces, for the life of the die (though it may vary by degree or sharpness). Many of the traditional varieties that a true collector will seek in other series to "cherry-pick," by examining a design closely and picking out differences, are unlikely to occur for the state quarters. One reason for this is that the production process has changed.

Bill Fivaz comments that focusing on letters of "Liberty" and looking for difference might work on Lincoln cents, but it is unlikely to work for the state quarters. In his book, *The Cherrypickers' Guide to Rare Die Varieties*, he writes, "To my knowledge, no significant die varieties have been reported, and chances are slim to none that there will ever be any since (1) the mint marks are now put on the galvano, eliminating repunched mint marks and/or over mint marks, and (2) the dies are now produced with a 'single squeeze' process, ostensibly taking doubled dies, etc. right out of the picture."

If the rush to make dies creates errors in the hubbing process, however, transferring one die from the master could cause varieties—it just either hasn't, yet, or it has not been noticed. Time will tell on this one.

Striking varieties (9) are widely known, and can be expensive. This is where the coin has the die strike in more than one location, causing multiple images to appear, and inevitably causing the coin to be misshaped in appearance. One of the most expensive ones to come to

light, so far, is a quadruple strike where strikes two, three, and four are about 35-percent off-center. The Pennsylvania quarter struck at least 26 times (15 main strikes, 11 secondary strikes) was recently quoted at more than $3,200.

Off-center strikes are also widely collected and known for all series of the state quarters. Depending on the degree a coin is off-center, it can have more or less value. *A Minor Off-Center* error is a coin struck between five- and 10-percent off center—easily visible to the eye— with areas of blank planchet visible.

To be a true off-center strike, some design elements must be missing. If no part of the design is missing, it is also collectible, but has a different name: a *broadstrike*. If the coin looks somewhat off-center, but has no design elements missing, it is considered an *uncentered broadstrike*. The broadstruck coins are popular but relatively inexpensive to acquire. (But finding one in pocket change generally will produce a $50 coin value).

"Live Free or Die" is the New Hampshire state motto seen on this rare off-center strike.

A major off-center error is similar to a minor one, except more of it is involved (generally 15 percent to 85 percent). For example, a 98-percent off-center state quarter (you can tell from the lettering that it is a state quarter and not the earlier Washington variety) is a $50 coin. A 10-percent off-center North Carolina is a $115 coin; a Virginia 20 percent off-center is a $250 item.

Some daily periodicals claim a *rotated reverse die* is worth thousands of dollars. A rotated reverse die is when a coin is viewed with its obverse design running from the 6 o'clock position to the 12 o'clock position. On coins, when the obverse is looked at, the lower portion is at 6 o'clock, upper portion at 12 o'clock. At the very same time, the reverse is oriented differently. If you turn the coin over sideways, right to left, the "top" of the design is at 6 o'clock, and the bottom at 12 o'clock. On the other hand, if you pick the coin up at 6 o'clock and flip upwards towards 12 o'clock, the reverse now can be seen in a correct rather than inverted view. (By contrast, a medal works in exactly the opposite way—when you rotate it, each side faces upward in the same direction).

Alan Herbert does offer a word of caution and urges that if someone wants to buy the mint errors, that they proceed cautiously—and with the advice of an expert dealer to assist them. "Better issue a stern warning not to buy coins, especially minting varieties on the lay auctions on the Internet. There is one right now asking a minimum bid of $350,000 for a 1943 cent which has been put on a buffing wheel until it is nearly unrecognizable as a coin. The buyer must demand certification, preferably by one of the . . . experts and not some of the third-party grading services, as they are still screwing up listings, mislabeling, and misattributing."

And of course there are other errors, too, for example: **Obverse clad missing/reverse clad missing.** Almost without exception, statehood quarters with one layer of cladding missing find their way into circulation. The coin side with the clad covering missing is usually a copper red and the coin is thinner and weighs less than its typical version. If you don't examine coins carefully, it's an error easy to miss. A state quarter without a level of cladding found in pocket change routinely sells in the secondary market for $300 or more and is detectable by sight, weight, and by

careful checking with a caliper. Missing cladding on the front or obverse (the Washington portrait) is worth about half of what a coin is valued at if the lack of cladding gives the reddish tinge to the statehood design.

Brockage is the technical term for multiple descriptions of what coins are called when two are in the coining chamber at the same time, either as struck coins or planchets, or as a combination (coin and planchet). **Struck through** coins covers objects or material that may come between the blank planchet and the die, and hence are struck into the surface of the coin. Cloth, thread, wire, dirt, and grease, or even a planchet fragment are included here. The worth of such a strike is modest (80 times face value is not a bad return, anyhow).

Herbert speaks to several more errors: "Filled dies are quite common, but no more so than on previous quarters. To have value they must be on uncirculated grade (MS-60 or higher) coins...." Visibility under intense magnification is also required, but as Herbert points out, "Many

BROCKAGE

'finds' have turned out to be either reflection doubling—caused by reflections off the newly minted surface—or machine doubling damage, from the die bouncing on the struck coin."

Fred Weinberg, the rare coin dealer (and error coin collector) who also specializes in selling error coins, offers his own interpretation: "In my opinion, to have value, the filled die area must be visible with the naked eye, and cover at least 25 to 35 percent of the coin (one side or the other, not combined)."

Regardless, have fun with this method of collecting—and watch and check your pocket change! You could find it truly worthwhile.

5

HOW TO COLLECT AND INVEST IN AMERICA'S STATE QUARTERS

Many people enjoy casually collecting America's state quarters from pocket change. But what if you want to collect the quarters for investment purposes? What do you need to know? Should you try to collect a set, or will individual acquisitions reap better rewards?

If you want to collect state quarters for investment purposes, acquiring them from pocket change—except for numismatic errors—is simply not the way to go. On the other hand, those interested in investing might want to look at high-grade state quarters in MS-68 and higher. Later in this book, I have rated all currently issued quarters and given my recommendations for investment partners.

To invest in coins you need to know mintage and survivability in a variety of conditions, principally those of MS-68 and above. For a modern series like state quarters, the number of coins certified by the major grading services is a substantial assistance. These are coins that should be acquired individually, not as a set, and it is obvious from the current price history that they have a bright future.

Really, there's no "correct" way to collect coins. When I started collecting coins nearly a half-century ago, I began because I found a 1906 Indian Head cent in pocket change and was fascinated by it. So when

1906 INDIAN HEAD CENT

the statehood quarters came along, I decided to collect from pocket change—but not in the traditional way of one of every date and mint-mark. I figured that one date and design was sufficient, so that a 50-coin collection would be complete.

To assist in the process, I bought a commercial album that had one slot for each state—50 in all—and began to fill them up. After awhile, I wanted to collect more and got a Littleton album that allowed me to put in both Philadelphia and Denver, and to have room for proof "S" San Francisco as well as silver proof coins. It's all about what you want to do and what you can afford.

Here are some general ways to group sets of state quarters:

- The complete set by date (56 coins), mintmark (168 coins), metal composition (additional 56 coins), method of strike (proofs, an additional 56 coins)

- Roll Sets (which come from the bank in $10 increments or 40 coins of one type and mintmark)

- By design, such as those showing state maps: Pennsylvania, Georgia, South Carolina, Ohio, Indiana, Louisiana, Illinois, Michigan, Texas, Minnesota, etc.

- By theme: natural phenomena, such as the Connecticut charter oak tree; New Hampshire's late Old Man of the Mountain; Vermont maple trees; animals, such as Delaware's horse bearing Caesar Rodney; South Carolina's Carolina wren; Louisiana's pelican; Wisconsin's cow; the California eagle; or historical figures, such as Delaware's Caesar Rodney, New Jersey's Washington crossing the Delaware, the Massachusetts Minuteman, Ohio's Neil Armstrong, Illinois' Lincoln, Alabama's Helen Keller, California's John Muir, etc.

- By designer (sculptor, engraver)

- By time frame (i.e., 2004–2005, or some other arrangement). One of the first modern coin collectors, Joseph Mickley, started out seeking coins from his birth year, 1799.

- By circulated coin issues (i.e., Philadelphia and Denver, a 100-coin set) or of a single mint

- By proof coin (such as "S" mint only; 50-coin set)

- By condition (say, MS-68 or proof 68, 69 or 70—the higher the more valuable)

- By error: there are an amazing number of double and triple struck state quarter coins, and a collection of them, although expensive to acquire, is fascinating to look at side by side.

- With other coins struck in honor of one or more of the 50 states. The U.S. Mint, at the behest of Congress, struck commemorative coins honoring the statehood of a number of states, ending with Iowa in 1946. These include: Alabama, Arkansas, California, Connecticut, Delaware, Illinois, Iowa, Maine, Maryland, Missouri, Oregon, Rhode Island, Texas, Vermont, and Virginia.

If your goal is to acquire a set of uncirculated MS-70 state quarters, one of each date and mintmark—the best of the best—unfortunately, you're probably in for a disappointment. The Professional Coin Grading Service (PCGS) has certified only 28 MS-70 coins of all dates and mintmarks *combined* for all statehood quarters minted 1999–2007; seven of them are Oregon, nine are California, the rest one coin here, one coin there. Numismatic Guaranty Corp. (NGC) has certified a handful as MS-70, as has ANACS. However, you can collect state quarters as certified coins of a certain grade. A set of "among the best" of the best available would cost more than $15,000, or an average of between $140 to $180 a coin.

A substantial and worthwhile collection of America's state quarters can be assembled from coins produced by the U.S. Mint as proof or specimen coinage, and also in high-grade (MS-66 and above) uncirculated issues. The proofs are intended primarily for coin collectors, and the uncirculated versions are taken carefully from circulation—but even if you aren't a collector, it's a series that you ought to give consideration to. Two different versions of proofs are available—one in copper-nickel clad, the other in coin silver (90 percent fine); each is sold initially only by the U.S. Mint at a fixed price. A substantial secondary market has developed, based primarily on the condition of the coins. These coins—and the very high-grade uncirculated pieces as well—have significant investment potential that some have already realized and others may seek to examine or at least consider in the coming years.

Created and sold by the Mint in sets, the coins have been broken out of the holders of issue and submitted to one or more independent grading services, where the better ones have been found to be Proof-65 at a minimum, all the way up to Proof-70 (the best grade). They have then been remarketed to the collecting public and those interested in making an investment choice in America's state quarters, at prices substantially in excess of the initial offering price from the Mint.

All proof coins are not created equal; most produced by the U.S. Mint today grade a minimum of Proof-65 on the grading scale (Proof-60 to Proof-70 is what is generally used; if a proof coin goes into circulation, it can grade Proof-58 or lower; none of the proof coins produced had entered circulation, and in any event, circulated modern proof coins are generally not collectible, absent a mint error to substantially enhance their value).

Prices for the proof coins being sold on the secondary market are extraordinary, not only in advertisements found in the commercial trade press such as *Numismatic News, Coin World, COINage* magazine, and *Coins* magazine, but also in online auctions such as Teletrade (the oldest service of its kind, which has more than 300 auctions involving more than 300,000 coins). The good news is, if you really want a "70," there are relatively large quantities in proof-70. Proof coins are more forgiving when it comes to perfection—and there are a six-figure worth of certified coins, where the uncirculated model, with hundreds of millions of coins to choose from, has few.

Storing Your Collection

Once you decided to collect America's state quarters, it's important to learn how to care for them. The reason for this is that the proper preservation of your quarters can have a substantial impact on their value.

Even coins that are put away in a desk drawer and never touched again can be damaged by the paper inside the drawer that begins to chemically decompose and let off the gaseous elements necessary to help along the tarnishing process. (Tarnish is metallic oxidation that actually damages the surface of a coin). Coins that are put into drawers, socks, or jars have a different problem—they can have nicks, dings, or scratches imparted onto their surface, resulting in a substantial diminution of value.

THE PROPER WAY TO HOLD A COIN—BETWEEN YOUR FINGERS.

Use of a coin holder may have its own problems, if you are not careful. There are some very fancy (and otherwise very fine) commercial holders that place the quarters in a solid cardboard frame with an acetate shield covering the coin to protect it from damage. That's all well and good, but if the quarter is not seated properly in the cardboard cutout, the acetate passing over the coin can cause a "slide mark" which can touch a high spot and cause minor but significant wear that lowers a quarter's value.

Or suppose you take a quarter out of its carefully crafted holder and drop it on the floor. That could cause soft metal to be moved (lowering the value of the coin). Perhaps when you pick up the quarter, you cannot grasp it by the edge, and instead allow your fingers to grasp the coin's surface. The natural oil from your fingers can impart onto the coin's surface, and eventually etch itself right in, damaging the coin. To avoid this, hold the quarter by the edge only, using your thumb and index finger.

So what can you do to preserve a quarter's condition? First, air and moisture are the enemy, and even high humidity in some areas of the country can cause damage to metal. If your coins are stored in a sealed container (such as a safe-deposit box), a moisture-absorbing packet can be very useful. (These are the same packages that are found in the stereo box that you just opened, or in some other electronic devices, to protect them until consumers open the package). They are available commercially at many hardware stores.

When handling quarters, do so either with fingertip sheaths on, or disposable polyethylene gloves. That avoids the possibility of fingerprints on the coin. Also, place beneath quarters that you are handling a soft velvet or foam pad; that way you won't suffer a serious economic loss if you drop a coin accidentally.

Short-term Storage

There are a number of popular albums available for housing the quarters as a series. An inexpensive cardboard die-cut without protection for the quarters costs around $4. Two popular brands are Whitman and Littleton. I would not recommend this for serious collectors—the quarters can be scratched by the cardboard and are exposed to the elements. However, for casual collecting, this is a solid option. I have one at home and one in the office, and am enjoying using it to collect the series out of pocket change without a lot of regard for condition.

For the more serious collector, there are a number of inexpensive commercial products that you can use to satisfactorily store your coins. There is the acid-free paper holder (2 inches by 2 inches square), which looks like a miniature envelope. These usually cost less than two to five cents apiece and can conveniently hold a coin without damaging it. You can write a description of the contents with a soft pencil.

There are also cardboard 2 × 2 holders with cellophane inserts that cover the quarter; they are usually held together with a staple (staple carefully—many a coin has been damaged by a staple mark that overshot the intended target). These are usually available at five to ten cents apiece, or less.

There are also soft vinyl holders. Be cautious that you do not place a state quarter in a soft vinyl holder that contains polyvinyl chloride (PVC). The chemicals in the PVC respond to heat and time, and can leach onto the surface of the coin, damaging it and destroying the value of an otherwise fine coin.

Some rigid vinyl-type holders in clear plastic have no PVC and work quite well in holding coins. They are 2 × 2 inches in size, and generally

STATE QUARTER IN HOLDER, STAPLED. THIS HOLDER COSTS ABOUT 2¢.

cost around 6 cents apiece. There are also vinyl pages that encase 2 × 2 holders (again watch for PCV that can leach onto the surface) as well as coin wallets with pockets that range from 18 to 60 coins.

There are inert plastic holders that fit tightly around the quarter, preventing air from getting in, and also protecting the surface of the coin. One of the better-known brands is the E&T Kointainer, made of Mylar, approximately 30 cents each. More rigid plastic containers, 2 × 2 in size and made from a mold that allows for the quarter to be fitted exactly, are available for around 70 cents apiece.

Commercially produced holders that the various grading services use are also available. The added benefit to purchasing one of these is that the quarter is also graded for you. There are a variety of rates that can be charged for this, but most are under $25.

The better the condition of the quarter you acquire, the better the holder should be to prevent it from being scratched or jostled— preferably some type of unsealed holder that can handle coins in quantity without damaging them. There are cardboard holders with a thin acetate covering the round hole that keeps coins sealed in called "flips"

1999 P 25C
DELAWARE
MS 68
1987538-002

NUMISMATIC GUARANTY CORPORATION

PCGS HOLDER. THE GRADING SERVICE CHARGES ABOUT $20 FOR GRADE AND HOLDER.

after the crease and fold in their design. You can keep statehood coins a in holder for quarters or use one for half- or large-sized dollars (either side). In an emergency, the new small-sized dollar holders for presidential dollars would also work—they are only about 3 millimeters larger than the Susan B. Anthony dollar, the Sacagawea coin, and its presidential successors.

Here is a summary of some of the holder alternatives available for statehood quarters, along with estimated unit cost:

- 2 × 2 paper holder   around 2–5¢ each in quantity

- 2 × 2 pocket flip vinyl   around 8–10¢ each in quantity

- screw top coin tube for rolls of 40   around 50¢ round; 75¢ square

- 2 × 2 staple-type holder   around 6¢ each in quantity

- 2 × 2 rigid plastic   around 75¢ each (individual)

Long-term Storage

If you're contemplating long-term storage, the chemical composition of your holder becomes important. First, some plastics—especially soft ones—leach onto a coin's surface. This is generally a soft plastics issue with PVC, or polyvinyl chloride.

There are a number of popular albums available to house the quarters as a series. A die cut album with acetate sleeves affords full protection, and costs around $25. Two popular brands, Whitman and Littleton, are good options.

The U.S. Mint did its part. Its 2004 annual report discloses that "During Financial Year 2004, the United States Mint signed new licensing agreements. . . . At the same time, we maintained existing licensing agreements with Whitman Publishing Company (formerly, H.E. Harris & Co.) to distribute Coin folders and holders for 50 State Quarters®, Golden Dollars and other coin-related products in outlets such as Borders, Walden Books, Wal-Mart, and Target; with Peak Capital Group to distribute albums that hold 50 State Quarters®; and with Wonderland Marketing to distribute various products that incorporate 50 State Quarters®, the 50 State Quarters® Logo and Greetings from America stamp images...." These library-style albums allow for convenient access to the state quarter coins and permit them to be substituted (a better conditioned coin for another) or even examined at close scrutiny to discover a minting error.

I maintain an inexpensive album (die-cut cardboard that folds up so that it is enclosed) in my office, so I can pick coins out of change and

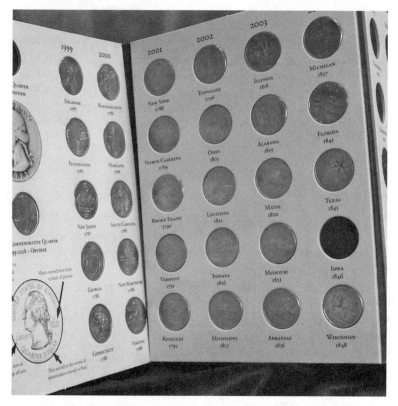

ONE METHOD OF STORAGE OF STATE QUARTERS IS THIS COIN ALBUM.

add them to my collection. This has space for a single design only, one date, one mintmark, and no specific mint errors. It has worked out fine. I also have a library-style album for a more complete set, with Philadelphia and Denver mint uncirculated coins.

One area that I focus on is error statehood quarters, including those specimens struck on the wrong planchet and double-struck coins. I have PCGS or NGC holders for most of those, and they are kept in a plastic box which in turn stays in safe-deposit boxes maintained at the bank.

The other state quarter coins that I have are generally kept in 2 × 2 envelopes with acetate that are stapled. Though quarter-size is available, I use old-fashioned silver dollar–size (1½ inches diameter, 38.1 mm). There's more than enough room left to write commentary or catalogue information. Though some use three staples so that the coin cannot exit, I generally prefer to staple the two open sides and allow the top to remain open and free. The coin can then easily be removed and there is no real fear of scratching the coin with the staple, or with a piece of cardboard punched through with a staple that is removed.

Again, for convenience, the 2 × 2 holders not from a grading service are all kept by me in cardboard boxes that are designed to hold the 2 × 2 holders. About 100 coin holders (and coins) generally can fit in a box which typically is between 7 and 8 inches long.

Storage in boxes should be pursuant to some methodology. You could, for example, do it alphabetically by state, by year, in the chronological order in which the coins were issued—any way that makes sense to *you* so that it can be retrieved quickly and conveniently should you need to do so.

You should also maintain a record of the coins you acquire and their condition (or third-party grade), either manually, on your personal computer as part of a word processing or spreadsheet program, or utilizing one of many collection maintenance programs, some of which include valuations. A copy should be retained in a safe place off the premises where the list is created, for security reasons such as robbery, fire, or clerical inadvertence.

6

STATE QUARTER LISTINGS

Template for the State Quarter Listings

In this chapter you'll find information on each of the 50 state quarters. We've utilized a common template to facilitate finding information. Below is the template with explanations for each section. A significant amount of technical data was obtained from The Statistical Abstract of the United States, an official publication of the Department of Commerce. Some of its data differ from encyclopedias, particularly as to the area of a state and how it ranks.

STATE, YEAR OF ISSUE: The subject state and the date of coinage as circulated. Coins struck in 1998 but issued in 1999 are listed as 1999.

State Information

YEAR OF STATEHOOD: year of entry into the Union

ORDER IN UNION: the numerical order (1–50) in which the state entered the Union

SIZE: square miles (rank out of 50 states)

POPULATION: estimated population as of April 2008 U.S. Census Bureau data

STATE MOTTO: motto (if the state has one)

STATE FLOWER: flower (if the state has one)

STATE BIRD: bird (if the state has one)

STATE TREE: tree (if the state has one)

Coin Specifications

MINTMARKS: the mint where the coin was issued, either "P" (Philadelphia), "D" (Denver), "S" (San Francisco), or "W" (West Point)

OBVERSE DESIGNER: name of the sculptor. This will be the same for all entries.

REVERSE DESIGNER: name of the sculptor (and designer when known).

OBVERSE DESIGN: portrait of George Washington, after Houdon, by John Flanagan, modified by William Cousins (1997). Above bust of Washington: United States of America. Beneath Washington's chin: "Liberty," which has appeared on every U.S. coin produced since the Mint Act of April 2, 1792. Beside Washington's hair braid: national motto "In God We Trust." Below neckline: "Quarter Dollar." On side of neckline: two initials, "JF" (John Flanagan), "WC" (William Cousins). (This information is the same for all entries, so we have only supplied it once here.)

REVERSE DESIGN: specifies design with certain common elements on every coin. At top: state name; beneath, date entered Union. At bottom: date of issue; beneath, motto "E Pluribus Unum" (Out of many, one), describing how the divided colonies became the United States of America. (Up to here, same for all entries.) State design: specified.

Design History

History of how the reverse design was chosen. The typical process for each state was as follows:

The state selects three to five concepts that are submitted to the U.S. Mint. Engravers at the Mint develop these into the design concepts. The CCCAC and the Fine Arts Commission review the three to five designs and make recommendations to the state. Following this process the designs are sent back to the state to make their final selection. It is up to the state how this final selection is made; some states let the public get involved in this final process while others just have the governor make the selection. This final selection is then sent back to the Secretary of Treasury for ratification. The legislative bill is very clear that the Secretary of Treasury will make the final selection. The U.S. Mint *must* receive unconditional rights to *all* elements in the design.

We also include in this section an illustration of one of the designs not selected.

Mintage Figures

PROOF initial mintages estimated

UNCIRCULATED "P" initial mintages approximated

UNCIRCULATED "D" initial mintages approximated

Price Record

The price record examines auction sales of coins (certified by PCGS, NGC, or other recognized grading services) that are conducted online or in a traditional auction sale. Two popular auctions are Heritage and Teletrade, which you will see indicated throughout. For the most part, the price records sought are for circulation strikes, rather than proofs. Every Philadelphia and Denver mint coin is covered (112 in all). The majority of sales are recent, and astonishingly, as of the beginning of 2008, a collection of highest-price circulation strikes combined exceeds $30,000; many of these coins are certified MS-69 or MS-70.

The breakdown will look like this:

PRICE:

DATE OF ISSUE:

GRADING SERVICE:

DATE OF SALE:

AUCTIONEER:

Common Errors and Values

All error coins have certain descriptive characteristics, and although the pricing varies from coin to coin, many coins have similar or equal values for a certain type of error. Error pricing in this book is courtesy of Fred Weinberg, who has priced many state quarters for the author's collection. He is competitive within the marketplace, and a renowned expert on all numismatic errors.

For each state quarter you will find error pricing for the following:

NOT STRUCK ON QUARTER PLANCHET: a statehood quarter design on the planchet of another denomination. On a nickel, or five-cent coin, the value might be about $850. There are other examples, frequently spectacular, with much higher prices.

DOUBLE STRUCK: struck twice. For statehood quarters, as well as other points, a doubly struck coin has high value, but not as high as a coin struck three or four times.

OBVERSE/REVERSE CLAD MISSING: either the top (nickel-colored) or core copper layer is missing

OFF CENTER: to those unacquainted with collecting errors, off-center coins are among the most striking and visually appealing. They are measured in degrees, for example 5-percent off-center, which is minor, whereas 35 percent is major. The major off-center strike is scarcer and priced accordingly.

ROTATED REVERSE: the reverse text/illustration does not match up with the positioning of the obverse side.

BROCKAGE: when an item gets in the way of the coin manufacture and alters the coin (i.e., a nail falls onto the machinery and becomes part of the coin)

BROADSIDE: the "pancake" effect

PARTIAL COLLAR: when only part of the rim is raised

STRUCK THROUGH: a hole in the coin

CLIPPED: part of the coin is cut off

Grading Hints

OBVERSE: the high points of the coin's obverse are prone to wear; the field off Washington's nose, and the area behind the head curls are prone to contact marks. Wear is most likely to be evident on the hair above Washington's ear and the cheekbones. (Same for all entries.)

REVERSE: At top: state name; beneath, date entered Union. At bottom, date of issue; beneath, motto "E Pluribus Unum" (Out of many, one), describing how the divided colonies became the United States of America. (Same for all entries.)

STATE DESIGN ON REVERSE: different on each.

Investment Potential

The investment potential for state quarters boils down to condition, mintage, the number of coins encapsulated in plastic ("slabbed"), and market scarcity. While past performance is no guarantee of future performance, and prices and other events change results, my formula for rating investment potential is as follows:

I have prepared an extensive analysis that involves ranking more than 90 state coins in mintage order. Using data from auction sales records from the beginning of the State Quarters program through today, I ranked the coins (P and D) in rarity according to the ratio of where they fell among the total number of coins surveyed. The closer the ranking is to 1, the higher the investment potential.

DELAWARE

STATE, YEAR OF ISSUE: Delaware, 1999

State Information

YEAR OF STATEHOOD: 1787
ORDER IN UNION: 1
SIZE: 2,396 sq. mi.
POPULATION: 864,000
STATE MOTTO: "Liberty and Independence"
STATE FLOWER: peach blossom
STATE BIRD: blue hen chicken
STATE TREE: American holly

Coin Specifications

MINTMARKS: P, D, S
OBVERSE DESIGNER: John Flanagan, modified by William Cousins (1997)
REVERSE DESIGNER: William Cousins, after a design by Eddy Seger
REVERSE DESIGN: At top: state name above date entered Union. At bottom: date of issue above motto "E Pluribus Unum," describing how the divided colonies became the United States of America. State design: "Caesar Rodney," Rodney astride his horse. Caesar Rodney's dash to Philadelphia, providing the decisive vote for a divided Delaware delegation and thus the key vote for American independence, is commemorated on this, the first of the state quarters. "The First State" appears at right, reflecting Delaware's historic role.

Design History

It was July 1776, and the weather was hot and humid. In Philadelphia, the delegates to the Continental Congress debated independence and were divided 6–6 on the next step to take. Tiny Delaware was also divided, one delegate favoring independence, the other favoring continuation of the fragile relationship with Great Britain. A third delegate, Caesar Rodney, was 80 miles away in Dover, Delaware. His two-day ride to Philadelphia changed the course of world history, as his decisive vote for American independence carried the day.

ALTERNATE DESIGN NOT
CHOSEN FOR DE QUARTER.

Through an Executive Order issued by Governor Tom Carper on February 2, 1998, state residents were encouraged to submit quarter design concepts to the Delaware Arts Council. The Council received more than 300 submissions. With the governor's approval, the Council forwarded several concepts to the U.S. Mint for review and execution of drawings.

The Citizens Commemorative Coin Advisory Committee met by conference call on April 9, 1998, to examine various design options and narrowed the choices for the reverse down to four designs:

- Caesar Rodney with a quill pen and the State of Delaware

- the blue hen

- a quill pen wrapped by "The First State" on a parchment scroll

- Goddess of Liberty holding State of Delaware, torch of Liberty, and "The First State"

The Committee suggested the following adjustments for the Rodney design: the state should be removed from the background and the figure of Caesar Rodney and his horse should be moved slightly to the left. The wording "The First State" should be moved to the right. Approval of the change in design to allow mottos to be moved was not approved by Congress until May 29.

The first-strike ceremony took place at the Philadelphia Mint on December 7, 1998. Inside the mint, a separate ceremony was held as Jules Reiver, a member of the Citizens Commemorative Coin Advisory Committee, and David Ganz were asked by Mint Director Philip Diehl to start other coining presses.

Mintage Figures

PROOF "S": 3.7 million
PROOF SILVER "S": 0.804 million
UNCIRCULATED "P": 373.4 million
UNCIRCULATED "D": 401.2 million

Price Record

PRICE: $2,300
DATE OF ISSUE: 1999 Mintmark P
GRADING SERVICE: PCGS MS-68
DATE OF SALE: 1/2008
AUCTIONEER: Teletrade

PRICE: $184
DATE OF ISSUE: 1999 Mintmark D
GRADING SERVICE: PCGS MS-67
DATE OF SALE: 9/2004
AUCTIONEER: Heritage

Of Note: Teletrade sold a 1999-S PCGS proof-70 deep mirror cameo Delaware quarter for $6,616 on March 29, 2007.

Common Errors and Values

NOT STRUCK ON QUARTER PLANCHET: $850

DOUBLE STRUCK: $550

STRUCK 3–4 TIMES: $750

OBVERSE CLAD MISSING: $375

REVERSE CLAD MISSING: $1,250

OFF CENTER MINOR: $125

OFF CENTER MAJOR: $250

ROTATED REVERSE: $250

BROCKAGE: $250

BROADSIDE: $75

STRUCK-THROUGH: $20

PARTIAL COLLAR: $45

CLIPPED "MINOR": $60

CLIPPED "MAJOR": $100

Grading Hints

OBVERSE: The high points of the coin's obverse are prone to wear; the field off Washington's nose, and the area behind the head curls, are prone to contact marks. Wear is most likely to be evident on the hair above Washington's ear and on the cheekbones. High-grade (MS-67 and above) coins will have no contact marks in the field.

REVERSE: This is the more important side for grade. High grade (above MS-67) has minimal (few if any) contact marks in the field. Knee, arm, horse's rump: all are high points that show wear and reduce the grade.

Investment Potential

Most "slabbed" Delaware state quarters are in MS-66 or better condition. Those that have gone up most in value and which have the greatest potential are graded MS-68 and better.

Past performance is no guarantee for the future, but among coins taken from circulation, the average (out of 56 states and territories), this book's analysis for P and D mint coins ranks these as follows: (P) 14 (out of 112 coins), (D) 100 (out of 112 coins). The coin is most available in MS-65 and MS-66, elusive in higher grades. Some of the coins just seem to have been struck circulated. Good potential for high grade.

PENNSYLVANIA

STATE, YEAR OF ISSUE: Pennsylvania, 1999

State Information

YEAR OF STATEHOOD: 1787
ORDER IN UNION: 2
SIZE: 46,058 sq. mi.
POPULATION: 12.4 million
STATE MOTTO: "Virtue, Liberty and Independence"
STATE FLOWER: mountain laurel
STATE BIRD: ruffled grouse
STATE TREE: hemlock

Coin Specifications

MINTMARKS: P, D, S
OBVERSE DESIGNER: John Flanagan, modified by William Cousins (1997)
REVERSE DESIGNER: William Cousins
REVERSE DESIGN: At top: state name above date entered Union. At bottom: date of issue above motto "E Pluribus Unum," describing how the divided colonies became the United States of America. State design: Outline of the Commonwealth of Pennsylvania, keystone at upper left. State motto at right. At center, an allegorical female figure of Commonwealth, depicted from atop the Capitol Dome at Harrisburg.

Design History

Selections for the Pennsylvania circulating quarter began on January 30, 1998. Pennsylvania Governor Tom Ridge issued a proclamation establishing a Commemorative Quarter Committee to review possible designs. The 14-member committee included representatives from major cultural, conservation, travel, and tourism organizations; a teacher; a high school student; the president of the state numismatic society; and the state treasurer. They went through more than 5,300 design submissions.

The winning design uses an allegorical figure based upon a 14-foot bronze sculpture that has been atop the Capitol Dome in Harrisburg since 1905. The state

ALTERNATE DESIGN NOT CHOSEN FOR PA QUARTER.

motto is also utilized in the design. The Citizens Commemorative Coin Advisory Committee met in May 1998 to review the designs. The designs considered included:

- the keystone, state flower, and bird

- an allegorical Liberty, state outline, and the keystone

- the state bird, flower, and words "Virtue, Liberty and Independence"

- William Penn and the Lenni Lenape Indians with keystone in background.

Rejected designs included the mountain laurel and the grouse. This was nixed by Chairman Carter Brown: "I don't think the grouse is going to mean anything to anybody." Thus the first of many state outlines was approved. The Pennsylvania quarter was released at a ceremony in Philadelphia in March 1999.

Mintage Figures

PROOF "S": 3.7 million
PROOF SILVER "S": 0.804 million
UNCIRCULATED "P": 349.0 million
UNCIRCULATED "D": 358.3 million

Price Record

PRICE: $48
DATE OF ISSUE: 1999 Mintmark P
GRADING SERVICE: PCGS MS-67
DATE OF SALE: 12/2003
AUCTIONEER: Heritage

PRICE: $218
DATE OF ISSUE: 1999 Mintmark D
GRADING SERVICE: PCGS MS-68
DATE OF SALE: 9/2005
AUCTIONEER: Heritage

Common Errors and Values

NOT STRUCK ON QUARTER
  PLANCHET: $1,500
DOUBLE STRUCK: $600
STRUCK 3–4 TIMES: $800
OBVERSE CLAD MISSING: $375
REVERSE CLAD MISSING: $1,000
OFF CENTER MINOR: $100
OFF CENTER MAJOR: $250

ROTATED REVERSE: $250
BROCKAGE: $250
BROADSIDE: $75
STRUCK-THROUGH: $20
PARTIAL COLLAR: $45
CLIPPED "MINOR": $60
CLIPPED "MAJOR": $100

Grading Hints

OBVERSE: The high points of the coin's obverse are prone to wear; the field off Washington's nose, and the area behind the head curls, are prone to contact marks. Wear is most likely to be evident on the hair above Washington's ear and on the cheekbones. High-grade (MS-67 and above) coins will have no contact marks in the field.

REVERSE: This is the more important side for grade. High grade (above MS-67) has minimal (few if any) contact marks in the field. The high points of the coin show wear first: statue's upraised arms and chest.

Investment Potential

Most "slabbed" state quarters are in MS-66 or better condition. Those that have gone up most in value and which have the greatest potential are MS-68 and better.

Past performance is no guarantee for the future, but from circulation the average (out of 56 states and territories) for P and D ranks 18. In 2008, based on auction sales records covering from the commencement of the State Quarters program to date, of more than 90 issues (P and D) taken from circulation, these coins ranked as follows: (P) 59, (D) 15. Strong recommendation for high grade.

NEW JERSEY

STATE, YEAR OF ISSUE: New Jersey, 1999

State Information

YEAR OF STATEHOOD: 1787
ORDER IN UNION: 3
SIZE: 8,215 sq. mi.
POPULATION: 8.6 million
STATE MOTTO: "Liberty and Prosperity"
STATE FLOWER: violet
STATE BIRD: eastern goldfinch
STATE TREE: dogwood

Coin Specifications

MINTMARKS: P, D, S
OBVERSE DESIGNER: John Flanagan, modified by William Cousins (1997)
REVERSE DESIGNER: Alfred Maletsky
REVERSE DESIGN: At top: state name above date entered Union. At bottom, date of issue above motto "E Pluribus Unum," describing how the divided colonies became the United States of America. State design: "Crossroads of the Revolution," Washington Crossing the Delaware, from the 1851 oil painting by Emmanuel Leutze.

Design History

New Jersey Governor Christine Todd Whitman moved rapidly to have a 15-person committee appointed to work on the design, which the Assembly and Senate promptly approved—astonishing considering it took years of debate before being able to designate the Jersey tomato as the state fruit or vegetable.

The selection process for the New Jersey quarter began November 17, 1997, when Assembly Joint Resolution Number 68 was passed to establish the New Jersey Commemorative Coin Design Commission. Setting the pattern, perhaps, for other states, a number of local numismatists were named to the design committee, as were people with backgrounds in art and history.

ALTERNATE DESIGN NOT CHOSEN FOR NJ QUARTER.

The Citizens Commemorative Coin Advisory Committee considered a few choices:

- Washington crossing the Delaware

- the horse and rider

- the outline of the state without "Trenton and the star" and Barnegat lighthouse over slightly to the right

- the Barnegat lighthouse and state motto

The committee met several times and issued a report on March 10, 1998, that stated: "a recurring suggestion was the use of a lighthouse to represent the state's shore and its attractions ... [but the members] decided against using a lighthouse ... since lighthouses may be more identifiable with Maine and North Carolina ..."

New Jersey is the first quarter to feature George Washington on both the obverse and reverse. The committee ultimately recommended a design after "Crossroads of the Revolution," Washington crossing the Delaware, from the 1851 oil painting by Emmanuel Leutze. This made perfect sense since more than 100 battles during the Revolutionary War were fought in the state, the most famous of which was Washington's Rout of the Hessians on Christmas Day 1776. Chairman J. Carter Brown remarked of the painting, "Although normally I think it's too much, the silhouette of this is so recognizable."

Governor Whitman struck the New Jersey quarter at a ceremony in Philadelphia in May 1999. This is the first of several colonial scenes on state quarters and noncirculating commemorative coin modern issues.

Mintage Figures

PROOF "S": 3.7 million
PROOF SILVER "S": 0.804 million
UNCIRCULATED "P": 363.2 million
UNCIRCULATED "D": 299.0 million

Price Record

PRICE: $100
DATE OF ISSUE: 1999 Mintmark P
GRADING SERVICE: PCGS MS-68
DATE OF SALE: 5/2005
AUCTIONEER: Teletrade

PRICE: $977
DATE OF ISSUE: 1999 Mintmark D
GRADING SERVICE: NGC MS-68
DATE OF SALE: 2/2008
AUCTIONEER: Heritage

Common Errors and Values

NOT STRUCK ON QUARTER PLANCHET: $1,500

DOUBLE STRUCK: $600

STRUCK 3–4 TIMES: $800

OBVERSE CLAD MISSING: $375

REVERSE CLAD MISSING: $1,000

OFF CENTER MINOR: $100

OFF CENTER MAJOR: $250

ROTATED REVERSE: $250

BROCKAGE: $250

BROADSIDE: $75

STRUCK-THROUGH: $20

PARTIAL COLLAR: $45

CLIPPED "MINOR": $60

CLIPPED "MAJOR": $100

Grading Hints

OBVERSE: The high points of the coin's obverse are prone to wear; the field off Washington's nose, and the area behind the head curls, are prone to contact marks. Wear is most likely to be evident on the hair above Washington's ear and on the cheekbones. High-grade (MS-67 and above) coins will have no contact marks in the field.

REVERSE: This is the more important side for grade. High grade (above MS-67) has minimal (few if any) contact marks in the field. The high points of the coin—standing Washington and boat's flag—will show wear first.

Investment Potential

Most "slabbed" state quarters are in MS-66 or better Condition. Those that have gone up most in value and which have the greatest potential are MS-68 and better.

Past performance is no guarantee for the future, but from circulation the average (out of 56 states and territories) for P and D ranks 19. In 2008, based on auction sales records covering from the commencement of the State Quarters program to date, of more than 90 issues (P and D) taken from circulation, these coins ranked as follows: (P) 40, (D) 26. High grade has strong possibilities.

GEORGIA

STATE, YEAR OF ISSUE: Georgia, 1999

State Information

YEAR OF STATEHOOD: 1787
ORDER IN UNION: 4
SIZE: 58,977 sq. mi.
POPULATION: 9.5 million
STATE MOTTO: "Wisdom, Justice, Moderation"
STATE FLOWER: Cherokee rose
STATE BIRD: brown thrasher
STATE TREE: live oak

Coin Specifications

MINTMARKS: P, D, S
OBVERSE DESIGNER: John Flanagan, modified by William Cousins (1997)
REVERSE DESIGNER: T. James Farrell
REVERSE DESIGN: At top: state name above date entered Union. At bottom, date of issue above motto "E Pluribus Unum," describing how the divided colonies became the United States of America. State design: outline of state of Georgia, peach, motto above. TJF designer initials at right.

Design History

Georgia was named for King George II of England (the name was chosen by James Oglethorpe, colonial administrator, in 1732). The selection process for the Georgia quarter was initiated when Georgia Governor Zell Miller gave responsibility to the Georgia Council for the Arts for the development and selection of the Georgia circulating quarter design. The council responded by submitting five design concepts to the U.S. Mint.

ALTERNATE DESIGN NOT CHOSEN FOR GA QUARTER.

The Citizens Commemorative Coin Advisory Committee meeting of May 1998 looked at recommending a choice of four designs:

- the outline of the state, book, and hands with scroll and sunburst, taking out the four stars and peach

- the outline of the state, peach, flowers, and state motto

- the state outline and a peach, and the words "Wisdom, Justice, Moderation," taking out the four stars

- the state bird and flower over the outline of the state.

The Federal Fine Arts Commission met May 21, 1998; its recommendations included "The state silhouette with the slogan 'Hope,' with symbols of recreation and education"; the second is the state bird . . . and the Cherokee rose, and the state map." The map outline with integration of the peach was preferred.

The Georgia quarter, the fourth state quarter, was unveiled at a press conference in Atlanta, Georgia, in July 1999. At the event, U.S. Treasurer Mary Ellen Withrow, Georgia Governor Roy Barnes, and others handed out this peach of a coin. Mint Director Philip Diehl was quoted as saying that he did not think that the use of the state outline was "a strong design element," but that overall the design framed the quarter quite nicely.

Mintage Figures

PROOF "S": 3.7 million
PROOF SILVER "S": 0.804 million
UNCIRCULATED "P": 451.8 million
UNCIRCULATED "D": 488.7 million

Price Record

PRICE: $977
DATE OF ISSUE: 1999 Mintmark P
GRADING SERVICE: NGC-MS-68
DATE OF SALE: 2/2008
AUCTIONEER: Teletrade

PRICE: $400
DATE OF ISSUE: 1999 Mintmark D
GRADING SERVICE: PCGS MS-67
DATE OF SALE: 6/2005
AUCTIONEER: Teletrade

Common Errors and Values

NOT STRUCK ON QUARTER PLANCHET: $1,750

DOUBLE STRUCK: $600

STRUCK 3–4 TIMES: $800

OBVERSE CLAD MISSING: $375

REVERSE CLAD MISSING: $850

OFF CENTER MINOR: $85

OFF CENTER MAJOR: $250

ROTATED REVERSE: $300

BROCKAGE: $250

BROADSIDE: $60

STRUCK-THROUGH: $20

PARTIAL COLLAR: $40

CLIPPED "MINOR": $50

CLIPPED "MAJOR": $75

Grading Hints

OBVERSE: The high points of the coin's obverse are prone to wear; the field off Washington's nose, and the area behind the head curls, are prone to contact marks. Wear is most likely to be evident on the hair above Washington's ear and on the cheekbones. High-grade (MS-67 and above) coins will have no contact marks in the field.

REVERSE: This is the more important side for grade. High grade (above MS-67) has minimal (few if any) contact marks in the field. The high points of the coin—rounded (inside) curve of the peach—will show wear first.

Investment Potential

Most "slabbed" state quarters are in MS-66 or better condition. Those that have gone up most in value and which have the greatest potential are MS-68 and better.

Past performance is no guarantee for the future, but from circulation the average (out of 56 states and territories) for P and D ranks 2. In 2008, based on auction sales records covering from the commencement of the State Quarters program to date, of more than 90 issues (P and D) taken from circulation, these coins ranked as follows: (P) 7, (D) 8. . Good upside potential for coins in grades MS-68 and above, and errors (few known).

CONNECTICUT

STATE, YEAR OF ISSUE: Connecticut, 1999

State Information

YEAR OF STATEHOOD: 1788
ORDER IN UNION: 5
SIZE: 5,544 sq. mi.
POPULATION: 3.5 million
STATE MOTTO: "Qui transtulit sustinet" (he who is transplanted still sustains)
STATE FLOWER: mountain laurel
STATE BIRD: American robin
STATE TREE: white oak

Coin Specifications

MINTMARKS: P, D, S
OBVERSE DESIGNER: John Flanagan, modified by William Cousins (1997)
REVERSE DESIGNER: T. James Farrell
REVERSE DESIGN: At top: state name above date entered Union. At bottom: date of issue above motto "E Pluribus Unum," describing how the divided colonies became the United States of America. State design: Charter Oak tree ("The Charter Oak"), designer initials TJF

Design History

One of Connecticut's most historic events involved the Charter Oak. On October 9, 1662, Connecticut formally received the charter won from King Charles II by Governor John Winthrop Jr., who had crossed the Atlantic for the purpose. Some 25 years later, with the succession of James II to the throne, Sir Edmund Andros, His Majesty's agent, arrived in Hartford with an armed force to seize the charter.

After hours of debate, with the charter on the table between the opposing parties, the candlelit room suddenly went dark. Moments later when the candles were relighted, the charter was gone. Captain Joseph Wadsworth is credited with having removed and secreted the charter in the majestic oak on the Wyllys estate. The tree finally fell during a great storm on August 21, 1856.

ALTERNATE DESIGN NOT CHOSEN FOR CT QUARTER.

In a press release issued February 3, 1998, Governor John G. Rowland announced the Connecticut Coin Design Competition. More than 112 citizens ranging from ages six to 87 from 46 cities and towns submitted design concept entries to the Connecticut Commission on the Arts. Nineteen entrants submitted renditions of the Charter Oak and five of those were selected and forwarded to the U.S. Mint.

Commentary from Citizens Commemorative Coin Advisory Committee considered the following designs:

- the Charter Oak and a brick wall

- the Charter Oak and a scroll

- the Charter Oak with the scroll removed

The Fine Arts hearing (May 21, 1998) has the Mint report: "Connecticut sent in one design concept, which was the Charter Oak, and they were quite adamant about incorporating that in the design."

Connecticut's "Charter Oak" quarter, the fifth and final quarter of 1999, was unveiled at a ceremony in Philadelphia in October 1999. The most artistic of the first year's designs, the Charter Oak previously appeared on the 1935 Connecticut tercentennial coin, authorized by Congress by the Act of June 21, 1934.

Mintage Figures

PROOF "S": 3.7 million
PROOF SILVER "S": 0.804 million
UNCIRCULATED "P": 688.7 million
UNCIRCULATED "D": 657.8 million

Price Record

PRICE: $1,380
DATE OF ISSUE: 1999 Mintmark P
GRADING SERVICE: PCGS MS-69
DATE OF SALE: 5/2007
AUCTIONEER: Heritage

PRICE: $253
DATE OF ISSUE: 1999 Mintmark D
GRADING SERVICE: PCGS MS-68
DATE OF SALE: 6/2006
AUCTIONEER: Heritage

Common Errors and Values

NOT STRUCK ON QUARTER
  PLANCHET: $1,750
DOUBLE STRUCK: $600
STRUCK 3–4 TIMES: $800
OBVERSE CLAD MISSING: $375
REVERSE CLAD MISSING: $750
OFF CENTER MINOR: $85
OFF CENTER MAJOR: $250

ROTATED REVERSE: $300
BROCKAGE: $250
BROADSIDE: $60
STRUCK-THROUGH: $20
PARTIAL COLLAR: $40
CLIPPED "MINOR": $50
CLIPPED "MAJOR": $75

Grading Hints

OBVERSE: The high points of the coin's obverse are prone to wear; the field off Washington's nose, and the area behind the head curls, are prone to contact marks. Wear is most likely to be evident on the hair above Washington's ear and on the cheekbones. High-grade (MS-67 and above) coins will have no contact marks in the field.

REVERSE: This is the more important side for grade. High grade (above MS-67) has minimal (few if any) contact marks in the field. The High points of the coin—especially the off-of-center main trunk (6 o'clock)—will show evidence of wear first.

Investment Potential

Most "slabbed" state quarters are in MS-66 or better condition. Those that have gone up most in value and which have the greatest potential are MS-68 and better.

Past performance is no guarantee of the future, but from circulation the average (out of 56 states and territories) for P and D ranks 12. In 2008, based on auction sales records covering from the commencement of the State Quarters program to date, of more than 90 issues (P and D) taken from circulation, these coins ranked as follows: (P) 28, (D) 14. Errors of this series are a real favorite of collectors.

MASSACHUSETTS

STATE, YEAR OF ISSUE: Massachusetts, 2000

State Information

YEAR OF STATEHOOD: 1788
ORDER IN UNION: 6
SIZE: 9,241 sq. mi.
POPULATION: 6.4 million
STATE MOTTO: "By the sword we seek peace, but peace only under liberty"
STATE FLOWER: mayflower
STATE BIRD: chickadee
STATE TREE: American elm

Coin Specifications

MINTMARKS: P, D, S
OBVERSE DESIGNER: John Flanagan, modified by William Cousins (1997)
REVERSE DESIGNER: Thomas D. Rogers Sr.
REVERSE DESIGN: At top: state name above date entered Union. At bottom: date of issue above motto "E Pluribus Unum," describing how the divided colonies became the United States of America. State design: map of Commonwealth of Massachusetts, "The Bay State," statue of the Minuteman, after the statue by Daniel Chester French at Lexington-Concord. (See the Lexington-Concord sesquicentennial half-dollar of 1925.) Initials TDR bottom left side of state map.

Design History

The state dog is the Boston terrier, the state beverage is cranberry juice, and the state fish is the cod. No wonder that historic symbol, "The Minuteman," is depicted on the Massachusetts quarter.

In February 1998, Governor Paul Cellucci initiated a unique contest encouraging Massachusetts elementary school students to submit designs for the state's commemorative quarter. A 10-member advisory Council would then narrow the finalist field to five proposals.

More than 25,000 schoolchildren throughout the Commonwealth participated in the first of many

ALTERNATE DESIGN NOT CHOSEN FOR MA QUARTER.

design competitions for state quarters. the favored result was a reproduction of Daniel Chester French's statue of "The Minuteman," which is located at Lexington-Concord and was previously depicted on the Lexington-Concord sesquicentennial half-dollar of 1925.

The Citizens Commemorative Coin Advisory Committee discussed the following designs:

- The USS *Constitution*

- The Minuteman

- The Sacred Cod

The committee made clear that "The Committee's preference was the US[S] *Constitution*, but there was concern in suggesting two coins with ships within the same year. However, they felt this was a very strong coin. The Fine Arts hearing (January 21, 1999) has Chairman Carter Brown wishing to "bag the fish" (The Sacred Cod), then adding: "That Minuteman is such a great soldier." Brown and the schoolchildren carried the day.

Mintage Figures

PROOF "S": 4.0 million
PROOF SILVER "S": 0.965 million
UNCIRCULATED "P": 628.6 million
UNCIRCULATED "D": 535.1 million

Price Record

PRICE: $87
DATE OF ISSUE: 2000 Mintmark P
GRADING SERVICE: PCGS MS-68
DATE OF SALE: 12/2003
AUCTIONEER: Heritage

PRICE: $60
DATE OF ISSUE: 2000 Mintmark D
GRADING SERVICE: PCGS MS-67
DATE OF SALE: 2/2000
AUCTIONEER: Heritage

Common Errors and Values

NOT STRUCK ON QUARTER PLANCHET: $1,750
DOUBLE STRUCK: $650
STRUCK 3–4 TIMES: $850
OBVERSE CLAD MISSING: $350
REVERSE CLAD MISSING: $600
OFF CENTER MINOR: $85
OFF CENTER MAJOR: $250

ROTATED REVERSE: N/A
BROCKAGE: $250
BROADSIDE: $50
STRUCK-THROUGH: $20
PARTIAL COLLAR: $40
CLIPPED "MINOR": $50
CLIPPED "MAJOR": $75

Note: Reported struck on another planchet (2000-P Sacagawea dollar on Mass. quarter), worth $15,000

Grading Hints

OBVERSE: The high points of the coin's obverse are prone to wear; the field off Washington's nose, and the area behind the head curls, are prone to contact marks. Wear is most likely to be evident on the hair above Washington's ear and on the cheekbones. High-grade (MS-67 and above) coins will have no contact marks in the field.

REVERSE: This is the more important side for grade. High grade (above MS-67) has minimal (few if any) contact marks in the field. The high points of the coin show wear first: Minuteman's head and rifle.

Investment Potential

Most "slabbed" state quarters are in MS-66 or better condition. Those that have gone up most in value and which have the greatest potential are MS-68 and better.

Past performance is no guarantee for the future, but from circulation the average (out of 56 states and territories) for P and D ranks 30. In 2008, based on auction sales records covering from the commencement of the State Quarters program to date, of more than 90 issues (P and D) taken from circulation, these coins ranked as follows: (P) 45, (D) 53.

Maryland

STATE, YEAR OF ISSUE: Maryland, 2000

State Information

YEAR OF STATEHOOD: 1788
ORDER IN UNION: 7
SIZE: 12,297 sq. mi.
POPULATION: 5.6 million
STATE MOTTO: "Manly deeds, womanly words"
STATE FLOWER: black-eyed Susan
STATE BIRD: Baltimore oriole
STATE TREE: white oak

Coin Specifications

MINTMARKS: P, D, S
OBVERSE DESIGNER: John Flanagan, modified by William Cousins (1997)
REVERSE DESIGNER: William J. Krawczewicz, designer; Thomas D. Rogers, sculptor-engraver
REVERSE DESIGN: At top: state name above date entered Union. At bottom: date of issue above motto "E Pluribus Unum," describing how the divided colonies became the United States of America. State design: Old State House Capitol Dome surrounded by white oak leaf clusters and the nickname "The Old Line State."

Design History

The Maryland State House is a distinctive building dating back to 1772 and features the country's largest wooden dome built without nails. Besides housing Maryland's colonial legislature from 1783–1784, the Maryland State House served as the nation's first peacetime capital. The Treaty of Paris was ratified here, officially ending the Revolutionary War. A treasure preserved, the State House continues as the country's oldest state capital building still in legislative use.

ALTERNATE DESIGN NOT CHOSEN FOR MD QUARTER.

On October 14, 1998, Governor Parris Glendening presented five state quarter design concepts to the U.S. Mint. These designs were the result of a statewide design contest. From the 280 submissions, five were chosen by the Maryland Commemorative Coin Committee, established specifically to evaluate quarter design submissions. The semifinal designs included:

- Maryland State House dome

- an outline of the State of Maryland

- the *Ark* and the *Dove*—ships that brought Lord Calvert to the new world

- Maryland State House

- Fort McHenry and the Star-Spangled Banner

Glendening favored the State House dome and chose that design on April 29, 1999. The winning designer is a graphic artist at the White House and lives in Maryland; he was also designer for the common reverse of the 1996 Atlanta Olympic Games $5 gold piece and the 1995 Atlanta $1 common reverse for the Olympics.

The minutes of the Citizens Commemorative Coin Advisory Committee also reflect a preference: "The Committee strongly endorsed the Ark and the Dove." The group also liked the Star-Spangled Banner version and thought building designs "lacked perspective." In the end, through its new quarter, the seventh state honors the Maryland State House. Leaf clusters from the official state tree, the white oak, and the nickname "The Old Line State" complete the selected design. Maryland's nickname honors its "troops of the line" who saved General Washington and his troops by holding firm during the Battle of Long Island in August 1776.

In April 2000, the U.S. Mint began selling the Maryland First Day Commemorative Coin Cover. This limited-edition cover—only 75,000 would be produced—features two Maryland quarters from the first day of mintage, February 28, 2000. Each cover includes quarters from both the Philadelphia and Denver mints on a handsome display card with the 33-cent flag-over-city postage stamp. The postmark of March 13, 2000, Annapolis, Maryland, marks the day Maryland quarters were first released to the Federal Reserve Bank and to the public.

Mintage Figures

PROOF "S": 4.0 million
PROOF SILVER "S": 0.965 million
UNCIRCULATED "P": 678.2 million
UNCIRCULATED "D": 556.5 million

Price Record

PRICE: $87
DATE OF ISSUE: 2000 Mintmark P
GRADING SERVICE: PCGS MS-68
DATE OF SALE: 12/2003
AUCTIONEER: Heritage

PRICE: $60
DATE OF ISSUE: 2000 Mintmark D
GRADING SERVICE: PCGS MS-67
DATE OF SALE: 2/2000
AUCTIONEER: Heritage

Common Errors and Values

NOT STRUCK ON QUARTER PLANCHET: $1,250
DOUBLE STRUCK: $600
STRUCK 3–4 TIMES: $800
OBVERSE CLAD MISSING: $350
REVERSE CLAD MISSING: $600
OFF CENTER MINOR: $95
OFF CENTER MAJOR: $250

ROTATED REVERSE: N/A
BROCKAGE: $250
BROADSIDE: $50
STRUCK-THROUGH: $20
PARTIAL COLLAR: $20
CLIPPED "MINOR": $50
CLIPPED "MAJOR": $75

Grading Hints

OBVERSE: The high points of the coin's obverse are prone to wear; the field off Washington's nose, and the area behind the head curls, are prone to contact marks. Wear is most likely to be evident on the hair above Washington's ear and on the cheekbones. High-grade (MS-67 and above) coins will have no contact marks in the field.

REVERSE: This is the more important side for grade. High grade (above MS-67) has minimal (few if any) contact marks in the field. The high points of the coin show wear first: middle rim of the dome and flag atop dome.

Investment Potential

Most "slabbed" state quarters are in MS-66 or better condition. Those that have gone up most in value and which have the greatest potential are MS-68 and better.

Past performance is no guarantee for the future, but from circulation the average (out of 56 states and territories) for P and D ranks 24. In 2008, based on auction sales records covering from the commencement of the State Quarters program to date, of more than 90 issues (P and D) taken from circulation, these coins ranked as follows: (P) 20, (D) 77.

SOUTH CAROLINA

STATE, YEAR OF ISSUE: South Carolina, 2000

State Information

YEAR OF STATEHOOD: 1788
ORDER IN UNION: 8
SIZE: 31,189 sq. mi.
POPULATION: 4.4 million
STATE MOTTO: "Prepared in mind and deed; while I breathe, I hope"
STATE FLOWER: yellow jessamine
STATE BIRD: Carolina wren
STATE TREE: palmetto

Coin Specifications

MINTMARKS: P, D, S
OBVERSE DESIGNER: John Flanagan, modified by William Cousins (1997)
REVERSE DESIGNER: Thomas D. Rogers Sr.
REVERSE DESIGN: At top: state name above date entered Union. At bottom: date of issue above motto "E Pluribus Unum," describing how the divided colonies became the United States of America. State design: map outlining state; "The Palmetto State" inside map; state tree and state bird perched on the state flower. Initials TDR to the right of palmetto tree base.

Design History

The South Carolina palmetto is classified by the U.S. Department of Agriculture as "Inodes Palmetto (also called Sabal Palmetto) and commonly known as the Cabbage Palmetto." It has long been closely associated with the history of South Carolina, and is represented on the state flag as well as on the state seal, where it is symbolic of the defeat of the British fleet by the fort, built of palmetto logs, on Sullivan's Island.

Beginning in 1998, the South Carolina Department of Parks, Recreation and Tourism accepted quarter design suggestions. From the many sent in by school-children and the South Carolina Numismatic Society, five emerged as semifinalist design concepts. The Citi-

ALTERNATE DESIGN NOT CHOSEN FOR SC QUARTER.

zens Commemorative Coin Advisory Committee and the Fine Arts Commission narrowed the five semifinalist design concepts down to three choices:

- Fort Moultrie (for a clearer design, the committee suggested removing the larger ship)

- the statehouse

- the state bird and flower (for this design the committee suggested removing the top of the branch and placing the bird to the left, away from the state)

At the Fine Arts hearing (January 21, 1999) Commissioner Barbaralee Dia-monstein-Spielvogel said, "I think we have to go with Palmetto State. . . ." The palmetto was adopted as the "Official State Tree of the State of South Carolina" by Joint Resolution No. 63, approved March 17, 1939.

Governor Jim Hodges then made his final decision, indicating that the palmetto tree represents South Carolina's strength; the Carolina wren's song symbolizes the hospitality of the state's people; and that the wren should be perched upon the state flower, the yellow jessamine.

Mintage Figures

PROOF "S": 4.0 million
PROOF SILVER "S": 0.965 million
UNCIRCULATED "P": 742.5 million
UNCIRCULATED "D": 566.2 million

Price Record

PRICE: $51
DATE OF ISSUE: 2000 Mintmark P
GRADING SERVICE: PCGS MS-68
DATE OF SALE: 5/2003
AUCTIONEER: Heritage

PRICE: $42
DATE OF ISSUE: 2000 Mintmark D
GRADING SERVICE: PCGS MS-67
DATE OF SALE: 9/2000
AUCTIONEER: Heritage

Common Errors and Values

NOT STRUCK ON QUARTER
PLANCHET: $1,500
DOUBLE STRUCK: $600
STRUCK 3–4 TIMES: $800
OBVERSE CLAD MISSING: $300
REVERSE CLAD MISSING: $550
OFF CENTER MINOR: $75
OFF CENTER MAJOR: $225

ROTATED REVERSE: N/A
BROCKAGE: $225
BROADSIDE: $50
STRUCK-THROUGH: $20
PARTIAL COLLAR: $20
CLIPPED "MINOR": $50
CLIPPED "MAJOR": $75

Grading Hints

OBVERSE: The high points of the coin's obverse are prone to wear; the field off Washington's nose, and the area behind the head curls, are prone to contact marks. Wear is most likely to be evident on the hair above Washington's ear and on the cheekbones. High-grade (MS-67 and above) coins will have no contact marks in the field.

REVERSE: This is the more important side for grade. High grade (above MS-67) has minimal (few if any) contact marks in the field. The high points of the coin show wear first: top and trunk of palmetto tree; wren's beak.

Investment Potential

Most "slabbed" state quarters are in MS-66 or better condition. Those that have gone up most in value and which have the greatest potential are MS-68 and better.

Past performance is no guarantee for the future, but from circulation the average (out of 56 states and territories) for P and D ranks 34. In 2008, based on auction sales records covering from the commencement of the state quarter program to date, of more than 90 issues (P and D) taken from circulation, these coins ranked as follows: (P) 57, (D) 64.

NEW HAMPSHIRE

STATE, YEAR OF ISSUE: New Hampshire, 2000

State Information

YEAR OF STATEHOOD: 1788
ORDER IN UNION: 9
SIZE: 9,283 sq. mi.
POPULATION: 1.3 million
STATE MOTTO: "Live free or die"
STATE FLOWER: purple lilac
STATE BIRD: purple finch
STATE TREE: white birch

Coin Specifications

MINTMARKS: P, D, S
OBVERSE DESIGNER: John Flanagan, modified by William Cousins (1997)
REVERSE DESIGNER: William Cousins
REVERSE DESIGN: At top: state name above date entered Union. At bottom: date of issue above motto "E Pluribus Unum," describing how the divided colonies became the United States of America. State design: "Old Man of the Mountain," a natural rock formation; state motto "Live Free or Die" in field; nine stars representing the ninth state admitted to the Union. Initials WC above "m" in Unum.

Design History

"The Old Man of the Mountain" was a natural rock formation found on Mount Cannon in northern New Hampshire. Composed of five layers of Conway red granite, it appears to show a distinct profile of an elderly man gazing eastward. Until recently, the formation, measuring over 40 feet high with a lateral distance of 25 feet, was held in place by cables and turnbuckles to prevent further slippage and possible destruction. This failed and on May 3, 2003, the Old Man slipped off the mountain.

ALTERNATE DESIGN NOT CHOSEN FOR NH QUARTER.

The New Hampshire quarter design began when Governor Jeanne Shaheen established a Commemorative Quarter Committee with representatives from among the Department of Cultural Affairs, arts educators, numismatists, historical societies, the Senate and House, and New Hampshire citizens. The committee opened a competition to all New Hampshire residents to submit design concepts for the New Hampshire quarter and even created a Web site to report on the selection process and other information about the program.

More than 300 designs and ideas were submitted to the committee for deliberation and selection. The designs were grouped by subject matter (e.g., Old Man, State Symbols, etc.). Three meetings were required to select the final five concepts, which were then sent to the U.S. Mint, with backup imagery and documentation, for transformation into finished artwork:

- The Old Man of the Mountain, with nine stars indicating New Hampshire's rank as the ninth state, the enabling vote for the Constitution of the United States, and the inscription "The Granite State"

- The Old Man of the Mountain with an eagle soaring beneath it, and the inscription "The Granite State"

- Robert Frost imagery based on his poem "The Road not Taken," including a forest scene with white birches (state tree) and a forked road

- A covered bridge with mountain/forest scenery, emblematic of the natural beauty of New Hampshire

- A town meeting house indicating New Hampshire's unique political structure of town government

The Fine Arts Commission held a hearing (January 21, 1999) at which Chairman J. Carter Brown said, "I agree that the 'Live Free or Die' is such a wonderful motto that I think that maybe we could make some recommendation that that is a plus." Commissioner Barbaralee Diamonstein-Spielvogel commented, "I think the meeting house is quite nice. This covered bridge . . . is somewhat lessened." Nonetheless, on January 28, Brown wrote to Mint director Diehl that "The covered bridge design (the one without the stone wall, birch trees, and quotation from Robert Frost) was the clear preference." He also made clear that "'The Meeting House' design was not approved."

In a March 11, 1999, letter to Mint director Philip Diehl, Fine Arts Commission Chairman J. Carter Brown revealed that "Two members did not like the New Hampshire 'Old Man of the Mountain' design; they did not find it attractive and they were concerned that without more relief than can be achieved on a coin, it would not be intelligible." However, the Old Man design won out.

On May 3, 2003, the "Old Man" collapsed in a rockslide. The New Hampshire state quarter is a permanent memorial to the geologic phenomenon.

Mintage Figures

PROOF "S": 4.0 million
PROOF SILVER "S": 0.965 million
UNCIRCULATED "P": 673.0 million
UNCIRCULATED "D": 495.9 million

Price Record

PRICE: $210
DATE OF ISSUE: 2000 Mintmark P
GRADING SERVICE: PCGS MS-68
DATE OF SALE: 11/2006
AUCTIONEER: Teletrade

PRICE: $525
DATE OF ISSUE: 2000 Mintmark D
GRADING SERVICE: PCGS MS-68
DATE OF SALE: 5/2007
AUCTIONEER: Teletrade

Common Errors and Values

NOT STRUCK ON QUARTER
PLANCHET: $1,500
DOUBLE STRUCK: $600
STRUCK 3–4 TIMES: $800
OBVERSE CLAD MISSING: $300
REVERSE CLAD MISSING: $550
OFF CENTER MINOR: $75
OFF CENTER MAJOR: $200

ROTATED REVERSE: N/A
BROCKAGE: $225
BROADSIDE: $50
STRUCK-THROUGH: $20
PARTIAL COLLAR: $20
CLIPPED "MINOR": $50
CLIPPED "MAJOR": $75

Grading Hints

OBVERSE: The high points of the coin's obverse are prone to wear; the field off Washington's nose, and the area behind the head curls, are prone to contact marks. Wear is most likely to be evident on the hair above Washington's ear and on the cheekbones. High-grade (MS-67 and above) coins will have no contact marks in the field.

REVERSE: This is the more important side for grade. High grade (above MS-67) has minimal (few if any) contact marks in the field. The high points of the coin, notably the Old Man's nose, show wear first.

Investment Potential

Most "slabbed" state quarters are in MS-66 or better condition. Those that have gone up most in value and which have the greatest potential are MS-68 and better.

Past performance is no guarantee of the future, but from circulation the average (out of 56 states and territories) for P and D ranks 23. In 2008, based on auction sales records covering from the commencement of the State Quarters program to date, of more than 90 issues (P and D) taken from circulation, these coins ranked as follows: (P) 19, (D) 78.

VIRGINIA

STATE, YEAR OF ISSUE: Virginia, 2000

State Information

YEAR OF STATEHOOD: 1788
ORDER IN UNION: 10
SIZE: 42,326 sq. mi.
POPULATION: 7.7 million
STATE MOTTO: "Sic semper tyrannis" (thus always to tyrants)
STATE FLOWER: dogwood
STATE BIRD: cardinal
STATE TREE: dogwood

Coin Specifications

MINTMARKS: P, D, S
OBVERSE DESIGNER: John Flanagan, modified by William Cousins (1997)
REVERSE DESIGNER: Edgar M. Stevens IV
REVERSE DESIGN: At top: state name above date entered Union. At bottom: date of issue above motto "E Pluribus Unum," describing how the divided colonies became the United States of America. State design: three ships—*Susan Constant, Godspeed,* and *Discovery*—which brought the first English settlers to Jamestown; "1607–2007," the "quadricentennial" anniversary of Jamestown; EMS initials on right of ocean at ship's right, near rim.

Design History

The selection of the design for Virginia's new quarter began when Governor James Gilmore III selected State Treasurer Susan F. Dewey to serve as liaison to the U.S. Mint for the 50 State Quarters program. Ideas were solicited from colleges, universities, museums, and state agencies.

Public comment was overwhelming, with thousands of responses received. Representatives from the Library of Virginia, the Department of Historic Resources, the Virginia Tourism Corporation, and the Department of General Services assisted the state treasurer in selecting design concepts for the Virginia quarter. The citizens of Virginia were encouraged to provide their comments.

ALTERNATE DESIGN NOT CHOSEN FOR VA QUARTER.

The Fine Arts Commission hearing (January 21, 1999) saw commissioners having no difficulty in choosing either

- Mount Vernon (two versions)
- Colonial Williamsburg

On January 28, Mint Director Philip Diehl received a letter from Fine Arts Chairman J. Carter Brown noting the "depiction of Mount Vernon with the dogwood branch was the first choice, with the 'Colonial capital, Williamsburg,' also being considered acceptable."

Virginia's governor went in a different direction, not surprising given the enormity of Jamestown, which received its own commemorative (noncirculating) coin in 2007 and a visit from Queen Elizabeth II.

Governor Gilmore then forwarded his final design concept recommendation, the Jamestown Quadricentennial, to the secretary of the treasury, who gave final approval.

Mintage Figures

PROOF "S": 4.0 million
PROOF SILVER "S": 0.965 million
UNCIRCULATED "P": 943.0 million
UNCIRCULATED "D": 651.6 million

Price Record

PRICE: $132
DATE OF ISSUE: 2000 Mintmark P
GRADING SERVICE: PCGS MS-68
DATE OF SALE: 9/2004
AUCTIONEER: Heritage

PRICE: $24
DATE OF ISSUE: 2000 Mintmark D
GRADING SERVICE: PCGS MS-67
DATE OF SALE: 6/2006
AUCTIONEER: Teletrade

Common Errors and Values

NOT STRUCK ON QUARTER
  PLANCHET: $1,500
DOUBLE STRUCK: $300
STRUCK 3–4 TIMES: $800
OBVERSE CLAD MISSING: $300
REVERSE CLAD MISSING: $550
OFF CENTER MINOR: $75
OFF CENTER MAJOR: $200

ROTATED REVERSE: N/A
BROCKAGE: $225
BROADSIDE: $50
STRUCK-THROUGH: $20
PARTIAL COLLAR: $20
CLIPPED "MINOR": $50
CLIPPED "MAJOR": $75

Grading Hints

OBVERSE: The high points of the coin's obverse are prone to wear; the field off Washington's nose, and the area behind the head curls, are prone to contact marks. Wear is most likely to be evident on the hair above Washington's ear and on the cheekbones. High-grade (MS-67 and above) coins will have no contact marks in the field.

REVERSE: This is the more important side for grade. High grade (above MS-67) has minimal (few if any) contact marks in the field. The high points of the coin show wear first—notably the right ship's center sail.

Investment Potential

Most "slabbed" state quarters are in MS-66 or better condition. Those that have gone up most in value and which have the greatest potential are MS-68 and better.

Past performance is no guarantee for the future, but from circulation the average (out of 56 states and territories) for P and D ranks 28. In 2008, based on auction sales records covering from the commencement of the State Quarters program to date, of more than 90 issues (P and D) taken from circulation, these coins ranked as follows: (P) 31, (D) 76.

NEW YORK

State Information

YEAR OF STATEHOOD: 1788
ORDER IN UNION: 11
SIZE: 53,989 sq. mi.
POPULATION: 19.2 million
STATE MOTTO: "Excelsior" (ever upward)
STATE FLOWER: rose
STATE BIRD: bluebird
STATE TREE: sugar maple

Coin Specifications

MINTMARKS: P, D, S
OBVERSE DESIGNER: John Flanagan, modified by William Cousins (1997)
REVERSE DESIGNER: Alfred Maletsky, sculptor-engraver; Daniel Carr, designer.
REVERSE DESIGN: At top: state name above date entered Union. At bottom: date of issue above motto "E Pluribus Unum," describing how the divided colonies became the United States of America. State design: state of New York map (including Long Island), with superimposed Statue of Liberty as seen from New Jersey view. The Erie Canal is plainly visible. "Gateway to Freedom" in upper right quadrant. Initials AFM at westernmost part of New York State map. Daniel Carr's design is widely seen as an artistic and inspirational triumph in minimalism.

Design History

Governor George Pataki's office requested design ideas from the residents of New York and received hundreds of suggestions from schoolchildren, history buffs, graphic artists, and coin collectors across the state. Pataki's office was flooded with sketches of state symbols, New York City landmarks, and even one donkey pulling a boat up the Erie Canal. On June 19, 2000, Governor Pataki unveiled the candidate designs, which included:

ALTERNATE DESIGN NOT CHOSEN FOR NY QUARTER.

- Henry Hudson and his ship, the *Half Moon*

- a rendering of the historic painting, *Battle of Saratoga*

- the Statue of Liberty

- the New York Federal Building

On February 17, 2000, the Fine Arts Commission panned designs showing the first U.S. Capitol in New York City and the Hudson ship *Half Moon*, but approved either a map of New York with the Statute of Liberty superimposed or a colonial scene of the victory at Saratoga. Fine Arts members preferred the map and Statue of Liberty; the Mint preferred the victory at Saratoga.

Saratoga was one of the major battles of the Revolutionary War, taking place September 19 through October 17, 1777. General Horatio Gates was the American commander; General John Burgoyne headed up the British forces, which lost 7,000 men to the Americans' mere 150 casualties. The surrender of Burgoyne led directly to French entry into the War for Independence. The New York coin faced the classic battle that has plagued New York state politics for years: whether to give credence to Upstate interests (Saratoga) or allow domination by New York City (Statue of Liberty) designs. Pataki, himself from Peekskill (Upstate) recommended Saratoga to the treasury secretary.

Ultimately, the state map with the Statue of Liberty was chosen and Pataki lobbied to insert the Erie Canal, which makes the design more successful. The design was made more poignant by the events of September 11, 2001, that affected New York City and the world.

Mintage Figures

PROOF "S": 3.0 million
PROOF SILVER "S": 0.889 million
UNCIRCULATED "P": 655.4 million
UNCIRCULATED "D": 619.6 million

Price Record

PRICE: $390
DATE OF ISSUE: 2001 Mintmark P
GRADING SERVICE: PCGS MS-66
DATE OF SALE: 5/2003
AUCTIONEER: Heritage

PRICE: $1,092
DATE OF ISSUE: 2001 Mintmark D
GRADING SERVICE: PCGS MS-68
DATE OF SALE: 12/2007
AUCTIONEER: Heritage

Common Errors and Values

NOT STRUCK ON QUARTER
   PLANCHET: $1,750
DOUBLE STRUCK: $650
STRUCK 3–4 TIMES: $850
OBVERSE CLAD MISSING: $350
REVERSE CLAD MISSING: $750
OFF CENTER MINOR: $100
OFF CENTER MAJOR: $750

ROTATED REVERSE: N/A
BROCKAGE: $275
BROADSIDE: $50
STRUCK-THROUGH: $20
PARTIAL COLLAR: $20
CLIPPED "MINOR": $50
CLIPPED "MAJOR": $75

Grading Hints

OBVERSE: The high points of the coin's obverse are prone to wear; the field off Washington's nose, and the area behind the head curls, are prone to contact marks. Wear is most likely to be evident on the hair above Washington's ear and on the cheekbones. High-grade (MS-67 and above) coins will have no contact marks in the field.

REVERSE: This is the more important side for grade. High grade (above MS-67) has minimal (few if any) contact marks in the field. The high points of the coin show wear first: upper torso and upraised arm of Statue of Liberty.

Investment Potential

Most "slabbed" state quarters are in MS-66 or better condition. Those that have gone up most in value and which have the greatest potential are MS-68 and better.

Past performance is no guarantee for the future, but from circulation the average (out of 56 states and territories) for P and D ranks 11. In 2008, based on auction sales records covering from the commencement of the State Quarters program to date, of more than 90 issues (P and D) taken from circulation, these coins ranked as follows: (P) 9, (D) 41.

NORTH CAROLINA

STATE, YEAR OF ISSUE: North Carolina, 2001

State Information

YEAR OF STATEHOOD: 1789
ORDER IN UNION: 12
SIZE: 52,672 sq. mi.
POPULATION: 9.06 million
STATE MOTTO: "Esse quam videri" (to be, rather than to seem)
STATE FLOWER: dogwood
STATE BIRD: cardinal
STATE TREE: pine

Coin Specifications

MINTMARKS: P, D, S
OBVERSE DESIGNER: John Flanagan, modified by William Cousins (1997)
REVERSE DESIGNER: John Mercanti
REVERSE DESIGN: At top: state name above date entered Union. At bottom: date of issue above motto "E Pluribus Unum," describing how the divided colonies became the United States of America. State design: Wilbur and Orville Wright at Kitty Hawk, December 1903, Orville piloting, Wilbur off the wing. Initials JM at ground-level, right.

Design History

Governor James B. Hunt appointed the North Carolina Department of Cultural Resources as the lead in the state's design concept process. The department established the North Carolina Commemorative Coin Committee, which consisted of members from Cultural Resources, the Division of Archives and History, and coin collectors. The committee solicited design ideas from the residents of North Carolina.

Hunt recommended a design honoring the first flight efforts of Wilbur and Orville Wright (The Wright Brothers) in 1903. Special commemoration of this was then already planned by the U.S. Mint with noncirculating legal-tender coins in 2003. The concept design viewed by the Fine Arts Commission (February 17, 2000) shows the open-air plane above the dunes of

ALTERNATE DESIGN NOT CHOSEN FOR NC QUARTER.

Kitty Hawk, where the Wright Brothers (of Ohio) first flew. The design is after a famous photo taken with a camera set by Orville Wright on December 17, 1903, with Orville piloting and Wilbur alongside the wings.

The Fine Arts Commission declined to approve two different drawings showing Cape Hatteras and the Cape's famous lighthouse, one with a pelican in flight. They definitely preferred the "first flight" theme. This was the subject of other noncirculating commemorative coins in 2003, and also the Ohio state quarter. Chairman J. Carter Brown termed "The Wright Brothers . . . just such an important event in the history of humankind, and Hatteras has all these negative connotations. . . ." On February 24, 2000, Brown wrote to Mint Director Philip Diehl that "The [first flight] design would work well on a coin."

Mintage Figures

PROOF "S": 3.0 million
PROOF SILVER "S": 0.889 million
UNCIRCULATED "P": 627.6 million
UNCIRCULATED "D": 427.8 million

Price Record

PRICE: $39
DATE OF ISSUE: 2001 Mintmark P
GRADING SERVICE: PCGS MS-68
DATE OF SALE: 12/2004
AUCTIONEER: Heritage

PRICE: $608
DATE OF ISSUE: 2001 Mintmark D
GRADING SERVICE: PCGS MS-68
DATE OF SALE: 7/2003
AUCTIONEER: Heritage

Common Errors and Values

NOT STRUCK ON QUARTER
  PLANCHET: $1,750
DOUBLE STRUCK: $600
STRUCK 3–4 TIMES: $800
OBVERSE CLAD MISSING: $300
REVERSE CLAD MISSING: $600
OFF CENTER MINOR: $75

OFF CENTER MAJOR: $250
ROTATED REVERSE: N/A
BROCKAGE: $250
BROADSIDE: $50
STRUCK-THROUGH: $20
PARTIAL COLLAR: $20
CLIPPED "MINOR": $50

Grading Hints

OBVERSE: The high points of the coin's obverse are prone to wear; the field off Washington's nose, and the area behind the head curls, are prone to contact marks. Wear is most likely to be evident on the hair above Washington's ear and on the cheekbones. High-grade (MS-67 and above) coins will have no contact marks in the field.

REVERSE: This is the more important side for grade. High grade (above MS-67) has minimal (few if any) contact marks in the field. The high points of the coin show wear first: Wilbur Wright (standing on beach dune) body and head.

Investment Potential

Most "slabbed" state quarters are in MS-66 or better condition. Those that have gone up most in value and which have the greatest potential are MS-68 and better.

Past performance is no guarantee for the future, but from circulation the average (out of 56 states and territories) for P and D ranks 26. In 2008, based on auction sales records covering from the commencement of the State Quarters program to date, of more than 90 issues (P and D) taken from circulation, these coins ranked as follows: (P) 66, (D) 30.

RHODE ISLAND

STATE, YEAR OF ISSUE: Rhode Island, 2001

State Information

YEAR OF STATEHOOD: 1790
ORDER IN UNION: 13
SIZE: 1,231 sq. mi.
POPULATION: 1.057 million
STATE MOTTO: "Hope"
STATE FLOWER: violet
STATE BIRD: Rhode Island red
STATE TREE: red maple

Coin Specifications

MINTMARKS: P, D, S
OBVERSE DESIGNER: John Flanagan, modified by William Cousins (1997)
REVERSE DESIGNER: Thomas D. Rogers Sr., sculptor-engraver; Daniel Carr, designer
REVERSE DESIGN: At top: state name above date entered Union. At bottom: date of issue above motto "E Pluribus Unum," describing how the divided colonies became the United States of America. State design: a vintage sailboat gliding through Narragansett Bay with Pell Bridge in the background. The image showcases Rhode Island's most popular water sport—sailing. Initials TDR located in waves at lower right.

Design History

Executive Order 99–4 was signed April 7, 1999, by Governor Lincoln Almond directing that the Rhode Island Council on the Arts organize a Coin Concept Advisory Panel whose membership included the president of the Rhode Island School of Design, the chairman of the Rhode Island Historical Preservation & Heritage Commission, a Rhode Island numismatist, "and Sen. John Chafee or designee in recognition of his original introduction of the Act in the United States Senate."

The aim was to give highest consideration to concepts which promote Rhode Island's rich heritage and

ALTERNATE DESIGN NOT CHOSEN FOR RI QUARTER.

recognize Rhode Island's historical significance among the original 13 colonies. Randall Rosenbaum, executive director of the Rhode Island State Council on the Arts, advises that "We solicited and received several hundred coin concepts from Rhode Island citizens."

More than 500 design concepts were submitted to the panel, and three finalists were chosen. Rhode Island residents were invited to vote for their favorite design at area libraries, the statehouse and via the Internet. The sailboat design was declared the winner, earning 57 percent of the 34,566 votes cast. Four concepts were selected for consideration by the Fine Arts Commission, two of which featured colonial minister Roger Williams, who sought religious freedom in Little Rhody. A third choice was a portrait of native son Gilbert Stuart, the talented artist, and the final version showed "The Ocean State," the choice of 16 million tourists a year who visit the 400 miles of beaches the state has to offer, and an idea drawing from the license plates produced by the state. Of the design ultimately chosen, the Fine Arts unit said, "The Roger Williams theme seemed the most appropriate." However, in the end, the Treasury chose the sailboat.

Mintage Figures

PROOF "S": 3.0 million
PROOF SILVER "S": 0.889 million
UNCIRCULATED "P": 423.0 million
UNCIRCULATED "D": 447.1 million

Price Record

PRICE: $75
DATE OF ISSUE: 2001 Mintmark P
GRADING SERVICE: PCGS MS-68
DATE OF SALE: 5/2005
AUCTIONEER: Teletrade

PRICE: $32
DATE OF ISSUE: 2001 Mintmark D
GRADING SERVICE: PCGS MS-67
DATE OF SALE: 3/2003
AUCTIONEER: Heritage

Common Errors and Values

NOT STRUCK ON QUARTER
PLANCHET: $2,000
DOUBLE STRUCK: $650
STRUCK 3–4 TIMES: $850
OBVERSE CLAD MISSING: $350
REVERSE CLAD MISSING: $650
OFF CENTER MINOR: $100
OFF CENTER MAJOR: N/A

ROTATED REVERSE: N/A
BROCKAGE: $300
BROADSIDE: $50
STRUCK-THROUGH: $20
PARTIAL COLLAR: $20
CLIPPED "MINOR": $50
CLIPPED "MAJOR": $75

Grading Hints

OBVERSE: The high points of the coin's obverse are prone to wear; the field off Washington's nose, and the area behind the head curls, are prone to contact marks. Wear is most likely to be evident on the hair above Washington's ear and on the cheekbones. High-grade (MS-67 and above) coins will have no contact marks in the field.

REVERSE: This is the more important side for grade. High grade (above MS-67) has minimal (few if any) contact marks in the field. The high points of the coin—here, the upper sail at 10 o'clock—show wear first.

Investment Potential

Most "slabbed" state quarters are in MS-66 or better condition. Those that have gone up most in value and which have the greatest potential are MS-68 and better.

Past performance is no guarantee of the future, but from circulation the average (out of 56 states and territories) for P and D ranks 32. In 2008, based on auction sales records covering from the commencement of the State Quarters program to date, of more than 90 issues (P and D) taken from circulation, these coins ranked as follows: (P) 46, (D) 70.

VERMONT

STATE, YEAR OF ISSUE: Vermont, 2001

State Information

YEAR OF STATEHOOD: 1791
ORDER IN UNION: 14
SIZE: 9,615 sq. mi.
POPULATION: 621,000
STATE MOTTO: "Freedom and unity"
STATE FLOWER: red clover
STATE BIRD: hermit thrush
STATE TREE: sugar maple

Coin Specifications

MINTMARKS: P, D, S
OBVERSE DESIGNER: John Flanagan, modified by William Cousins (1997)
REVERSE DESIGNER: T. James Farrell
REVERSE DESIGN: At top: state name above date entered Union. At bottom: date of issue above motto "E Pluribus Unum," describing how the divided colonies became the United States of America. State design: Camel's Hump Mountain with an image of maple trees with sap buckets in the foreground. Initials TJF below "ty" in "Unity."

Design History

As a result of Executive Order 02–99, the Vermont Arts Council oversaw the solicitation of design concepts for the state quarter. They organized a Coin Concept Advisory panel consisting of the state archivist, the director of the Vermont Historical Society, the director of the Vermont Crafts Council, the director of the Vermont Department of Historical Preservation, the Vermont state treasurer, the Vermont state curator, a representative of the Vermont Department of Tourism and Marketing, the director of the Vermont Museum and Gallery Alliance, and a private citizen.

The goal of the design was to promote Vermont's rich heritage and recognize Vermont's historical significance among the 13 original colonies. Several

ALTERNATE DESIGN NOT CHOSEN FOR VT QUARTER.

people independently suggested that the profile of Camel's Hump should be the main feature of the design. Others suggested a variety of views of the White River along Route 107. Still others suggested a variety of views of Holstein cows. In the end, the State Coin Selection Committee (designated in the executive order) was permitted to decide to combine any or all of these elements into a single concept, and forward that on to the governor for his review.

The Vermont designs appeared before Fine Arts Commission on February 17, 2000, and two designs were selected: a single snowflake with the state motto on either side, or homage to the state's maple sugar industry with a single farmer tapping into three trees (also with the state motto). Multiple snowflakes and a ski bobcat were rejects. On February 24, Fine Arts Chairman J. Carter Brown wrote to Mint Director Philip Diehl that "The design with multiple snowflakes superimposed on a mountain was not acceptable." Brown wrote, "Either the design depicting the gathering of maple syrup or the one with the single snowflake were considered good choices." Maple syrup it was.

Mintage Figures

PROOF "S": 3.0 million
PROOF SILVER "S": 0.889 million
UNCIRCULATED "P": 423.0 million
UNCIRCULATED "D": 459.4 million

Price Record

PRICE: $43
DATE OF ISSUE: 2001 Mintmark P
GRADING SERVICE: PCGS MS-67
DATE OF SALE: 9/2006
AUCTIONEER: Teletrade

PRICE: $18
DATE OF ISSUE: 2001 Mintmark D
GRADING SERVICE: PCGS MS-66
DATE OF SALE: 10/2002
AUCTIONEER: Heritage

Common Errors and Values

NOT STRUCK ON QUARTER
  PLANCHET: $2,000
DOUBLE STRUCK: $700
STRUCK 3–4 TIMES: $850
OBVERSE CLAD MISSING: $350
REVERSE CLAD MISSING: $650
OFF CENTER MINOR: $100
OFF CENTER MAJOR: N/A

ROTATED REVERSE: N/A
BROCKAGE: $300
BROADSIDE: $50
STRUCK-THROUGH: $20
PARTIAL COLLAR: $20
CLIPPED "MINOR": $50
CLIPPED "MAJOR": $75

Grading Hints

OBVERSE: The high points of the coin's obverse are prone to wear; the field off Washington's nose, and the area behind the head curls, are prone to contact marks. Wear is most likely to be evident on the hair above Washington's ear and on the cheekbones. High-grade (MS-67 and above) coins will have no contact marks in the field.

REVERSE: This is the more important side for grade. High grade (above MS-67) has minimal (few if any) contact marks in the field. The high points of the coin show wear first: tree trunk at right; sugar tapper's arm and shoulder.

Investment Potential

Most "slabbed" state quarters are in MS-66 or better condition. Those that have gone up most in value and which have the greatest potential are MS-68 and better.

Past performance is no guarantee for the future, but from circulation the average (out of 56 states and territories) for P and D ranks 35. In 2008, based on auction sales records covering from the commencement of the State Quarters program to date, of more than 90 issues (P and D) taken from circulation, these coins ranked as follows: (P) 46, (D) 81.

KENTUCKY

STATE, YEAR OF ISSUE: Kentucky, 2001

State Information

YEAR OF STATEHOOD: 1792
ORDER IN UNION: 15
SIZE: 40,411 sq. mi.
POPULATION: 4.2 million
STATE MOTTO: "United we stand; divided we fall"
STATE FLOWER: goldenrod
STATE BIRD: cardinal
STATE TREE: tulip poplar

Coin Specifications

MINTMARKS: P, D, S
OBVERSE DESIGNER: John Flanagan, modified by William Cousins (1997)
REVERSE DESIGNER: T. James Farrell
REVERSE DESIGN: At top: state name above date entered Union. At bottom: date of issue above motto "E Pluribus Unum," describing how the divided colonies became the United States of America. State design: "My Old Kentucky Home," Thoroughbred in front of fence. Initials TJF at lower right fence.

Design History

In 1997, Kentucky had the fourth-largest number of farms in the nation. The state's 88,000 farms averaged 159 acres. Kentucky's first lady Judi Patton headed up the Kentucky Quarter Project Committee, which received nearly 1,800 design concepts from people across the state. The committee then narrowed the submissions to a smaller pool, from which Governor and Mrs. Patton chose 12 finalists for the public to vote on.

The final designs were displayed in the front lobby of the state capitol and on the Internet from June 15 through 17, 1999. More than 50,000 residents of Kentucky cast votes for their favorite. Four designs were forwarded to the U.S. Mint in June 1999:

ALTERNATE DESIGN NOT CHOSEN FOR KY QUARTER.

- "My Old Kentucky Home"

- a horse and jockey

- Abraham Lincoln's birthplace

- Daniel Boone with his dog

Governor Paul Patton preferred a Thoroughbred racehorse standing in front of a farmhouse ("My Old Kentucky Home"). Also approved: Daniel Boone with his dog, crouching position. Rejected: Boone at the Cumberland Gap and Lincoln's birthplace. The Commission of Fine Arts met February 17, 2000; Barbara Bradford of the U.S. Mint apprised the committee that "[Old Kentucky Home"] was very much the preferential design. . . ." Carter Brown, the chair, thought "Daniel Boone is pretty terrific" and that "For a stronger design historically, Lincoln is a more important event than any of these. . . ." He found Cumberland Gap "a nonstarter." But it was "Old Kentucky Home" that won in the end.

Mintage Figures

PROOF "S": 3.0 million
PROOF SILVER "S": 0.889 million
UNCIRCULATED "P": 353.0 million
UNCIRCULATED "D": 370.5 million

Price Record

PRICE: $1,840
DATE OF ISSUE: 2001 Mintmark P
GRADING SERVICE: PCGS MS-69
DATE OF SALE: 12/2007
AUCTIONEER: Heritage

PRICE: $210
DATE OF ISSUE: 2001 Mintmark D
GRADING SERVICE: PCGS MS-68
DATE OF SALE: 5/2003
AUCTIONEER: Heritage

Common Errors and Values

NOT STRUCK ON QUARTER
  PLANCHET: $2,000
DOUBLE STRUCK: $700
STRUCK 3–4 TIMES: $850
OBVERSE CLAD MISSING: $350
REVERSE CLAD MISSING: $650
OFF CENTER MINOR: $100
OFF CENTER MAJOR: N/A

ROTATED REVERSE: N/A
BROCKAGE: $300
BROADSIDE: $50
STRUCK-THROUGH: $20
PARTIAL COLLAR: $20
CLIPPED "MINOR": $50
CLIPPED "MAJOR": $75

Grading Hints

OBVERSE: The high points of the coin's obverse are prone to wear; the field off Washington's nose, and the area behind the head curls, are prone to contact marks. Wear is most likely to be evident on the hair above Washington's ear and on the cheekbones. High-grade (MS-67 and above) coins will have no contact marks in the field.

REVERSE: This is the more important side for grade. High grade (above MS-67) has minimal (few if any) contact marks in the field. The high points of the coin show wear first: horse's head and butt.

Investment Potential

Most "slabbed" state quarters are in MS-66 or better condition. Those that have gone up most in value and which have the greatest potential are MS-68 and better. Past performance is no guarantee for the future, but from circulation the average (out of 56 states and territories) for P and D ranks 10. In 2008, based on auction sales records covering from the commencement of the State Quarters program to date, of more than 90 issues (P and D) taken from circulation, these coins ranked as follows: (P) 75, (D) 18.

TENNESSEE

STATE, YEAR OF ISSUE: Tennessee, 2002

State Information

YEAR OF STATEHOOD: 1796
ORDER IN UNION: 16
SIZE: 42,146 sq. mi.
POPULATION: 6.1 million
STATE MOTTO: "Agriculture and commerce"
STATE FLOWER: iris
STATE BIRD: mockingbird
STATE TREE: tulip poplar

Coin Specifications

MINTMARKS: P, D, S
OBVERSE DESIGNER: John Flanagan, modified by William Cousins (1997)
REVERSE DESIGNER: Donna Weaver, engraver; Shawn Stookey, designer
REVERSE DESIGN: At top: state name above date entered Union. At bottom: date of issue above motto "E Pluribus Unum," describing how the divided colonies became the United States of America. State design incorporates musical instruments and a score with the inscription "Musical Heritage." Three stars represent Tennessee's three regions, and the instruments symbolize each region's distinct musical style. The fiddle represents the Appalachian music of east Tennessee, the trumpet stands for the blues of west Tennessee for which Memphis is famous, and the guitar is for central Tennessee, home to Nashville, the capital of country music. Initials DW above ribbon, right side at edge.

Design History

Governor Don Sundquist announced a statewide contest for students, artisans, and citizens to choose the Tennessee quarter in March 2000. "I am excited about the designs that Tennesseans will come up with in representing the Volunteer State," Sundquist said. "There are many creative and talented people who will make us proud." The Tennessee Coin Commission, appointed by Sundquist, would oversee the project.

ALTERNATE DESIGN NOT CHOSEN FOR TN QUARTER.

On April 10, 2001, the Commission of Fine Arts reviewed reverse designs for Tennessee:

- musical instruments and a score with the inscription "Musical Heritage"

- another version of design #1

- women in early-20th-century garb at the ballot box. The coin was entitled "Ratification of the 19th amendment"

- Sequoia and the written alphabet or "talking leaves" Cherokee

On April 30, Fine Arts Commission Vice Chair Harry Robinson III wrote to Jay Johnson, director of the Mint, that "The Commission selected the Musical Heritage theme and preferred version #2 as it was less crowded than #1. There was not much enthusiasm for either design #3 or #4."

Mintage Figures

PROOF "S" 3.0 million
PROOF SILVER "S" 0.892 million
UNCIRCULATED "P" 361.6 million
UNCIRCULATED "D" 286.4 million

Price Record

PRICE: $56
DATE OF ISSUE: 2002 Mintmark P
GRADING SERVICE: PCGS MS-68
DATE OF SALE: 1/2003
AUCTIONEER: Heritage

PRICE: $130
DATE OF ISSUE: 2002 Mintmark D
GRADING SERVICE: PCGS MS-68
DATE OF SALE: 4/2005
AUCTIONEER: Teletrade

Common Errors and Values

NOT STRUCK ON QUARTER
  PLANCHET: $2,000
DOUBLE STRUCK: $750
STRUCK 3–4 TIMES: $850
OBVERSE CLAD MISSING: $350
REVERSE CLAD MISSING: $650
OFF CENTER MINOR: $100
OFF CENTER MAJOR: N/A

ROTATED REVERSE: N/A
BROCKAGE: $300
BROADSIDE: $50
STRUCK-THROUGH: $20
PARTIAL COLLAR: $20
CLIPPED "MINOR": $50
CLIPPED "MAJOR": $75

Grading Hints

OBVERSE: The high points of the coin's obverse are prone to wear; the field off Washington's nose, and the area behind the head curls, are prone to contact marks. Wear is most likely to be evident on the hair above Washington's ear and on the cheekbones. High-grade (MS-67 and above) coins will have no contact marks in the field.

REVERSE: This is the more important side for grade. High grade (above MS-67) has minimal (few if any) contact marks in the field. The high points of the coin show wear first: guitar body, strings, frets.

Investment Potential

Most "slabbed" state quarters are in MS-66 or better condition. Those that have gone up most in value and which have the greatest potential are MS-68 and better.

Past performance is no guarantee for the future, but from circulation the average (out of 56 states and territories) for P and D ranks 21. In 2008, based on auction sales records covering from the commencement of the State Quarters program to date, of more than 90 issues (P and D) taken from circulation, these coins ranked as follows: (P) 55, (D) 32.

OHIO

STATE, YEAR OF ISSUE: Ohio, 2002

State Information

YEAR OF STATEHOOD: 1803
ORDER IN UNION: 17
SIZE: 44,828 sq. mi.
POPULATION: 11.4 million
STATE MOTTO: "With God, all things are possible"
STATE FLOWER: scarlet carnation
STATE BIRD: cardinal
STATE TREE: buckeye

Coin Specifications

MINTMARKS: P, D, S
OBVERSE DESIGNER: John Flanagan, modified by William Cousins (1997)
REVERSE DESIGNER: Donna Weaver
REVERSE DESIGN: At top: state name above date entered Union. At bottom: date of issue above motto "E Pluribus Unum," describing how the divided colonies became the United States of America. State design honors Ohio's contribution to the history of aviation, depicting an early aircraft and an astronaut, super-imposed on a map outlining the state. the design also includes the inscription "Birthplace of Aviation Pioneers." Initials DW below "on" in "Pioneer."

Design History

Ohio's bicentennial was celebrated in 2003, and this made the quarter's appearance a part of the celebration. The Ohio Bicentennial Commission accepted quarter designs to be reviewed by an 11-member Ohio Commemorative Quarter Program Committee announced by Governor Bob Taft. The deadline for submissions was May 25, 2000.

The committee selected several representative designs that were displayed on the state Web site from June 20 through June 22, 2000. Visitors were able to point and click to register their opinions on their favorite designs. The top three to five designs were sent to a graphic artist for fine-tuning before

ALTERNATE DESIGN NOT CHOSEN FOR OH QUARTER.

making their final journey to the U.S. Mint. The Mint's Citizens Commemorative Coin Advisory Committee reviewed the drawings and recommended candidate designs to the U.S. Fine Arts Commission.

The 11-member Committee of the Ohio Bicentennial Commission selected 10 design ideas (from 7,300 suggestions), which were developed into designs by artists at Ohio State, Kent State, and Bowling Green State universities:

- An outline of the state with Lake Erie, aviation, and invention symbols, including Thomas Edison's lightbulb

- an outline of the state with the state bird, the cardinal, and buckeye leaves

- the statehouse with aviation symbols

- Marblehead's 1822 lighthouse and the Lake Erie shore

- a celebration of the spirit of invention that would honor Edison and state contributions to air and space travel

- pioneers of flight, showing the lunar landing, John Glenn's Friendship 7 space capsule circling the Earth, and the Wright Brothers' airplane

- Johnny Appleseed

- Serpent Mound superimposed on a relief map of Ohio. (The quarter-mile-long mound in Adams County was built by the Adena people between 800 B.C. and A.D. 100; it was a favorite of schoolchildren who submitted designs.)

- the Underground Railroad

- transportation, in a design that includes canal boats, riverboats, and the National Road, which was cut through Ohio in the 1830s.

The Commission of Fine Arts met April 19, 2001, in Washington, On April 30, Harry G. Robinson III, vice chairman, wrote to Mint Director Jay Johnson: "Noting Governor Taft's preference for the aviation theme, the Commission chose the pioneers of aviation design. It was recommended that 'Pioneers (rather than Heroes) of Aviation' or simply 'Aviation Pioneers' be added within the state boundaries, just below the airplane; 'Birthplace of Aviation' was not considered acceptable because of the historical conflict with North Carolina."

The commission went on to acknowledge that "We should like to note here the letters from members of the Ohio Bicentennial Commission protesting the

Mint's changes and additions to the Ohio designs as submitted. In design #1, for example, there was criticism of the addition of the stars on both sides and of the astronaut's overly-detailed spacesuit. The Commission would hope that the Mint and the Ohio commission can arrive at mutually acceptable modifications to the design if it is the one finally chosen."

The commission had other choices, however. "As an alternative to the aviation theme, there was great enthusiasm for design #3, showing the state bird and tree superimposed on the outline of the state. The rendition of the cardinal and the buckeye branch is very strong and would show up well on a coin, and the state's motto is a nice addition. The design including the Edison lightbulb did not have any supporters."

One minor change that the local state committee effected: they changed the direction in which that the biplane was flying.

Mintage Figures

PROOF "S": 3.0 million
PROOF SILVER "S": 0.892 million
UNCIRCULATED "P": 217.2 million
UNCIRCULATED "D": 414.8 million

Price Record

PRICE: $379
DATE OF ISSUE: 2002 Mintmark P
GRADING SERVICE: PCGS MS-69
DATE OF SALE: 12/2003
AUCTIONEER: Heritage

PRICE: $126
DATE OF ISSUE: 2002 Mintmark D
GRADING SERVICE: PCGS MS-66
DATE OF SALE: 3/2003
AUCTIONEER: Heritage

Common Errors and Values

NOT STRUCK ON QUARTER
 PLANCHET: $2,000
DOUBLE STRUCK: $750
STRUCK 3–4 TIMES: $850
OBVERSE CLAD MISSING: $350
REVERSE CLAD MISSING: $650
OFF CENTER MINOR: $100

OFF CENTER MAJOR: N/A
ROTATED REVERSE: N/A
BROCKAGE: $300
BROADSIDE: $50
STRUCK-THROUGH: $20
PARTIAL COLLAR: $20
CLIPPED "MINOR": $50

Grading Hints

OBVERSE: The high points of the coin's obverse are prone to wear; the field off Washington's nose, and the area behind the head curls, are prone to contact marks. Wear is most likely to be evident on the hair above Washington's ear and on the cheekbones. High-grade (MS-67 and above) coins will have no contact marks in the field.

REVERSE: This is the more important side for grade. High grade (above MS-67) has minimal (few if any) contact marks in the field. The high points of the coin show wear first: spaceman's helmet and legs.

Investment Potential

Most "slabbed" state quarters are in MS-66 or better condition. Those that have gone up most in value and which have the greatest potential are MS-68 and better.

Past performance is no guarantee for the future, but from circulation the average (out of 56 states and territories) for P and D ranks 25. In 2008, based on auction sales records covering from the commencement of the State Quarters program to date, of more than 90 issues (P and D) taken from circulation, these coins ranked as follows: (P) 10, (D) 34.

LOUISIANA

STATE, YEAR OF ISSUE: Louisiana, 2002

State Information

YEAR OF STATEHOOD: 1812

ORDER IN UNION: 18

SIZE: 49,651 sq. mi.

POPULATION: 4. .2 million

STATE MOTTO: "Union, justice, confidence"

STATE FLOWER: magnolia

STATE BIRD: eastern brown pelican

STATE TREE: cypress

Coin Specifications

MINTMARKS: P, D, S

OBVERSE DESIGNER: John Flanagan, modified by William Cousins (1997)

REVERSE DESIGNER: John Mercanti

REVERSE DESIGN: At top: state name above date entered Union. At bottom: date of issue above motto "E Pluribus Unum," describing how the divided colonies became the United States of America. State design outlines the United States, shows the extent of the Louisiana Purchase (1803) by Jefferson, and the size of Louisiana (upraised outline). Also shown: images of Louisiana's state bird—the pelican—a trumpet with musical notes, and alongside the map the inscription "Louisiana Purchase." The trumpet on the coin is a tribute to the state's heritage of jazz music; four notes are being played in staccato fashion. Initials JM in Florida panhandle on map.

Design History

In July 1999, Mike Foster Jr., the governor of Louisiana, established the 18-member Louisiana Commemorative Coin Advisory Commission. It consisted of the governor, or the governor's designee; the state treasurer or his designee; a collector of Louisiana currency printed subsequent to Louisiana's admittance into the Union in 1812; a collector of coins minted at the New Orleans Mint; and a minimum of seven and a maximum of 14 citizens of the state of Louisiana knowledgeable about rare coins

ALTERNATE DESIGN NOT CHOSEN FOR LA QUARTER.

and/or the geography, flora, fauna, history, political development, and/or natural heritage of the state of Louisiana, selected from the seven congressional districts of Louisiana.

The governor was looking for a design theme that contained an enduring symbol, representation, or emblem of Louisiana that would inform a viewer about the state.

The following designs were ultimately submitted to the Commission of Fine Arts:

- A pelican and paddle-wheel steamboat superimposed on an outline of the state

- A pelican flying over a paddle-wheel steamboat

- The Louisiana Purchase territory outlined on a map of the United States

- A flying pelican superimposed on the state outline, and the inscription "The Bayou State"

On April 30, 2001, commission chairman J. Carter Brown wrote Mint Director Jay Johnson that #1 was the winner. Design #2 came in second, and #4 came in third.

Mintage Figures

PROOF "S": 3.0 million
PROOF SILVER "S": 0.892 million
UNCIRCULATED "P": 362.0 million
UNCIRCULATED "D": 402.2 million

Price Record

PRICE: $494
DATE OF ISSUE: 2002 Mintmark P
GRADING SERVICE: PCGS MS-69
DATE OF SALE: 5/2003
AUCTIONEER: Heritage

PRICE: $70
DATE OF ISSUE: 2002 Mintmark D
GRADING SERVICE: PCGS MS-68
DATE OF SALE: 8/2005
AUCTIONEER: Teletrade

Common Errors and Values

NOT STRUCK ON QUARTER
  PLANCHET: $2,000
DOUBLE STRUCK: $800
STRUCK 3–4 TIMES: $950
OBVERSE CLAD MISSING: $350
REVERSE CLAD MISSING: $650
OFF CENTER MINOR: $100
OFF CENTER MAJOR: N/A

ROTATED REVERSE: N/A
BROCKAGE: $300
BROADSIDE: $50
STRUCK-THROUGH: $20
PARTIAL COLLAR: $20
CLIPPED "MINOR": $50
CLIPPED "MAJOR": $75

Grading Hints

OBVERSE: The high points of the coin's obverse are prone to wear; the field off Washington's nose, and the area behind the head curls, are prone to contact marks. Wear is most likely to be evident on the hair above Washington's ear and on the cheekbones. High-grade (MS-67 and above) coins will have no contact marks in the field.

REVERSE: This is the more important side for grade. High grade (above MS-67) has minimal (few if any) contact marks in the field. The high points of the coin—the pelican's head and body—show wear first.

Investment Potential

Most "slabbed" state quarters are in MS-66 or better condition. Those that have gone up most in value and which have the greatest potential are MS-68 and better.

Past performance is no guarantee of the future, but from circulation the average (out of 56 states and territories) for P and D ranks 5. In 2008, based on auction sales records covering from the commencement of the State Quarters program to date, of more than 90 issues (P and D) taken from circulation, these coins ranked as follows: (P) 5, (D) 47.

INDIANA

STATE, YEAR OF ISSUE: Indiana, 2002

State Information

YEAR OF STATEHOOD: 1816
ORDER IN UNION: 19
SIZE: 36,420 sq. mi.
POPULATION: 6.3 million
STATE MOTTO: "The crossroads of America"
STATE FLOWER: peony
STATE BIRD: cardinal
STATE TREE: tulip tree

Coin Specifications

MINTMARKS: P, D, S
OBVERSE DESIGNER: John Flanagan, modified by William Cousins (1997)
REVERSE DESIGNER: Donna Weaver, engraver; Josh Harvey, designer
REVERSE DESIGN: At top: state name above date entered Union. At bottom: date
of issue above motto "E Pluribus Unum," describing how the divided colonies
became the United States of America. State design: the image of an Indi-
anapolis Speedway race car superimposed on an outline of the state with the
inscription "Crossroads of America." The design includes 19 stars signifying
Indiana as the 19th state admitted into the Union. Initials DW below "RI" in
"America."

Design History

When Indiana first lady Judy O'Bannon announced the call for design concepts for Indiana's commemorative quarter, few could have anticipated the
submission of more than 3,700 design ideas. The
designs were reviewed by a selection committee
impaneled by the Indiana Arts Commission, which
made recommendations to the governor regarding
preliminary designs. Entries had to be postmarked no
later than December 10, 1999.

The design response was impressive, but even more
impressive was the public's response when given the
opportunity to weigh in with their opinions. From Feb-

ALTERNATE DESIGN NOT
CHOSEN FOR IN QUARTER.

ruary 7–25, people could register votes for their favorite design themes by visiting the Indiana Arts Commission (IAC) Web site. They could also vote by ballots printed in several newspapers throughout the state. "When online voting concluded, nearly 155,000 votes had been registered," said IAC Executive Director Dorothy L. Ilgen. "Almost 2,100 ballots were submitted by the postmark deadline." The "Crossroads of America" theme was prominent, as were historic and tour sites.

Some of the final designs were as follows:

- A portrait of Chief Little Turtle surrounded by tulip poplars

- A portrait of Chief Little Turtle with the state outline beside the torch and stars from the state flag

- A race car and athlete showcasing the racing and basketball program providing state championship recognition

- The state outline with a cardinal, 19 stars, and the Crossroads of America logo.

When the Commission of Fine Arts surveyed the designs, they commented by letter (April 30, 2001) to Mint Director Jay Johnson that "Design #2, showing Chief Little Turtle with the state outline, enclosed by stars on either side, was the first choice. The same design enclosed by stylized tulip poplars (#1) was second, although it was pointed out that the leaves should be rendered so they look like real tulip poplar leaves. Design #3, which we understand is the governor's choice, was acceptable, but #4, although also featuring a racing car, was not acceptable from a design point of view." The design chosen had more fluidity of motion.

Mintage Figures

PROOF "S": 3.0 million
PROOF SILVER "S": 0.892 million
UNCIRCULATED "P": 362.6 million
UNCIRCULATED "D": 327.2 million

Price Record

PRICE: $690
DATE OF ISSUE: 2002 Mintmark P
GRADING SERVICE: PCGS MS-69
DATE OF SALE: 11/2003
AUCTIONEER: Heritage

PRICE: $70
DATE OF ISSUE: 2002 Mintmark D
GRADING SERVICE: PCGS MS-67
DATE OF SALE: 4/2006
AUCTIONEER: Heritage

Common Errors and Values

NOT STRUCK ON QUARTER PLANCHET: $2,000
DOUBLE STRUCK: $800
STRUCK 3–4 TIMES: $950
OBVERSE CLAD MISSING: $350
REVERSE CLAD MISSING: $650
OFF CENTER MINOR: $100
OFF CENTER MAJOR: N/A

ROTATED REVERSE: N/A
BROCKAGE: $300
BROADSIDE: $50
STRUCK-THROUGH: $20
PARTIAL COLLAR: $20
CLIPPED "MINOR": $50
CLIPPED "MAJOR": $75

Grading Hints

OBVERSE: The high points of the coin's obverse are prone to wear; the field off Washington's nose, and the area behind the head curls, are prone to contact marks. Wear is most likely to be evident on the hair above Washington's ear and on the cheekbones. High-grade (MS-67 and above) coins will have no contact marks in the field.

REVERSE: This is the more important side for grade. High grade (above MS-67) has minimal (few if any) contact marks in the field. The high points of the coin show wear first: race car body and front tires (both sides).

Investment Potential

Most "slabbed" state quarters are in MS-66 or better condition. Those that have gone up most in value and which have the greatest potential are MS-68 and better.

Past performance is no guarantee for the future, but from circulation the average (out of 56 states and territories) for P and D ranks 3. In 2008, based on auction sales records covering from the commencement of the state quarter program to date, of more than 90 issues (P and D) taken from circulation, these coins ranked as follows: (P) 2, (D) 80.

MISSISSIPPI

STATE, YEAR OF ISSUE: Mississippi, 2002

State Information

YEAR OF STATEHOOD: 1817
ORDER IN UNION: 20
SIZE: 48,286 sq. mi.
POPULATION: 2.9 million
STATE MOTTO: "Virtute et armis" (by virtue and arms)
STATE FLOWER: magnolia
STATE BIRD: mockingbird
STATE TREE: magnolia

Coin Specifications

MINTMARKS: P, D, S
OBVERSE DESIGNER: John Flanagan, modified by William Cousins (1997)
REVERSE DESIGNER: Donna Weaver

REVERSE DESIGN: At top: state name above date entered Union. At bottom: date of issue above motto "E Pluribus Unum," describing how the divided colonies became the United States of America. State design utilizes the beauty and elegance of the state flower, combining the blossoms and leaves of two magnolias with the inscription "The Magnolia State." Initials DW incused in lower right magnolia leaf.

Design History

Although there are several varieties of magnolia found throughout the world, it is the southern magnolia, or *Magnolia grandiflora,* that is native to the southeastern United States. Boasting large, showy white flowers as big as 15 inches across, they are named for the famed 18th-century French botanist Pierre Magnol. The magnolia is the state flower of Mississippi.

The Citizens Commemorative Coin Advisory Committee met in Salt Lake City on March 8, 2001, to consider designs for the Mississippi state quarter. Governor Ronnie Musgrove had submitted three designs:

ALTERNATE DESIGN NOT CHOSEN FOR MS QUARTER.

- a magnolia flower with a branch

- a mockingbird

- "Mississippi—The Magnolia State."

They next went to the the Commission of Fine Arts which met in Washington on April 19. Harry G. Robinson III wrote to Mint Director Jay Johnson that "Design #1 was considered by everyone to be a fine design, with the suggestion that making the flower element slightly smaller would avoid the crowding seen when looking at the coin-size rendition. Design #2 was a distant second choice, and #3 was not acceptable."

Mintage Figures

PROOF "S": 3.08 million
PROOF SILVER "S": 0.892 million
UNCIRCULATED "P": 290 million
UNCIRCULATED "D": 289.6 million

Price Record

PRICE: $130
DATE OF ISSUE: 2002 Mintmark P
GRADING SERVICE: PCGS MS-68
DATE OF SALE: 5/2005
AUCTIONEER: Teletrade

PRICE: $150
DATE OF ISSUE: 2002 Mintmark D
GRADING SERVICE: PCGS MS-68
DATE OF SALE: 5/2005
AUCTIONEER: Teletrade

Common Errors and Values

NOT STRUCK ON QUARTER
  PLANCHET: $2,000
DOUBLE STRUCK: $800
STRUCK 3–4 TIMES: $950
OBVERSE CLAD MISSING: $350
REVERSE CLAD MISSING: $650
OFF CENTER MINOR: $100
OFF CENTER MAJOR: N/A

ROTATED REVERSE: N/A
BROCKAGE: $300
RROADSIDE: $50
STRUCK-THROUGH: $20
PARTIAL COLLAR: $20
CLIPPED "MINOR": $50
CLIPPED "MAJOR": $75

Grading Hints

OBVERSE: The high points of the coin's obverse are prone to wear; the field off Washington's nose, and the area behind the head curls, are prone to contact marks. Wear is most likely to be evident on the hair above Washington's ear and on the cheekbones. High-grade (MS-67 and above) coins will have no contact marks in the field.

REVERSE: This is the more important side for grade. High grade (above MS-67) has minimal (few if any) contact marks in the field. The high points of the coin show wear first: lower portion of flower (6 to 8 o'clock).

Investment Potential

Most "slabbed" state quarters are in MS-66 or better condition. Those that have gone up most in value and which have the greatest potential are MS-68 and better.

Past performance is no guarantee for the future, but from circulation the average (out of 56 states and territories) for P and D ranks 17. In 2008, based on auction sales records covering from the commencement of the State Quarters program to date, of more than 90 issues (P and D) taken from circulation, these coins ranked as follows: (P) 33, (D) 27.

ILLINOIS

STATE, YEAR OF ISSUE: Illinois, 2003

State Information

YEAR OF STATEHOOD: 1818
ORDER IN UNION: 21
SIZE: 57,918 sq. mi.
POPULATION: 12. .8 million
STATE MOTTO: "State sovereignty, national union"
STATE FLOWER: violet
STATE BIRD: cardinal
STATE TREE: oak

Coin Specifications

MINTMARKS: P, D, S
OBVERSE DESIGNER: John Flanagan, modified by William Cousins (1997)
REVERSE DESIGNER: Donna Weaver
REVERSE DESIGN: At top: state name above date entered Union. At bottom: date of issue above motto "E Pluribus Unum," describing how the divided colonies became the United States of America. State design: an outline of the state in map form; within, a young Abraham Lincoln. A farm scene and the Chicago skyline appear on the left and to the right of the state's outline. There are 21 stars bordering the coin, signifying Illinois as the 21st state to be admitted into the Union on December 3, 1818. Initials DW to right of map.

Design History

The Illinois commemorative quarter committee was chaired by Governor George H. Ryan and first lady Lura Lynn Ryan. The committee considered many designs featured around the themes of history, agriculture, and Lincoln. They forwarded five designs to the Mint for review:

- state symbols (bird, butterfly, leaf) over an outline of the state-nominated "Land of Lincoln"

- "Land of Lincoln," "21st Century State"; state outline with farm and city skyline silhouetted

ALTERNATE DESIGN NOT CHOSEN FOR IL QUARTER.

- a mature Lincoln with his lawbooks sitting beside the state where he practiced law for many years

- a farmer plowing "The Prairie State"

- skyscraper in foreground, growing corn in the background, and the Lincoln motto together with "The 21st State" and "The Prairie State"

On March 12, 2002, Mint Director Henrietta Holsman Fore transmitted the designs to Carter Brown, chairman of the Commission of Fine Arts. She asked for review of the enclosed designs at the March 21 meeting. Brown wrote Fore on April 5 that although there was some appreciation for design number four depicting a farmer plowing with his horse, there was unanimous agreement that design number three, showing a seated Lincoln with his lawbooks, best represented the "Land of Lincoln." Ultimately chosen: a young Abraham Lincoln surrounded by the outline of the state. A farm scene and a city skyline appear on the left and right of the outline.

"This design is one of the most distinctive of the series. It is the first U.S. coin to feature a young Abraham Lincoln, and thus it is a numismatic first," said Henrietta Holsman Fore at the Illinois quarter launch in 2003.

Mintage Figures

PROOF "S": 3.4 million
PROOF SILVER "S":1.125 million
UNCIRCULATED "P": 225.8 million
UNCIRCULATED "D": 237.4 million

Price Record

PRICE: $500
DATE OF ISSUE: 2003 Mintmark P
GRADING SERVICE: PCGS MS-68
DATE OF SALE: 11/2006
AUCTIONEER: Teletrade

PRICE: $33
DATE OF ISSUE: 2003 Mintmark D
GRADING SERVICE: PCGS MS-67
DATE OF SALE: 6/2005
AUCTIONEER: Teletrade

Common Errors and Values

NOT STRUCK ON QUARTER PLANCHET: $1,750

DOUBLE STRUCK: $900

STRUCK 3–4 TIMES: $1,100

OBVERSE CLAD MISSING: $350

REVERSE CLAD MISSING: $650

OFF CENTER MINOR: $115

OFF CENTER MAJOR: N/A

ROTATED REVERSE: N/A

BROCKAGE: $300

BROADSIDE: $50

STRUCK-THROUGH: $20

PARTIAL COLLAR: $20

CLIPPED "MINOR": $50

CLIPPED "MAJOR": $75

Grading Hints

OBVERSE: The high points of the coin's obverse are prone to wear; the field off Washington's nose, and the area behind the head curls, are prone to contact marks. Wear is most likely to be evident on the hair above Washington's ear and on the cheekbones. High-grade (MS-67 and above) coins will have no contact marks in the field.

REVERSE: This is the more important side for grade. High grade (above MS-67) has minimal (few if any) contact marks in the field. The high points of the coin show wear first: Lincoln's right arm, elbow, and left knee.

Investment Potential

Most "slabbed" state quarters are in MS-66 or better condition. Those that have gone up most in value and which have the greatest potential are MS-68 and better.

Past performance is no guarantee for the future, but from circulation the average (out of 56 states and territories) for P and D ranks 7. In 2008, based on auction sales records covering from the commencement of the State Quarters program to date, of more than 90 issues (P and D) taken from circulation, these coins ranked as follows: (P) 4, (D) 69.

ALABAMA

STATE, YEAR OF ISSUE: Alabama, 2003

State Information

YEAR OF STATEHOOD: 1819
ORDER IN UNION: 22
SIZE: 52,237 sq. mi.
POPULATION: 4.6 million
STATE MOTTO: "We dare defend our rights"
STATE FLOWER: camellia
STATE BIRD: yellowhammer
STATE TREE: southern pine

Coin Specifications

MINTMARKS: P, D, S
OBVERSE DESIGNER: John Flanagan, modified by William Cousins (1997)
REVERSE DESIGNER: Norman E. Nemeth
REVERSE DESIGN: At top: state name above date entered Union. At bottom: date of issue above motto "E Pluribus Unum," describing how the divided colonies became the United States of America. State design: seated image of Helen Keller with her name in English, and in a reduced-size version of braille. The Alabama quarter is the first U.S. circulating coin to feature braille. An Alabama long leaf pine branch and magnolias grace the sides of the design, and a "Spirit of Courage" banner underlines the central image. Initials NEN beneath "Spirit."

Design History

Helen Keller was born at "Ivy Green" in Tuscumbia, Alabama, in 1880. When she was a small child, an illness destroyed her sight, hearing, and speech. Despite her disabilities, Helen Keller learned to speak and read using the raised and manual alphabets, as well as braille.

In January 2001, Governor Don Siegelman announced a statewide competition for Alabama schools to submit concepts for the Alabama quarter. Siegelman asked participants to follow the theme, "Education: Link to the Past, Gateway to the Future."

ALTERNATE DESIGN NOT CHOSEN FOR AL QUARTER.

The idea behind the contest was to give students the opportunity to exercise their creativity and to encourage research into Alabama's rich history.

More than 450 drawings and design suggestions were received from Alabama schoolchildren. Submitted designs included moon rockets and space shuttles representing Alabama's contribution to the U.S. space program; a statue of Vulcan symbolizing Alabama's heritage of iron production; depictions of the beautiful Alabama State Capitol; Native American Cherokee Indian Chief Sequoyah; and various state symbols.

The governor and his staff decided the finalists were:

- the state capitol

- Helen Keller

- a design depicting various symbols of Alabama's history, including Cherokee Indian Chief Sequoyah, on a historical time line

- Alabama's state bird, the yellowhammer

On April 5, 2002, the Commission of Fine Arts wrote to the Mint that "Design No. 4, showing the yellowhammer, pine branch, and state outline, had the most votes, although No. 1, showing the state capitol flanked by branches of pine and camellia, was a close second. The design featuring a likeness of Helen Keller, which we understand is the governor's choice, did not seem particularly appropriate because although born in Alabama, Miss Keller spent most of her life in New England and is associated with that part of the country."

However, the final selection of Helen Keller, "Spirit of Courage," was ultimately made by the Governor's office. The Alabama quarter is the first U.S. circulating coin to feature braille. An Alabama long leaf pine branch and magnolias grace the sides of the design, and a "Spirit of Courage" banner underlines the central image.

Mintage Figures

PROOF "S": 3.4 million
PROOF SILVER "S":1.125 million
UNCIRCULATED "P": 225.0 million
UNCIRCULATED "D": 232.4 million

Price Record

PRICE: $90
DATE OF ISSUE: 2003 Mintmark P
GRADING SERVICE: PCGS MS-68
DATE OF SALE: 11/2006
AUCTIONEER: Teletrade

PRICE: $170
DATE OF ISSUE: 2003 Mintmark D
GRADING SERVICE: PCGS MS-68
DATE OF SALE: 5/2005
AUCTIONEER: Teletrade

Common Errors and Values

NOT STRUCK ON QUARTER
  PLANCHET: $2,000
DOUBLE STRUCK: $800
STRUCK 3–4 TIMES: $1,000
OBVERSE CLAD MISSING: $350
REVERSE CLAD MISSING: $650
OFF CENTER MINOR: $115
OFF CENTER MAJOR: N/A

ROTATED REVERSE: N/A
BROCKAGE: $300
BROADSIDE: $50
STRUCK-THROUGH: $20
PARTIAL COLLAR: $20
CLIPPED "MINOR": $50
CLIPPED "MAJOR": $75

Grading Hints

OBVERSE: The high points of the coin's obverse are prone to wear; the field off Washington's nose, and the area behind the head curls, are prone to contact marks. Wear is most likely to be evident on the hair above Washington's ear and on the cheekbones. High-grade (MS-67 and above) coins will have no contact marks in the field.

REVERSE: This is the more important side for grade. High grade (above MS-67) has minimal (few if any) contact marks in the field. The high points of the coin show wear first: head and right arm of Helen Keller; machine top.

Investment Potential

Most "slabbed" state quarters are in MS-66 or better condition. Those that have gone up most in value and which have the greatest potential are MS-68 and better.

Past performance is no guarantee of the future, but from circulation the average (out of 56 states and territories) for P and D ranks 20. In 2008, based on auction sales records covering from the commencement of the State Quarters program to date, of more than 90 issues (P and D) taken from circulation, these coins ranked as follows: (P) 43, (D) 24.

MAINE

State Information

YEAR OF STATEHOOD: 1820
ORDER IN UNION: 23
SIZE: 33,741 sq. mi.
POPULATION: 1.3 million
STATE MOTTO: "Dirigo" (I direct)
STATE FLOWER: white pinecone and tassel
STATE BIRD: chickadee
STATE TREE: eastern white pine

Coin Specifications

MINTMARKS: P, D, S
OBVERSE DESIGNER: John Flanagan, modified by William Cousins (1997)
REVERSE DESIGNER: Donna Weaver, engraver; Daniel Carr, designer
REVERSE DESIGN: At top: state name above date entered Union. At bottom: date of issue above motto "E Pluribus Unum," describing how the divided colonies became the United States of America. State design: the Pemaquid Point Light atop a granite coast and a schooner at sea. Initials DW incused on left shore (rocky edge).

Design History

Pemaquid Point Light is located in New Harbor, Maine, and marks the entrance to Muscongus Bay and Johns Bay. Since the beginning of ship activity in the area, a shoal created hazardous navigation conditions, causing many shipwrecks. As maritime trade increased in the area, so did the need for a lighthouse. In 1826, Congress appropriated funds to build a lighthouse at Pemaquid Point. Although the original building was replaced in 1835, and the original ten lamps in 1856, the light is still a beacon for ships and remains one of Maine's most popular tourist attractions.

The process for choosing a design for the quarter began in March 2001, when Governor Angus King established the seven-member Commission on the

ALTERNATE DESIGN NOT CHOSEN FOR ME QUARTER.

Maine State Quarter Design. The commission was headed by State Treasurer Dale McCormick, who launched a design contest open to all full- and part-time Maine residents and scheduled to conclude on May 11, 2001.

The commission examined about 200 concepts and drawings from the Maine public. Finalists were forwarded to King for his review on June 6, 2001. King selected three of the five concepts presented to him:

- the Pemaquid Point Light and a three-masted schooner navigating the rocky Maine coast. These elements reflected Maine's maritime history. Also included was a young white pine tree, the official state tree, representing the state's forestry product industries.

- Maine's Mount Katahdin, including the original Penobscot Indian spelling, "Ktaadn." Mount Katahdin, located in Maine's north woods, is the highest mountain in Maine (5,267 feet above sea level) and marks the northern end of the Appalachian Trail. Henry David Thoreau's *The Maine Woods* was written about Mount Katahdin.

- an outline of the state with the sun rising above a body of water with 16 rays emanating from the sun to indicate Maine's 16 counties. The North Star, a part of Maine's state seal, was depicted to the left of the rising sun.

Governor King suggested a fourth idea similar to the third but incorporating different design elements. It included the elements of the rising sun and white pine and a representation of the West Quoddy Head Light in Lubec, Maine. The distinctively shaped West Quoddy Head Light is known for its red and white horizontal stripes. These four design concepts were submitted to the U.S. Mint.

The Commission of Fine Arts wrote to the Mint that "There was unanimous agreement that design No. 1, showing a rocky coast, lighthouse, and sailing ship, most clearly said "Maine." The governor's preferred concept, design #3, is an intriguing one, but hard to represent graphically on a coin."

Mintage Figures

PROOF "S": 3.4 million
PROOF SILVER "S":1.125 million
UNCIRCULATED "P": 217.4 million
UNCIRCULATED "D": 231.4 million

Price Record

PRICE: $525
DATE OF ISSUE: 2003 Mintmark P
GRADING SERVICE: PCGS MS-68
DATE OF SALE: 11/2006
AUCTIONEER: Teletrade

PRICE: $1,092
DATE OF ISSUE: 2003 Mintmark D
GRADING SERVICE: PCGS MS-68
DATE OF SALE: 12/2007
AUCTIONEER: Heritage

Common Errors and Values

NOT STRUCK ON QUARTER PLANCHET: $2,000
DOUBLE STRUCK: $800
STRUCK 3–4 TIMES: $1,100
OBVERSE CLAD MISSING: $350
REVERSE CLAD MISSING: $650
OFF CENTER MINOR: $115
OFF CENTER MAJOR: N/A

ROTATED REVERSE: N/A
BROCKAGE: $300
BROADSIDE: $50
STRUCK-THROUGH: $20
PARTIAL COLLAR: $20
CLIPPED "MINOR": $50
CLIPPED "MAJOR": $75

Grading Hints

OBVERSE: The high points of the coin's obverse are prone to wear; the field off Washington's nose, and the area behind the head curls, are prone to contact marks. Wear is most likely to be evident on the hair above Washington's ear and on the cheekbones. High-grade (MS-67 and above) coins will have no contact marks in the field.

REVERSE: This is the more important side for grade. High grade (above MS-67) has minimal (few if any) contact marks in the field. The high points of the coin show wear first: ship on water, rocks at bottom, lighthouse.

Investment Potential

Most "slabbed" state quarters are in MS-66 or better condition. Those that have gone up most in value and which have the greatest potential are MS-68 and better.

Past performance is no guarantee for the future, but from circulation the average (out of 56 states and territories) for P and D ranks 6. In 2008, based on auction sales records covering from the commencement of the State Quarters program to date, of more than 90 issues (P and D) taken from circulation, these coins ranked as follows: (P) 3, (D) 79.

MISSOURI

STATE, YEAR OF ISSUE: Missouri, 2003

State Information

YEAR OF STATEHOOD: 1821
ORDER IN UNION: 24
SIZE: 69,709 sq. mi.
POPULATION: 5.8 million
STATE MOTTO: "The welfare of the people shall be supreme law"
STATE FLOWER: hawthorne
STATE BIRD: bluebird
STATE TREE: dogwood

Coin Specifications

MINTMARKS: P, D, S
OBVERSE DESIGNER: John Flanagan, modified by William Cousins (1997)
REVERSE DESIGNER: Alfred Maletsky, engraver; Paul Jackson, designer
REVERSE DESIGN: At top: state name above date entered Union. At bottom: date of issue above motto "E Pluribus Unum," describing how the divided colonies became the United States of America. State design: Lewis and Clark's historic return to St. Louis down the Missouri River, mingled with the new: the Jefferson National Expansion Memorial (Gateway Arch) in the background. The quarter is inscribed "Corps of Discovery 1804–2004" to mark the bicentennial. Initials AFM at lower right in water.

Design History

In February 2001, Governor Bob Holden announced the selection of the Missouri Commemorative Quarter Design Committee and requested statewide design submissions. During the month of March, the state received more than 3,000 concept submissions. The committee, composed of a team of experts, selected 12 finalists.

Lori Holden, first lady of Missouri, was placed in charge of the state quarter program. "I am so pleased to send back to the U.S. Mint the designs chosen by Missourians," she said. "And I am even more pleased that the citizens of Missouri had an opportunity to

ALTERNATE DESIGN NOT CHOSEN FOR MO QUARTER.

become part of history by choosing the design they felt best represents this state's long and diverse history."

The state submitted five design concepts to the U.S. Mint, who made some adaptations to ensure the best-looking quarter possible. The winning concept, depicting the explorers Louis and Clark, was created by Paul Jackson, an artist from Columbia.

However, the artist had a concern with the revised design that came back from the Mint: it was a historically inaccurate rendering that drew from his design but departed radically from it.

John Darkow, an editorial cartoonist for the *Columbia Daily Tribune*, captured the controversy of the Paul Jackson design for the Missouri state quarters. *Reproduction courtesy of John Darkow and the* Columbia Daily Tribune

Jackson wrote to Lori Holden to protest the lack of integrity given his work. "Not only is [the revised design] a weak, cluttered design, but is far from historically accurate, and doesn't convey any great feeling of Missouri pride." Jackson dubbed the change in designs "Quarter gate."

Jackson added in a correspondence to me, "Over the past 20 years as an artist I've entered hundreds of competitions, but none so inequitable or misleading. I've never once been forced to surrender all copyright interest, even when I won. And I am appalled that the Mint won't credit or recognize the state artist's contribution to the process in any way. There is historical precedent for two sets of initials, designer and engraver. Only with this program has that fact been forgotten."

On November 22, the Mint's revised version of Jackson's concept was announced as the winner. The winning design features the St. Louis Arch and three men paddling down the river in a canoe. Jackson created paper stickers that could be pasted over the existing quarters—a way to show what his design would have looked like. More than 100,000 were put into circulation despite Mint official's threats, and claims that the Secret Service would seize them. (They didn't.)

As a result of this situation, the Treasury Department revised the rules for future state quarter competitions so that the state committees were required to send written descriptions of the designs to the Mint for the designers at the Mint to render.

Mintage Figures

PROOF "S": 3.4 million
PROOF SILVER "S": 1.125 million
UNCIRCULATED "P": 225.0 million
UNCIRCULATED "D": 228.2 million

Price Record

PRICE: $4,312
DATE OF ISSUE: 2003 Mintmark P
GRADING SERVICE: PCGS MS-68
DATE OF SALE: 12/2007
AUCTIONEER: Heritage

PRICE: $120
DATE OF ISSUE: 2003 Mintmark D
GRADING SERVICE: PCGS MS-68
DATE OF SALE: 6/2005
AUCTIONEER: Teletrade

Common Errors and Values

NOT STRUCK ON QUARTER
PLANCHET: $2,000
DOUBLE STRUCK: $850
STRUCK 3–4 TIMES: $1,250
OBVERSE CLAD MISSING: $350
REVERSE CLAD MISSING: $650
OFF CENTER MINOR: $115
OFF CENTER MAJOR: N/A

ROTATED REVERSE: N/A
BROCKAGE: $300
BROADSIDE: $50
STRUCK-THROUGH: $20
PARTIAL COLLAR: $20
CLIPPED "MINOR": $50
CLIPPED "MAJOR": $75

Grading Hints

OBVERSE: The high points of the coin's obverse are prone to wear; the field off Washington's nose, and the area behind the head curls, are prone to contact marks. Wear is most likely to be evident on the hair above Washington's ear and on the cheekbones. High-grade (MS-67 and above) coins will have no contact marks in the field.

REVERSE: This is the more important side for grade. High grade (above MS-67) has minimal (few if any) contact marks in the field. The high points of the coin show wear first: longboat, tops of trees (right and left).

Investment Potential

Most "slabbed" state quarters are in MS-66 or better condition. Those that have gone up most in value and which have the greatest potential are MS-68 and better.

Past performance is no guarantee for the future, but from circulation the average (out of 56 states and territories) for P and D ranks 13. In 2008, based on auction sales records covering from the commencement of the State Quarters program to date, of more than 90 issues (P and D) taken from circulation, these coins ranked as follows: (P) 17, (D) 36.

ARKANSAS

STATE, YEAR OF ISSUE: Arkansas, 2003

State Information

YEAR OF STATEHOOD: 1836
ORDER IN UNION: 25
SIZE: 53,182 sq. mi
POPULATION: 2.8 million
STATE MOTTO: "The people rule"
STATE FLOWER: apple blossom
STATE BIRD: mockingbird
STATE TREE: pine

Coin Specifications

MINTMARKS: P, D, S
OBVERSE DESIGNER: John Flanagan, modified by William Cousins (1997)
REVERSE DESIGNER: John Mercanti, engraver; Dortha Scott, designer
REVERSE DESIGN: At top: state name above date entered Union. At bottom: date of issue above motto "E Pluribus Unum," describing how the divided colonies became the United States of America. State design: image of rice stalks, a diamond, and a mallard flying above a lake. Initials JM incused on water detail at right.

Design History

In January 2001, Governor Mike Huckabee announced the Arkansas Quarter Challenge as a statewide competition. A two-week media tour promoting the challenge resulted in 9,320 design entries. A committee then narrowed the designs down to the top 100, which were displayed at the state capitol in Little Rock. Huckabee selected 11 judges from across the state to review those entries and chose the best dozen, which were narrowed down to three by the governor to send to the U.S. Mint for review:

- an outline of the state, a pine tree, apple blossoms, ducks in flight, mountains, and a banner reading "Natural State"

ALTERNATE DESIGN NOT CHOSEN FOR AR QUARTER.

- the state capitol with a mockingbird and pine branches in the foreground

- a diamond, ducks, lakes, mountains, and rice

These final designs were modified by the U.S. Mint and returned to the governor, who made the final choice. On October 7, 2002, Huckabee announced that design #3 was the winner, and the official release of the coin was on October 28, 2003, at Crater of Diamonds State Park.

On October 29, 2003, U.S. Representative Mike Ross inserted remarks in the Congressional Record which explain the choice:

"Our Quarter incorporates several elements that truly reflect Arkansas. This is a coin that helps everyone in our nation understand why Arkansas is so proudly called 'The Natural State.' the background of the Quarter represents the abundance of natural resources that our state encompasses. Elements of the Quarter, including a mallard duck soaring above the water with trees in the background, symbolizes Arkansas's reputation as one of the most popular states in the country for hunting and fishing, and as a state with a high-abundance of forest land. The rice on the left side of the Quarter signifies the important role rice and other agricultural crops play in Arkansas's economy.

"The centerpiece of the Quarter is a diamond, representing the Crater of Diamonds State Park near Murfreesboro, home to the largest diamond ever to be unearthed in the United States and the only diamond mine in the world where the public can search for diamonds."

Mintage Figures

PROOF "S": 3.4 million
PROOF SILVER "S": 1.125 million
UNCIRCULATED "P": 228.0 million
UNCIRCULATED "D": 229.8 million

Price Record

PRICE: $460
DATE OF ISSUE: 2003 Mintmark P
GRADING SERVICE: PCGS MS-68
DATE OF SALE: 12/2007
AUCTIONEER: Heritage

PRICE: $120
DATE OF ISSUE: 2003 Mintmark D
GRADING SERVICE: PCGS MS-68
DATE OF SALE: 11/2006
AUCTIONEER: Teletrade

Common Errors and Values

NOT STRUCK ON QUARTER
PLANCHET: $2,000
DOUBLE STRUCK: $850
STRUCK 3–4 TIMES: $1,250
OBVERSE CLAD MISSING: $350
REVERSE CLAD MISSING: $650
OFF CENTER MINOR: $115
OFF CENTER MAJOR: N/A

ROTATED REVERSE: N/A
BROCKAGE: $300
BROADSIDE: $50
STRUCK-THROUGH: $20
PARTIAL COLLAR: $20
CLIPPED "MINOR": $50
CLIPPED "MAJOR": $75

Grading Hints

OBVERSE: The high points of the coin's obverse are prone to wear; the field off Washington's nose, and the area behind the head curls, are prone to contact marks. Wear is most likely to be evident on the hair above Washington's ear and on the cheekbones. High-grade (MS-67 and above) coins will have no contact marks in the field.

REVERSE: This is the more important side for grade. High grade (above MS-67) has minimal (few if any) contact marks in the field. The high points of the coin show wear first: diamond (top third), mallard's body.

Investment Potential

Most "slabbed" state quarters are in MS-66 or better condition. Those that have gone up most in value and which have the greatest potential are MS-68 and better.

Past performance is no guarantee for the future, but from circulation the average (out of 56 states and territories) for P and D ranks 16. In 2008, based on auction sales records covering from the commencement of the State Quarters program to date, of more than 90 issues (P and D) taken from circulation, these coins ranked as follows: (P) 25, (D) 35.

MICHIGAN

STATE, YEAR OF ISSUE: Michigan, 2004

State Information

YEAR OF STATEHOOD: 1837
ORDER IN UNION: 26
SIZE: 96,705 sq. mi.
POPULATION: 10.07 million
STATE MOTTO: "If you seek a pleasant peninsula, look about you"
STATE FLOWER: apple blossom
STATE BIRD: robin
STATE TREE: white pine

Coin Specifications

MINTMARKS: P, D, S
OBVERSE DESIGNER: John Flanagan, modified by William Cousins (1997)
REVERSE DESIGNER: Donna Weaver
REVERSE DESIGN: At top: state name above date entered Union. At bottom: date of issue above motto "E Pluribus Unum," describing how the divided colonies became the United States of America. State design: outline of the state, upper and lower peninsula, and map of the Great Lakes, inscribed "Great Lakes State." Initials DW on the Ohio shore of Lake Erie.

Design History

As was the case with several designs, the Michigan coin spanned two gubernatorial administrations. On November 28, 2001, Governor John Engler established the 25-member Michigan Quarter Commission. Commission members consisted of individuals from the fields of education, art, history, and numismatics. The commission solicited recommendations for design concepts from the residents of the state. Engler said, "It is not too soon to begin thinking about a design that honors our unique history, traditions, and symbols. Who should submit ideas for our Michigan quarter? I hope that this wonderful opportunity energizes people of all ages all across our state—school children,

ALTERNATE DESIGN NOT CHOSEN FOR MI QUARTER.

their teachers and parents, history buffs, coin collectors, all who love the Great Lakes State." They received more than 4,300 suggestions.

The commission narrowed the entries down to five candidate concepts that were approved by Engler, and forwarded them to the U.S. Mint on May 10, 2002:

- Michigan state outline, with Great Lakes and state icons
- Michigan state outline, with Great Lakes and the Mackinac Bridge
- Michigan state outline, with the Mackinac Bridge and automobile
- Michigan state outline, with Great Lakes and automobile
- Michigan state outline with Great Lakes

The June 24 meeting of the Citizens Coin Advisory Committee in Washington, D.C., reviewed designs for the Michigan state quarter. The consensus preferred a merging of two of the five presented designs, favoring the image to show a state outline with the words "Great Lakes State" without including the outline of all five lakes.

On July 14, 2003, Mint Director Henrietta Holsman Fore forwarded Michigan quarter designs to the Commission of Fine Arts for review, asking that the July 17, 2003, meeting of the commission take up the five transmitted designs.

On July 17, the CFA met and Barbara Bradford of the Mint showed the Michigan designs first, noting that they had already been seen by the CCCAC. All five designs showed outlines of the state, most showed it bordered by the Great Lakes. Bradford pointed out the topographical finish added to the two peninsulas, a request of the state, so that they would be differentiated from the water areas. One design incorporated several small icons of historic or architectural relevance; other showed the Mackinac Bridge and/or an early automobile design. She said the CCCAC had preferred design #3, without the bridge and using the automobile from #4. There was a discussion about the various designs, with the consensus being "the simpler the better," and so #1 became the first choice, with the request that the lettering of "Great Lakes State" be made slightly smaller, and, if possible, the image of the state and the lakes be enlarged.

In September 2003, following a consultation with the Michigan Quarter Commission, Governor Jennifer Granholm selected the Great Lakes State design.

Mintage Figures

PROOF "S": 2.7 million
PROOF SILVER "S": 1.7 million
UNCIRCULATED "P": 233.8 million
UNCIRCULATED "D": 225.8 million

Price Record

PRICE: $42
DATE OF ISSUE: 2004 Mintmark P
GRADING SERVICE: PCGS MS-68
DATE OF SALE: 1/2006
AUCTIONEER: Heritage

PRICE: $552
DATE OF ISSUE: 2004 Mintmark D
GRADING SERVICE: PCGS MS-69
DATE OF SALE: 12/2007
AUCTIONEER: Heritage

Common Errors and Values

NOT STRUCK ON QUARTER PLANCHET: $2,000
DOUBLE STRUCK: $850
STRUCK 3–4 TIMES: $1,500
OBVERSE CLAD MISSING: $350
REVERSE CLAD MISSING: $650
OFF CENTER MINOR: $115
OFF CENTER MAJOR: $1,250

ROTATED REVERSE: N/A
BROCKAGE: $300
BROADSIDE: $50
STRUCK-THROUGH: $20
PARTIAL COLLAR: $20
CLIPPED "MINOR": $50
CLIPPED "MAJOR": $75

Grading Hints

OBVERSE: The high points of the coin's obverse are prone to wear; the field off Washington's nose, and the area behind the head curls, are prone to contact marks. Wear is most likely to be evident on the hair above Washington's ear and on the cheekbones. High-grade (MS-67 and above) coins will have no contact marks in the field.

REVERSE: This is the more important side for grade. High grade (above MS-67) has minimal (few if any) contact marks in the field. The high points of the coin—state of Michigan (lower peninsula)—show wear first.

Investment Potential

Most "slabbed" state quarters are in MS-66 or better condition. Those that have gone up most in value and which have the greatest potential are MS-68 and better.

Past performance is no guarantee for the future, but from circulation the average (out of 56 states and territories) for P and D ranks 31. In 2008, based on auction sales records covering from the commencement of the State Quarters program to date, of more than 90 issues (P and D) taken from circulation, these coins ranked as follows: (P) 65, (D) 42.

FLORIDA

STATE, YEAR OF ISSUE: Florida, 2004

State Information

YEAR OF STATEHOOD: 1845
ORDER IN UNION: 27
SIZE: 59,928 sq. mi.
POPULATION: 18.2 million
STATE MOTTO: "In God we trust"
STATE FLOWER: orange blossom
STATE BIRD: mockingbird
STATE TREE: white Sabal palmetto palm

Coin Specifications

MINTMARKS: P, D, S
OBVERSE DESIGNER: John Flanagan, modified by William Cousins (1997)
REVERSE DESIGNER: T. James Farrell, engraver; Ralph Butler, designer
REVERSE DESIGN: At top: state name above date entered Union. At bottom: date of issue above motto "E Pluribus Unum," describing how the divided colonies became the United States of America. State design: incorporates a 16th-century Spanish galleon, a space shuttle, and the inscription "Gateway to Discovery." A strip of land with Sabal palm trees is also depicted.

Design History

On April 9, 2002, Governor Jeb Bush appointed a nine-person Florida Commemorative Quarter Committee that included a numismatist, an anthropologist, a landscape artist, teachers, and various political and cultural leaders. In May 2002, the committee reviewed more than 1,500 design concepts and narrowed the candidates to 26. Committee members met via video teleconference on June 7 to narrow the finalists to ten designs, which were presented to the governor. He selected five concepts to go to the Mint:

ALTERNATE DESIGN NOT CHOSEN FOR FL QUARTER.

- A heron standing in the Everglades

- "Gateway to Discovery," depicting Ponce de Leon's flagship and the space shuttle over palm trees

- "Fishing Capital of the World," depicting a swordfish and palm tree

- A design commemorating Castillo de San Marcos in St. Augustine, the nation's oldest city

- "America's Spaceport," depicting a map outline of the state with the shuttle positioned in the field

In a three-week public vote, a total of 424,346 votes were cast. Floridians chose "Gateway to Discovery" as the winning design. A design with a heron standing in the Everglades—which won Bush's vote—came in third.

Henrietta Holsman Fore, Mint director, wrote to Harry G. Robinson III, chair of the Commission of Fine Arts on January 21, 2003, that "neither the CFA nor the CCCAC endorsed the "Gateway to Discovery" or "America's Spaceport" design, as they were deemed too cluttered and commercial in appearance." There was political involvement, however, and "Governor Bush's office has requested that renditions of these themes be returned to the state as candidate designs. We have, therefore, revised both of these designs and would appreciate the CFA's review and comment on both. . . ."

On January 22, 2003, historian Sue Kohler of the CFA wrote to its members: "I hate to bother you with these Florida designs again, but the Mint has made some changes to simplify the ones you did not find acceptable and would like to have your thoughts on them." The selected design reflects the power of the voting public.

Mintage Figures

PROOF "S": 2.7 million
PROOF SILVER "S": 1.7 million
UNCIRCULATED "P": 240.2 million
UNCIRCULATED "D": 241.6 million

Price Record

PRICE: $320	PRICE: $345
DATE OF ISSUE: 2004 Mintmark P	DATE OF ISSUE: 2004 Mintmark D
GRADING SERVICE: PCGS MS-69	GRADING SERVICE: PCGS MS-68
DATE OF SALE: 5/2005	DATE OF SALE: 12/2007
AUCTIONEER: Teletrade	AUCTIONEER: Heritage

Common Errors and Values

NOT STRUCK ON QUARTER PLANCHET: $2,000	ROTATED REVERSE: N/A
	BROCKAGE: $300
DOUBLE STRUCK: $900	BROADSIDE: $50
STRUCK 3–4 TIMES: $1,500	STRUCK-THROUGH: $20
OBVERSE CLAD MISSING: $350	PARTIAL COLLAR: $20
REVERSE CLAD MISSING: $750	CLIPPED "MINOR": $50
OFF CENTER MINOR: $115	CLIPPED "MAJOR": $75
OFF CENTER MAJOR: $1,250	

Grading Hints

OBVERSE: The high points of the coin's obverse are prone to wear; the field off Washington's nose, and the area behind the head curls, are prone to contact marks. Wear is most likely to be evident on the hair above Washington's ear and on the cheekbones. High-grade (MS-67 and above) coins will have no contact marks in the field.

REVERSE: This is the more important side for grade. High grade (above MS-67) has minimal (few if any) contact marks in the field. The high points of the coin show wear first: tail of space shuttle, mainsail of ship (8 o'clock).

Investment Potential

Most "slabbed" state quarters are in MS-66 or better condition. Those that have gone up most in value and which have the greatest potential are MS-68 and better.

Past performance is no guarantee for the future, but from circulation the average (out of 56 states and territories) for P and D ranks this: 9. In 2008, based on auction sales records covering from the commencement of the State Quarters program to date, of more than 90 issues (P and D) taken from circulation, these coins ranked as follows: (P) 11, (D) 16.

TEXAS

STATE, YEAR OF ISSUE: Texas, 2004

State Information

YEAR OF STATEHOOD: 1845
ORDER IN UNION: 28
SIZE: 267,277 sq. mi.
POPULATION: 23.9 million
STATE MOTTO: "Friendship"
STATE FLOWER: bluebonnet
STATE BIRD: mockingbird
STATE TREE: pecan

Coin Specifications

MINTMARKS: P, D, S
OBVERSE DESIGNER: John Flanagan, modified by William Cousins (1997)
REVERSE DESIGNER: Norman E. Nemeth, engraver; Daniel Miller, designer
REVERSE DESIGN: At top: state name above date entered Union. At bottom: date of issue above motto "E Pluribus Unum," describing how the divided colonies became the United States of America. State design: matte outline of the state with a lone star superimposed on the outline and the inscription "The Lone Star State." The lariat encircling the design is symbolic of the cattle and cowboy history of Texas, as well as its frontier spirit.

Design History

On August 14, 2000, Governor George W. Bush appointed the 15-member Texas Quarter Dollar Coin Design Advisory Committee. The committee authorized the Texas Numismatic Association to conduct a statewide design contest on its behalf with the caveat that all designers must be Texans. Nearly 2,600 candidate design concepts were submitted, and from those design concepts, 17 finalists were selected and presented to the advisory committee for review.

The committee further narrowed the submissions to the five designs that were most representative and emblematic of the state. These included:

ALTERNATE DESIGN NOT CHOSEN FOR TX QUARTER.

- the Lone Star State map outline with five-pointed star inside, slightly off center

- the five-pointed star enlarged at center with small state map below

- map with star surrounded by fauna, plants, and flowers

- state map outline with five-pointed star, map highlighted in rope-style

- a second variation of the state map outline

Mint Director Henrietta Fore sent the potential designs to Harry Robinson III, CFA chairman. Robinson wrote back that "At its meeting on 22 April the Commission of Fine Arts reviewed designs for the Texas state quarter. Although there were no specific objections to the preferred design, marked No. 1, the members unanimously agreed that design No. 2, with the large star in the Center, was more unusual with its emphasis on a single element making a much stronger coin design. It was requested, however, that the small outline of the state at the bottom be deleted . . . an afterthought. . . ."

Governor Rick Perry submitted the preferred design of the outline of Texas beneath the Lone Star and encircled by a lariat, which was approved by the Secretary of the Treasury (appointed by President George W. Bush) on August 26, 2003.

Mintage Figures

PROOF "S": 2.7 million
PROOF SILVER "S":1.7 million
UNCIRCULATED "P": 278.8 million
UNCIRCULATED "D": 263.0 million

Price Record

PRICE: $50
DATE OF ISSUE: 2004 Mintmark P
GRADING SERVICE: PCGS MS-68
DATE OF SALE: 11/2006
AUCTIONEER: Teletrade

PRICE: $546
DATE OF ISSUE: 2004 Mintmark D
GRADING SERVICE: PCGS MS-69
DATE OF SALE: 12/2007
AUCTIONEER: Heritage

Common Errors and Values

NOT STRUCK ON QUARTER
PLANCHET: $2,500
DOUBLE STRUCK: $1,000
STRUCK 3–4 TIMES: $2,500
OBVERSE CLAD MISSING: $400
REVERSE CLAD MISSING: $750
OFF CENTER MINOR: $125
OFF CENTER MAJOR: N/A

ROTATED REVERSE: N/A
BROCKAGE: $300
BROADSIDE: $50
STRUCK-THROUGH: $20
PARTIAL COLLAR: $20
CLIPPED "MINOR": $50
CLIPPED "MAJOR": $75

Grading Hints

OBVERSE: The high points of the coin's obverse are prone to wear; the field off Washington's nose, and the area behind the head curls, are prone to contact marks. Wear is most likely to be evident on the hair above Washington's ear and on the cheekbones. High-grade (MS-67 and above) coins will have no contact marks in the field.

REVERSE: This is the more important side for grade. High grade (above MS-67) has minimal (few if any) contact marks in the field. The high points of the coin—notably the center point of the lone star—show wear first.

Investment Potential

Most "slabbed" state quarters are in MS-66 or better condition. Those that have gone up most in value and which have the greatest potential are MS-68 and better.

Past performance is no guarantee for the future, but from circulation the average (out of 56 states and territories) for P and D ranks 37. In 2008, based on auction sales records covering from the commencement of the State Quarters program to date, of more than 90 issues (P and D) taken from circulation, these coins ranked as follows: (P) 58, (D) 72.

IOWA

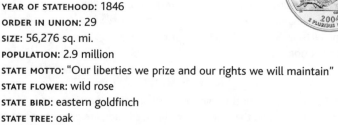

STATE, YEAR OF ISSUE: Iowa, 2004

State Information

YEAR OF STATEHOOD: 1846
ORDER IN UNION: 29
SIZE: 56,276 sq. mi.
POPULATION: 2.9 million
STATE MOTTO: "Our liberties we prize and our rights we will maintain"
STATE FLOWER: wild rose
STATE BIRD: eastern goldfinch
STATE TREE: oak

Coin Specifications

MINTMARKS: P, D, S
OBVERSE DESIGNER: John Flanagan, modified by William Cousins (1997)
REVERSE DESIGNER: John Mercanti (after a Grant Wood painting)
REVERSE DESIGN: At top: state name above date entered Union. At bottom: date of issue above motto "E Pluribus Unum," describing how the divided colonies became the United States of America. State design: one-room schoolhouse with a teacher and students planting a tree, and the inscriptions "Foundation in Education" and "Grant Wood." The design is based after *Arbor Day*, a paint-ing by Grant Wood, who was born near Anamosa, Iowa. Initials JM opposite side of "Grant Wood."

Design History

In May 2002, Governor Thomas J. Vilsack established the 16-member Iowa Quarter Commission, which worked with libraries, banks, and credit unions to solicit ideas and concepts for the state quarter design.
The commission received nearly 2,000 submissions, which were narrowed to five candidate themes, including:

- "American Gothic," based on Grant Wood's most famous painting

- "Foundation in Education," after the Grant Wood painting *Arbor Day*

ALTERNATE DESIGN NOT CHOSEN FOR IA QUARTER.

- "Feeding the World," featuring pigs, cattle, and corn superimposed over a map of the state

- "Sullivan Brothers," after five brothers who died aboard ship in World War II

- "Beautiful Land," depicting "young corn" after the Grant Wood painting

The U.S. Mint did not approve two of the quarter designs. "American Gothic" was rejected by the Mint because of legal issues over rights to the image. "The Five Sullivan Brothers," based on the five Sullivan brothers of Waterloo who were killed serving on the same U.S. Navy ship during World War II, was not approved because of rules that prohibit certain representations, such as a "head and shoulder portrait or bust of any person, living or dead."

In July 2003, the Mint forwarded five approved candidate designs to Governor Vilsack for final recommendation. Three designs were emblematic of the "Feeding the World" theme, and the other two represented the "Young Corn" and "Foundation in Education" concepts.

"From the one-room schoolhouse to the virtual classroom, Iowa has a strong foundation in education," Governor Vilsack said. "The Iowa quarter will be a symbol to the rest of the nation of Iowa's values: that we are committed to our responsibility to educating our young people, that we respect our agricultural heritage and work to protect our environment, that we are dedicated to helping people secure a brighter future and contribute to their communities, and that we are determined to create opportunity for all Iowans."

The panel voted 8–0 in favor of "American Gothic" during a special teleconference meeting, which was called after a New York company that claims to have rights to the painting raised concerns about its use on a coin.

The CFA's preferred choice was an outline of the state embossed "Feeding the World," with pig and cattle beneath, corn and soybeans bracketing either side of Iowa.

Governor Vilsack chose the "Foundation in Education" design, which was approved by the Secretary of the Treasury on August 26, 2003.

Mintage Figures

PROOF "S": 2.7 million   UNCIRCULATED "P": 213.8 million
PROOF SILVER "S": 1.7 million   UNCIRCULATED "D": 251.8 million

Price Record

PRICE: $1,035	**PRICE:** $1,840
DATE OF ISSUE: 2004 Mintmark P	**DATE OF ISSUE:** 2004 Mintmark D
GRADING SERVICE: PCGS MS-68	**GRADING SERVICE:** PCGS MS-68
DATE OF SALE: 12/2007	**DATE OF SALE:** 12/2007
AUCTIONEER: Heritage	**AUCTIONEER:** Heritage

Common Errors and Values

NOT STRUCK ON QUARTER PLANCHET: $2,500	**ROTATED REVERSE:** N/A
	BROCKAGE: $300
DOUBLE STRUCK: $1,000	**BROADSIDE:** $50
STRUCK 3–4 TIMES: $2,500	**STRUCK-THROUGH:** $20
OBVERSE CLAD MISSING: $400	**PARTIAL COLLAR:** $20
REVERSE CLAD MISSING: $750	**CLIPPED "MINOR":** $50
OFF CENTER MINOR: $125	**CLIPPED "MAJOR":** $75
OFF CENTER MAJOR: N/A	

Grading Hints

OBVERSE: The high points of the coin's obverse are prone to wear; the field off Washington's nose, and the area behind the head curls, are prone to contact marks. Wear is most likely to be evident on the hair above Washington's ear and on the cheekbones. High-grade (MS-67 and above) coins will have no contact marks in the field.

REVERSE: This is the more important side for grade. High grade (above MS-67) has minimal (few if any) contact marks in the field. The high points of the coin show wear first: roof line, right side (front).

Investment Potential

Most "slabbed" state quarters are in MS-66 or better condition. Those that have gone up most in value and which have the greatest potential are MS-68 and better.

Past performance is no guarantee for the future, but from circulation the average (out of 56 states and territories) for P and D ranks 4. In 2008, based on auction sales records covering from the commencement of the State Quarters program to date, of more than 90 issues (P and D) taken from circulation, these coins ranked as follows: (P) 12, (D) 13.

WISCONSIN

STATE, YEAR OF ISSUE: Wisconsin, 2004

State Information

YEAR OF STATEHOOD: 1848
ORDER IN UNION: 30
SIZE: 65,499 sq. mi.
POPULATION: 5.6 million
STATE MOTTO: "Forward"
STATE FLOWER: wood violet
STATE BIRD: robin
STATE TREE: sugar maple

Coin Specifications

MINTMARKS: P, D, S
OBVERSE DESIGNER: John Flanagan, modified by William Cousins (1997)
REVERSE DESIGNER: Alfred Maletsky
REVERSE DESIGN: At top: state name above date entered Union. At bottom: date of issue above motto "E Pluribus Unum," describing how the divided colonies became the United States of America. State design: agricultural theme featuring a cow, a cut round of cheese, and an ear of corn. The design also bears an inscription of the State motto, "Forward." Initials ALF under "d" in "Forward" beneath ribbon.

Design History

Wisconsin is considered "America's Dairy Land," producing more than 15 percent of the nation's milk. Wisconsin also produces more than 350 different varieties, types, and styles of award-winning cheeses—more than any other state. The state has approximately 17,000 dairy farms, with just over one million cows that produce an average of 17,306 gallons of milk each per year. Wisconsin adopted the state motto "Forward" in 1851, reflecting Wisconsin's continuous drive to be a national leader.

Beginning in 2003, potential designs for the state quarter were sent in from all over Wisconsin. Competing designs included alternative dairyland themes, out-

ALTERNATE DESIGN NOT CHOSEN FOR WI QUARTER.

door hunting and fishing, and celebrations of the frontier period. After a statewide vote, Governor Scott McCallum submitted five design concepts to the U.S. Mint:

- a cow in a farm scene
- scenic Wisconsin (featuring deer and fish)
- Native American with trapper and canoe
- cow, cheese, and corn representing the state's agriculture
- a priest with a Native American in a canoe

In 2003, Governor Jim Doyle coordinated a statewide vote to select the final design, in which design #4 was the popular choice.

On July 14, 2003, Mint Director Henrietta Fore sent a letter to David M. Childs, chair of the Commission of Fine Arts, asking that designs of Michigan be dealt with at the June 24 meeting. A penciled note on the commission copy says, "The Mint apparently forgot to send a similar letter re the Wisconsin coins," though four quarter designs were returned. It turned out not to be a problem. On July 24, Childs wrote Fore that "There was no enthusiasm for any of the designs." The CFA suggested that "The theme 'cultural interaction' as depicted on designs #3 and #5 could be more fully developed with an eye toward simplicity."

The fourth design won out. This design was approved by the secretary of the treasury on October 9, 2003.

Mintage Figures

PROOF "S": 2.7 million
PROOF SILVER "S":1.7 million
UNCIRCULATED "P": 226.4 million
UNCIRCULATED "D": 226.8 million

Price Record

PRICE: $150
DATE OF ISSUE: 2004 Mintmark P
GRADING SERVICE: PCGS MS-68
DATE OF SALE: 5/2005
AUCTIONEER: Teletrade

PRICE: $2,530
DATE OF ISSUE: 2004 Mintmark D
GRADING SERVICE: PCGS MS-66
DATE OF SALE: 09/2006
AUCTIONEER: Heritage

Common Errors and Values

NOT STRUCK ON QUARTER PLANCHET: $2,500

DOUBLE STRUCK: $1,000

STRUCK 3–4 TIMES: $2,500

OBVERSE CLAD MISSING: $400

REVERSE CLAD MISSING: $750

OFF CENTER MINOR: $125

OFF CENTER MAJOR: N/A

ROTATED REVERSE: N/A

BROCKAGE: $300

BROADSIDE: $50

STRUCK-THROUGH: $20

PARTIAL COLLAR: $20

CLIPPED "MINOR": $50

CLIPPED "MAJOR": $75

Grading Hints

OBVERSE: The high points of the coin's obverse are prone to wear; the field off Washington's nose, and the area behind the head curls, are prone to contact marks. Wear is most likely to be evident on the hair above Washington's ear and on the cheekbones. High-grade (MS-67 and above) coins will have no contact marks in the field.

REVERSE: This is the more important side for grade. High grade (above MS-67) has minimal (few if any) contact marks in the field. The high points of the coin show wear first: cow's snout, round of cheese (bottom portion).

Investment Potential

Most "slabbed" state quarters are in MS-66 or better condition. Those that have gone up most in value and which have the greatest potential are MS-68 and better.

Past performance is no guarantee for the future, but from circulation the average (out of 56 states and territories) for P and D ranks 1. In 2008, based on auction sales records covering from the commencement of the State Quarters program to date, of more than 90 issues (P and D) taken from circulation, these coins ranked as follows: (P) 29, (D) 1. The errors remain the most active market item, with good upside potential.

CALIFORNIA

STATE, YEAR OF ISSUE: California, 2005

State Information

YEAR OF STATEHOOD: 1850
ORDER IN UNION: 31
SIZE: 158,869 sq. mi.
POPULATION: 36.55 million
STATE MOTTO: "Eureka" (I have found it)
STATE FLOWER: golden poppy
STATE BIRD: California valley quail
STATE TREE: California redwood

Coin Specifications

MINTMARKS: P, D, S
OBVERSE DESIGNER: John Flanagan, modified by William Cousins (1997)
REVERSE DESIGNER: Don Everhart II, engraver; Garrett Burke, designer
REVERSE DESIGN: At top: state name above date entered Union. At bottom: date of issue above motto "E Pluribus Unum," describing how the divided colonies became the United States of America. State design: naturalist and conservationist John Muir admiring Yosemite Valley's monolithic granite head wall known as "Half Dome"; design also contains a soaring California condor. Inscriptions include "John Muir," "Yosemite Valley." Initials DE incused in Sierra Nevada hills at lower right.

Design History

Governor Gray Davis wanted the citizens of California to come up with the design idea for the state's quarter. To involve the public in the design process, the governor directed then–California State Librarian Kevin Starr and his staff to create and facilitate a statewide outreach program that invited every native and resident Californian to send a quarter design to Sacramento.

The State Library launched the California Quarter Project via brochure and Web site, promoting the program at press conferences, on radio and TV talk shows,

ALTERNATE DESIGN NOT CHOSEN FOR CA QUARTER.

in privately funded public service announcements, and in many of California's leading newspapers.

The library received more than 8,000 separate designs. The project commission forwarded 20 design concepts to Davis's office for further consideration, from which five were chosen as finalists and sent for final review to the U.S. Mint. Davis, meanwhile, was recalled from office by the voters, and his successor, Arnold Schwarzenegger, chose the final selection. The design concepts included:

- "Gold Miner," with a '49er panning for gold, with natural resources at 2, 4, 9, and 10 o'clock in the field

- John Muir/Yosemite Valley

- "Waves and Sun," a modernistic rendering

- the "Giant Sequoia" design showing the tree and an eagle

- The Golden Gate Bridge

The Citizens Coinage Advisory Committeemet on November 18, 2003, to discuss the California design and had several suggestions. They recommended design #3, showing the "Waves and Sun" (three members opposed) and design #2, showing the John Muir/Yosemite Valley, as second choice (one opposed). The committee recommended to "clear up the design and remove some of the busyness."

Mint Director Henrietta Fore then asked the Commission of Fine Arts to review the designs. They did, and promptly opposed the The CCAC. The CFA "preferred design #5 which featured the Golden Gate Bridge. However [they recommended] that the trees on both sides be removed, leaving just the poppies."

The Department of the Treasury approved the "John Muir/Yosemite Valley" design on April 15, 2004.

Mintage Figures

PROOF "S": 3.2 million
PROOF SILVER "S":1.6 million
UNCIRCULATED "P": 257.2 million
UNCIRCULATED "D": 263.2 million

Price Record

PRICE: $1,840
DATE OF ISSUE: 2005 Mintmark P
GRADING SERVICE: PCGS MS-70
DATE OF SALE: 12/2007
AUCTIONEER: Heritage

PRICE: $190
DATE OF ISSUE: 2005 Mintmark D
GRADING SERVICE: PCGS MS-69
DATE OF SALE: 2/2007
AUCTIONEER: Teletrade

Common Errors and Values

NOT STRUCK ON QUARTER PLANCHET: $2,500
DOUBLE STRUCK: $900
STRUCK 3–4 TIMES: $2,250
OBVERSE CLAD MISSING: $400
REVERSE CLAD MISSING: $950
OFF CENTER MINOR: $115
OFF CENTER MAJOR: N/A

ROTATED REVERSE: N/A
BROCKAGE: $300
BROADSIDE: $50
STRUCK-THROUGH: $20
PARTIAL COLLAR: $20
CLIPPED "MINOR": $50
CLIPPED "MAJOR": $125

Grading Hints

OBVERSE: The high points of the coin's obverse are prone to wear; the field off Washington's nose, and the area behind the head curls, are prone to contact marks. Wear is most likely to be evident on the hair above Washington's ear and on the cheekbones. High-grade (MS-67 and above) coins will have no contact marks in the field.

REVERSE: This is the more important side for grade. High grade (above MS-67) has minimal (few if any) contact marks in the field. The high points of the coin show wear first: John Muir's right arm and shoulder.

Investment Potential

Most "slabbed" state quarters are in MS-66 or better condition. Those that have gone up most in value and which have the greatest potential are MS-68 and better.

Past performance is no guarantee for the future, but from circulation the average (out of 56 states and territories) for P and D ranks: 15. In 2008, based on auction sales records covering from the commencement of the State Quarters program to date, of more than 90 issues (P and D) taken from circulation, these coins ranked as follows: (P) 39, (D) 31.

MINNESOTA

STATE, YEAR OF ISSUE: Minnesota, 2005

State Information

YEAR OF STATEHOOD: 1858
ORDER IN UNION: 32
SIZE: 86,943 sq. mi.
POPULATION: 5.19 million
STATE MOTTO: "L'etoile du nord" (the star of the north)
STATE FLOWER: pink-and-white lady's slipper
STATE BIRD: common loon
STATE TREE: red pine

Coin Specifications

MINTMARKS: P, D, S
OBVERSE DESIGNER: John Flanagan, modified by William Cousins (1997)
REVERSE DESIGNER: Charles L. Vickers
REVERSE DESIGN: At top: state name above date entered Union. At bottom: date of issue above motto "E Pluribus Unum," describing how the divided colonies became the United States of America. State design: tree-lined lake with two people fishing, a loon on the water, and a textured outline of the state surrounding its nickname, "Land of 10,000 Lakes." Initials CLV at extreme right side in loon's wake.

Design History

Minnesota, the "Land of 10,000 Lakes," actually contains more than 15,000 such bodies of water whose total shoreline exceeds 90,000 miles—more than California, Hawaii, and Florida combined. Equally renowned as the home of the headwaters of the mighty Mississippi River, the name Minnesota is derived from the Dakota Sioux word for "cloudy water."

Governor Tim Pawlenty established the Governor's State Quarter Commission in May 2003 and charged it with selecting five design narratives. The finalists were:

- map outline over plow, mallard, snowflake

- "Land of 10,000 Lakes" with outline, fisherman, mallard, trees

ALTERNATE DESIGN NOT CHOSEN FOR MN QUARTER.

- "Headwaters of the Mississippi" (from mountains to bridge)

- lakes: fishermen and mallard

- lakes: map, fishermen, mallard

It is interesting to note that Minnesota was the first state that did not submit actual pictorial designs to the U.S. Mint. They instead used narrative descriptions; the Mint took these descriptions and rendered a design.

On February 12, 2004, Mint Director Henrietta Fore forwarded the chosen designs to the Commission of Fine Arts. On February 27, Charles Atherton, CFA secretary, wrote Fore that "Design #4 was approved with the recommendation that the trees in the background be removed, leaving only the men in the canoe, and the loon in the foreground." He also noted, "It was thought that the water could be studied further, to give it more definition.

The governor announced the winning design at the 2004 Governor's Fishing Opener. By selecting the "Land of 10,000 Lakes" design, Governor Pawlenty chose the design recommended to him by the Minnesota State Quarter Commission.

Minnesota was the first state that did not submit actual pictorial designs to the U.S. Mint. They instead used narrative descriptions; the Mint took these descriptions and rendered a design.

Mintage Figures

PROOF "S": 3.2 million
PROOF SILVER "S":1.6 million
UNCIRCULATED "P": 239.6 million
UNCIRCULATED "D": 248.4 million

Price Record

PRICE: $1,610
DATE OF ISSUE: 2005 Mintmark P
GRADING SERVICE: ANACS MS-70
DATE OF SALE: 12/2007
AUCTIONEER: Heritage

PRICE: $30
DATE OF ISSUE: 2005 Mintmark D
GRADING SERVICE: PCGS MS-67
DATE OF SALE: 6/2005
AUCTIONEER: Teletrade

Common Errors and Values

NOT STRUCK ON QUARTER PLANCHET: $2,250

DOUBLE STRUCK: $900

STRUCK 3–4 TIMES: $2,000

OBVERSE CLAD MISSING: $400

REVERSE CLAD MISSING: $950

OFF CENTER MINOR: $115

OFF CENTER MAJOR: N/A

ROTATED REVERSE: N/A

BROCKAGE: $300

BROADSIDE: $50

STRUCK-THROUGH: $20

PARTIAL COLLAR: $20

CLIPPED "MINOR": $50

CLIPPED "MAJOR": $125

Grading Hints

OBVERSE: The high points of the coin's obverse are prone to wear; the field off Washington's nose, and the area behind the head curls, are prone to contact marks. Wear is most likely to be evident on the hair above Washington's ear and on the cheekbones. High-grade (MS-67 and above) coins will have no contact marks in the field.

REVERSE: This is the more important side for grade. High grade (above MS-67) has minimal (few if any) contact marks in the field. The highpoints of the coin show wear first: mallard in the foreground

Investment Potential

Most "slabbed" state quarters are in MS-66 or better condition. Those that have gone up most in value and which have the greatest potential are MS-68 and better.

Past performance is no guarantee for the future, but from circulation the average (out of 56 states and territories) for P and D ranks 33. In 2008, based on auction sales records covering from the commencement of the State Quarters program to date, of more than 90 issues (P and D) taken from circulation, these coins ranked as follows: (P) 50, (D) 73.

OREGON

STATE, YEAR OF ISSUE: Oregon, 2005

State Information

YEAR OF STATEHOOD: 1859
ORDER IN UNION: 33
SIZE: 97,132 sq. mi.
POPULATION: 3.7 million
STATE MOTTO: "She flies with her own wings"
STATE FLOWER: Oregon grape
STATE BIRD: western meadowlark
STATE TREE: Douglas fir

Coin Specifications

MINTMARKS: P, D, S
OBVERSE DESIGNER: John Flanagan, modified by William Cousins (1997)
REVERSE DESIGNER: Donna Weaver
REVERSE DESIGN: At top: state name above date entered Union. At bottom: date of issue above motto "E Pluribus Unum," describing how the divided colonies became the United States of America. State design: a portion of Crater Lake, the deepest lake in the United States, formed 7,700 years ago and here viewed from the south-southwest rim. The design incorporates Wizard Island, as well as Watchman and Hillman Peaks on the lake's rim, and conifers. Bears the inscription "Crater Lake." Initials DW beneath lowest pine tree branch, right side.

Design History

Executive Order 03–06 established an Oregon Commemorative Coin Commission of which the governor and state treasurer were co-chairs. Over the course of several months, they collected and voted on many designs. Those carefully considered included:

- Crater Lake viewed from the south

- a prairie schooner on the Oregon Trail moving past Native American dwellings toward mountains

ALTERNATE DESIGN NOT CHOSEN FOR OR QUARTER.

- Mt. Hood viewed from the east with the Columbia River

- a wild chinook salmon jumping up a waterfall

On May 24, 2004, after more than seven months of researching, discussing, tweaking, and debating, the commission made a 10–8 recommendation for the design for the state quarter. Design #1 was favored both by the commission and Governor Ted Kulongoski. Design #3 was voted a close second.

On February 19, 2004, Commission of Fine Arts Secretary Charles H. Atherton wrote Mint Director Henrietta Fore that "a variation of Design #4 was approved, using just large fish in the Center of the coin."

Design #1 won out in the end, and the Department of the Treasury approved the "Crater Lake" design on July 13, 2004.

Mintage Figures

PROOF "S": 3.2 million
PROOF SILVER "S":1.6 million
UNCIRCULATED "P": 316.2 million
UNCIRCULATED "D": 404.0 million

Price Record

PRICE: $60
DATE OF ISSUE: 2005 Mintmark P
GRADING SERVICE: PCGS MS-69
DATE OF SALE: 8/2005
AUCTIONEER: Teletrade

PRICE: $287.50
DATE OF ISSUE: 2005 Mintmark D
GRADING SERVICE: PCGS MS-68
DATE OF SALE: 12/2007
AUCTIONEER: Heritage

Common Errors and Values

NOT STRUCK ON QUARTER
  PLANCHET: $2,500
DOUBLE STRUCK: $900
STRUCK 3–4 TIMES: $2,000
OBVERSE CLAD MISSING: $350
REVERSE CLAD MISSING: $800
OFF CENTER MINOR: $115
OFF CENTER MAJOR: N/A

ROTATED REVERSE: N/A
BROCKAGE: $300
BROADSIDE: $50
STRUCK-THROUGH: $20
PARTIAL COLLAR: $20
CLIPPED "MINOR": $50
CLIPPED "MAJOR": $125

Grading Hints

OBVERSE: The high points of the coin's obverse are prone to wear; the field off Washington's nose, and the area behind the head curls, are prone to contact marks. Wear is most likely to be evident on the hair above Washington's ear and on the cheekbones. High-grade (MS-67 and above) coins will have no contact marks in the field.

REVERSE: This is the more important side for grade. High grade (above MS-67) has minimal (few if any) contact marks in the field. The high points of the coin—loon in lower quarter of lake—show wear first.

Investment Potential

Most "slabbed" state quarters are in MS-66 or better condition. Those that have gone up most in value and which have the greatest potential are MS-68 and better.

Past performance is no guarantee for the future, but from circulation the average (out of 56 states and territories) for P and D ranks 27. In 2008, based on auction sales records covering from the commencement of the State Quarters program to date, of more than 90 issues (P and D) taken from circulation, these coins ranked as follows: (P) 52, (D) 38.

KANSAS

STATE, YEAR OF ISSUE: Kansas, 2005

State Information

YEAR OF STATEHOOD: 1861
ORDER IN UNION: 34
SIZE: 82,282 sq. mi.
POPULATION: 2.7 million
STATE MOTTO: "Ad astra per aspera" (to the stars through difficulties)
STATE FLOWER: native sunflower
STATE BIRD: western meadowlark
STATE TREE: cottonwood

Coin Specifications

MINTMARKS: P, D, S
OBVERSE DESIGNER: John Flanagan, modified by William Cousins (1997)
REVERSE DESIGNER: Norman E. Nemeth
REVERSE DESIGN: At top: state name above date entered Union. At bottom: date of issue above motto "E Pluribus Unum," describing how the divided colonies became the United States of America. State design: buffalo (facing right) and sunflower motif at left. Initials NEM at left beneath buffalo.

Design History

The buffalo (the state animal of Kansas) and the sunflower (which has been the state flower for more than 100 years) are emblematic symbols of the heartland's rich history, natural beauty, and bright future. It was only natural that they would play a role in the state quarter design.

"We first asked Kansans to send in their ideas for the Kansas quarter back in July 2003," Governor Kathleen Sawbills reported. "We were looking for a way to represent our state's heritage, our traditions, our past and future, all in a space a little less than an inch in diameter. But Kansans are creative, and we received more than 1,500 submissions from people young and old."

ALTERNATE DESIGN NOT CHOSEN FOR KS QUARTER.

The 16-member Kansas Commemorative Coin Commission narrowed the search for Kansas' quarter design to four finalists:

- buffalo, the state animal, and sunflower, the state flower

- image of the statue that sits atop the state capitol—an Native American archer aiming his bow skyward, toward the North Star

- a single sunflower

- sunflower with wheat

Commission of Fine Arts Secretary Charles H. Atherton wrote to Mint Director Henrietta Fore on February 27, 2004, that "Design #3 with only a larger sunflower in the Center of the coin and no other elements was approved."

The winning design was then recommended by the state's high school students in a statewide vote and approved by the governor in the spring of 2004. It features a buffalo, the state animal, and a sunflower, the state flower. The Treasury Department approved the "Buffalo and Sunflower" design on July 13, 2004.

Mintage Figures

PROOF "S": 3.2 million
PROOF SILVER "S": 1.6 million
UNCIRCULATED "P": 263.4 million
UNCIRCULATED "D": 300.0 million

Price Record

PRICE: $42
DATE OF ISSUE: 2005 Mintmark P
GRADING SERVICE: PCGS MS-69
DATE OF SALE: 5/2006
AUCTIONEER: Heritage

PRICE: $29
DATE OF ISSUE: 2005 Mintmark D
GRADING SERVICE: PCGS MS-68
DATE OF SALE: 12/2005
AUCTIONEER: Heritage

Common Errors and Values

NOT STRUCK ON QUARTER
  PLANCHET: $2,500
DOUBLE STRUCK: $1,250
STRUCK 3–4 TIMES: $2,500
OBVERSE CLAD MISSING: $350
REVERSE CLAD MISSING: $800
OFF CENTER MINOR: $120
OFF CENTER MAJOR: N/A

ROTATED REVERSE: N/A
BROCKAGE: $300
BROADSIDE: $50
STRUCK-THROUGH: $20
PARTIAL COLLAR: $20
CLIPPED "MINOR": $50
CLIPPED "MAJOR": $125

Grading Hints

OBVERSE: The high points of the coin's obverse are prone to wear; the field off Washington's nose, and the area behind the head curls, are prone to contact marks. Wear is most likely to be evident on the hair above Washington's ear and on the cheekbones. High-grade (MS-67 and above) coins will have no contact marks in the field.

REVERSE: This is the more important side for grade. High grade (above MS-67) has minimal (few if any) contact marks in the field. The high points of the coin show wear first: bison shoulder, at center.

Investment Potential

Most "slabbed" state quarters are in MS-66 or better condition. Those that have gone up most in value and which have the greatest potential are MS-68 and better.

Past performance is no guarantee for the future, but from circulation the average (out of 56 states and territories) for P and D ranks 40. In 2008, based on auction sales records covering from the commencement of the State Quarters program to date, of more than 90 issues (P and D) taken from circulation, these coins ranked as follows: (P) 60, (D)74.

WEST VIRGINIA

STATE, YEAR OF ISSUE: West Virginia, 2005

State Information

YEAR OF STATEHOOD: 1863
ORDER IN UNION: 35
SIZE: 24,231 sq. mi.
POPULATION: 1.8 million
STATE MOTTO: "Montani semper liberi" (mountaineers are always free)
STATE FLOWER: big rhododendron
STATE BIRD: cardinal
STATE TREE: sugar maple

Coin Specifications

MINTMARKS: P, D, S
OBVERSE DESIGNER: John Flanagan, modified by William Cousins (1997)
REVERSE DESIGNER: John Mercanti
REVERSE DESIGN: At top: state name above date entered Union. At bottom: date of issue above motto "E Pluribus Unum," describing how the divided colonies became the United States of America. State design: the New River and the New River Gorge Bridge, bearing the inscription "New River Gorge." Initials JM at right of water in Gorge.

Design History

The design chosen to represent West Virginia combines the natural physical beauty of the state and the triumph of the human intellect exemplified by the engineering wonder that is the New River Gorge Bridge. At 3,030 feet long and 69 feet wide, the bridge is the world's largest steel span and the second highest bridge in the United States, rising 876 feet above the New River Gorge in southern West Virginia. In 1978, 53 miles of the New River was added to the National Park System as the New River Gorge National River.

The governor announced that a design contest would be held for West Virginia's entry to the state-

ALTERNATE DESIGN NOT CHOSEN FOR WV QUARTER.

hood quarter field. More than 1,800 design concepts were submitted from around the state, and students from the Governor's School for the Arts (a high school) narrowed the field to five finalists:

- "Appalachian Warmth," a quilt in the shape of a map of West Virginia

- Bridge Day New River Gorge, with parachutist going off bridge

- New River Gorge Bridge with raftsmen below

- New River Gorge with bridge

- Anna Jarvis (founder of Mother's Day) with state outline

On November 18, 2003, the designs were presented to the CCAC. Susan Smallplant from the governor's office, stated that "the governor had no preference for any of the designs." Most members expressed support for design #1, whereas #2 received no support. They decided to recommend #4, showing the New River Gorge Bridge, as the committee's first choice. Design #1, showing the Appalachian quilt, was the committee's second choice.

David Childs, chairman of the CFA wrote to Mint Director Henrietta Fore (December 1, 2003) that "The unanimous choice here was design #4, the New River Gorge. No changes were recommended."

On March 31, 2004, West Virginia Governor Bob Wise announced his selection of the New River Gorge as the design he would submit for final approval. The Department of the Treasury approved the design on May 4, 2004. On October 14, 2005, Governor Joe Manchin and first lady Gayle Manchin joined nearly 4,000 citizens during a ceremony to mark the official introduction of the West Virginia state quarter and the completion of the State Capitol Dome restoration project. Congress created a Mother's Day commemorative coin in June 2008 based on the Anna Jarvis design.

Mintage Figures

PROOF "S": 3.2 million
PROOF SILVER "S":1.6 million
UNCIRCULATED "P": 365.4 million
UNCIRCULATED "D": 356.2 million

Price Record

PRICE: $42

DATE OF ISSUE: 2005 Mintmark P

GRADING SERVICE: PCGS MS-68

DATE OF SALE: 1/2006

AUCTIONEER: Heritage

PRICE: $31

DATE OF ISSUE: 2005 Mintmark D

GRADING SERVICE: PCGS MS-68

DATE OF SALE: 12/2005

AUCTIONEER: Heritage

Common Errors and Values

NOT STRUCK ON QUARTER PLANCHET: $2,500

DOUBLE STRUCK: $1,250

STRUCK 3–4 TIMES: $2,500

OBVERSE CLAD MISSING: $350

REVERSE CLAD MISSING: $800

OFF CENTER MINOR: $120

OFF CENTER MAJOR: N/A

ROTATED REVERSE: N/A

BROCKAGE: $300

BROADSIDE: $50

STRUCK-THROUGH: $20

PARTIAL COLLAR: $20

CLIPPED "MINOR": $50

CLIPPED "MAJOR": $125

Grading Hints

OBVERSE: The high points of the coin's obverse are prone to wear; the field off Washington's nose, and the area behind the head curls, are prone to contact marks. Wear is most likely to be evident on the hair above Washington's ear and on the cheekbones. High-grade (MS-67 and above) coins will have no contact marks in the field.

REVERSE: This is the more important side for grade. High grade (above MS-67) has minimal (few if any) contact marks in the field. The high points of the coin show wear first: mountain tops, beneath bridge.

Investment Potential

Most "slabbed" state quarters are in MS-66 or better condition. Those that have gone up most in value and which have the greatest potential are MS-68 and better.

Past performance is no guarantee of the future, but from circulation the average (out of 56 states and territories) for P and D ranks 38. In 2008, based on auction sales records covering from the commencement of the State Quarters program to date, of more than 90 issues (P and D) taken from circulation, these coins ranked as follows: (P) 61, (D) 71.

NEVADA

STATE, YEAR OF ISSUE: Nevada, 2006

State Information

YEAR OF STATEHOOD: 1864
ORDER IN UNION: 36
SIZE: 110,567 sq. mi.
POPULATION: 2.5 million
STATE MOTTO: "All for our country"
STATE FLOWER: sagebrush
STATE BIRD: mountain bluebird
STATE TREE: single-leaf piñon bristlecone pine

Coin Specifications

MINTMARKS: P, D, S
OBVERSE DESIGNER: John Flanagan, modified by William Cousins (1997)
REVERSE DESIGNER: Don Everhart II
REVERSE DESIGN: At top: state name above date entered Union. At bottom: date of issue above motto "E Pluribus Unum," describing how the divided colonies became the United States of America. State design: trio of wild mustangs, the sun rising behind snowcapped mountains, bordered by sagebrush and a banner that reads "The Silver State." Initials DE near ribbon tip, lower right.

Design History

When the Nevada State Quarter Commission was getting ready to select final quarter designs, Mint officials made clear that there were a number of themes not acceptable, including any gambling icon, a slot machine or a show-girl, as part of the design. Political statements were also banned, including a nuclear mushroom cloud or anything to do with Yucca Mountain.

On behalf of Governor Kenny Guinn and State Treasurer Brian K. Krolicki, the commission accepted design concepts from the public in the summer of 2004. The 17-member commission reviewed all submissions, and forwarded five recommendations:

ALTERNATE DESIGN NOT
CHOSEN FOR NV QUARTER.

- motto "The Silver State" with a miner holding pick and shovel in front of a Comstock mine

- motto "The Silver State" with a pair of crossed pickaxes fronted by a stylized star, representing Nevada's entry into the Union

- head and shoulders of a bighorn sheep above a snowcapped mountain

- three galloping wild horses, sagebrush, the sun rising behind snow-capped mountains, and "The Silver State," inside a banner

- petroglyph and native artifacts emphasizing Nevada's Native American heritage

The citizens of Nevada voted on the designs. More than 60,000 votes were cast, and the people of Nevada favored the galloping horses design, "The Silver State," which received 32 percent of the vote.

On January 20, 2005, the Citizens Coinage Advisory Committee met to discuss the potential designs. The committee's preferred design for Nevada was #2 (desert bighorn sheep), with #1 (miner with pick and shovel) also receiving considerable support. Members were very enthusiastic about design #2, which was widely praised as both innovative and aesthetically appealing. Members suggested that if Nevada wanted to incorporate recognition as "The Silver State" into the design, that motto could be used in place of "All for Our Country." For design #1, members recommended removing the shovel and moving the pick from the miner's right shoulder to the left, toward the right rim. It was further suggested that the size of the miner should be reduced, and the mountains in the background should be enlarged. There was little support for designs #3, #4, or #5.

The CFA unanimously approved design #3, with the recommendation that the sheep be slightly smaller so that the Sierra Nevada mountain range at the bottom of the coin could be made larger, and that the motto, "All for Our Country" be removed.

On July 20, 2005, the Department of the Treasury approved the design of the three wild horses (#4). A U.S. Bureau of Land Management survey last year found that 19,000 of the nation's 37,000 wild horses live in Nevada. "The Silver State" motto recognizes the Comstock Lode of years past and acknowledges that even today, 30 percent of U.S. silver production comes from this state. The magnificent sculpturing by artist-engraver Don Everhart II makes this coin a winner in every sense of the word.

Mintage Figures

PROOF "S": 3.2 million
PROOF SILVER "S":1.5 million
UNCIRCULATED "P": 277.0 million
UNCIRCULATED "D": 312.8 million

Price Record

PRICE: $414
DATE OF ISSUE: 2006 Mintmark P
GRADING SERVICE: PCGS MS-69
DATE OF SALE: 11/2007
AUCTIONEER: Teletrade

PRICE: $36
DATE OF ISSUE: 2006 Mintmark D
GRADING SERVICE: PCGS MS-67
DATE OF SALE: 5/2006
AUCTIONEER: Teletrade

Common Errors and Values

NOT STRUCK ON QUARTER
  PLANCHET: N/A
DOUBLE STRUCK: $1,500
STRUCK 3–4 TIMES: $2,500
OBVERSE CLAD MISSING: $400
REVERSE CLAD MISSING: $800
OFF CENTER MINOR: $120
OFF CENTER MAJOR: N/A

ROTATED REVERSE: N/A
BROCKAGE: $400
BROADSIDE: $75
STRUCK-THROUGH: $20
PARTIAL COLLAR: $35
CLIPPED "MINOR": $75
CLIPPED "MAJOR": $125

Grading Hints

OBVERSE: The high points of the coin's obverse are prone to wear; the field off Washington's nose, and the area behind the head curls, are prone to contact marks. Wear is most likely to be evident on the hair above Washington's ear and on the cheekbones. High-grade (MS-67 and above) coins will have no contact marks in the field.

REVERSE: This is the more important side for grade. High grade (above MS-67) has minimal (few if any) contact marks in the field. The high points of the coin show wear first: mustang rump at left, mustang body at center.

Investment Potential

Most "slabbed" state quarters are in MS-66 or better condition. Those that have gone up most in value and which have the greatest potential are MS-68 and better.

Past performance is no guarantee for the future, but from circulation the average (out of 56 states and territories) for P and D ranks 39. In 2008, based on auction sales records covering from the commencement of the State Quarters program to date, of more than 90 issues (P and D) taken from circulation, these coins ranked as follows: (P) 67, (D) 68.

NEBRASKA

STATE, YEAR OF ISSUE: Nebraska, 2006

State Information

YEAR OF STATEHOOD: 1867
ORDER IN UNION: 37
SIZE: 77,358 sq. mi.
POPULATION: 1.7 million
STATE MOTTO: "Equality before the law"
STATE FLOWER: goldenrod
STATE BIRD: western meadowlark
STATE TREE: cottonwood

Coin Specifications

MINTMARKS: P, D, S
OBVERSE DESIGNER: John Flanagan, modified by William Cousins (1997)
REVERSE DESIGNER: Charles L. Vickers
REVERSE DESIGN: At top: state name above date entered Union. At bottom: date of issue above motto "E Pluribus Unum," describing how the divided colonies became the United States of America. State design: oxen-drawn covered wagon carrying pioneers in the foreground, and Chimney Rock, the natural wonder that rises 445 feet from the valley of North Platte River. The sun is in full view behind the wagon. Initials CLV beneath "k" in "Rock."

Design History

An eight-person Quarter Design Committee was appointed in Nebraska in order to determine the state quarter design. They met monthly to examine designs and soon found themselves in a quandary; minutes of that meeting reveal: "The Committee reviewed the design preferential poll noting that no one design was the strong majority winner." Voting continued eliminating concept by concept. From 6,500 submissions, it whittled down slowly to 25. Finally, four of these were forwarded to the U.S. Mint:

ALTERNATE DESIGN NOT CHOSEN FOR NE QUARTER.

- Sower statue atop the state capitol
- state capitol building in Lincoln
- Chimney Rock formation along the western trail of Conestoga; wagon pulled by pioneer's oxen
- Standing Bear, a Native American rights advocate, holding an ax

On January 25, 2005, the CCAC met and considered the remaining designs. They recommended either design #2 or #4. Members described the image on design #3 as both meaningful and historic. In response to concerns from some members, the CCAC advised verification of the anatomical accuracy of the oxen. Regarding design #4, members suggested modifying the design to make it clear that the ax is a pipe ax rather than a regular straight ax. In particular, it was suggested that the ax/pipe be turned so that the bowl of the pipe could be seen, thereby identifying it as a pipe at the lower end.

The minutes reveal that "Members also wanted to ensure that the portrait is historically accurate, and to enlarge the image of Standing Bear as much as possible while remaining consistent with the Mint's policy against head-and-shoulders portraits on state quarters. Regarding the other designs, #1 was considered to be an unsuccessful rendering in part due to the image being cut off at the knees, and there was little enthusiasm for the image of the state capitol on design #2."

The Commission of Fine Arts commented that their choice was for the state capitol because of its architectural significance, although the Chief Standing Bear design was also considered a good one.

Nebraska Governor Dave Heineman announced his recommendation of "Chimney Rock" on June 1, 2005. The Department of the Treasury approved the design on July 20, 2005.

Mintage Figures

PROOF "S": 2.8 million
PROOF SILVER "S":1.5 million
UNCIRCULATED "P": 318.0 million
UNCIRCULATED "D": 273.0 million

Price Record

PRICE: $57

DATE OF ISSUE: 2006 Mintmark P

GRADING SERVICE: PCGS MS-69

DATE OF SALE: 1/2007

AUCTIONEER: Heritage

PRICE: $475

DATE OF ISSUE: 2006 Mintmark D

GRADING SERVICE: PCGS MS-68

DATE OF SALE: 8/2006

AUCTIONEER: Teletrade

Common Errors and Values

NOT STRUCK ON QUARTER PLANCHET: N/A

DOUBLE STRUCK: $1,500

STRUCK 3–4 TIMES: $2,500

OBVERSE CLAD MISSING: $400

REVERSE CLAD MISSING: $800

OFF CENTER MINOR: $120

OFF CENTER MAJOR: N/A

ROTATED REVERSE: N/A

BROCKAGE: $400

BROADSIDE: $75

STRUCK-THROUGH: $20

PARTIAL COLLAR: $35

CLIPPED "MINOR": $75

CLIPPED "MAJOR": $125

Grading Hints

OBVERSE: The high points of the coin's obverse are prone to wear; the field off Washington's nose, and the area behind the head curls, are prone to contact marks. Wear is most likely to be evident on the hair above Washington's ear and on the cheekbones. High grade (MS-67 and above) Coins will have no contact marks in the field.

REVERSE: This is the more important side for grade. High grade (above MS-67) has minimal (few if any) contact marks in the field. The high points of the coin show wear first: sun (left), top of wagon, top of Chimney Rock.

Investment Potential

Most "slabbed" state quarters are in MS-66 or better condition. Those that have gone up most in value and which have the greatest potential are MS-68 and better.

Past performance is no guarantee for the future, but from circulation the average (out of 56 states and territories) for P and D ranks 8. In 2008, based on auction sales records covering from the commencement of the State Quarter program to date, of more than 90 issues (P and D) taken from circulation, these coins ranked as follows: (P) 6, (D) 54.

COLORADO

STATE, YEAR OF ISSUE: Colorado, 2006

State Information

YEAR OF STATEHOOD: 1876
ORDER IN UNION: 38
SIZE: 104,100 sq. mi.
POPULATION: 4 .8 million
STATE MOTTO: "Nil sine numine" (nothing without providence)
STATE FLOWER: Rocky Mountain columbine
STATE BIRD: lark bunting
STATE TREE: Colorado blue spruce

Coin Specifications

MINTMARKS: P, D, S
OBVERSE DESIGNER: John Flanagan, modified by William Cousins (1997)
REVERSE DESIGNER: Norman E. Nemeth
REVERSE DESIGN: At top: state name above date entered Union. At bottom: date of issue above motto "E Pluribus Unum," describing how the divided colonies became the United States of America. State design: sweeping vista of the Rocky Mountains with evergreen trees and a banner carrying the inscription "Colorful Colorado" is shown. Initials NEM in lower right pine trees.

Design History

On February 4, 2004, the Colorado Commemorative Quarter Advisory Commission was formed by Governor Bill Owens. Colorado first lady Frances Owens served as commission chair, and design suggestions were requested from citizens. Five designs were chosen to send to the U.S. Mint:

- Rocky Mountains with the inscription "Colorful Colorado"

- Cliff Palace, mountains, and blue spruce trees with the inscription "Mesa Verde"

ALTERNATE DESIGN NOT CHOSEN FOR CO QUARTER.

- mountains with the inscription "Birthplace of the 10th Mountain Division" paying tribute to the Army's famous division and showing a skier wearing military gear of the 1940s

- mountains in the background with a large letter "C" entwined with a columbine, the state flower, and the inscription, "The Centennial State," as Colorado was the only state admitted to the Union in 1876

- Pike's Peak, the inscription "Pike's Peak or Bust," a miner's crossed pick and shovel, and two snowflakes, representing the state's famous winter weather

On March 15, 2005, the Citizens Coinage Advisory Committee held a public meeting at U.S. Mint headquarters in Washington, D.C. The result: "The CCAC recommends design #4 for Colorado. Members considered this design to be appealing and very representative of the state. There was a consensus that on design #4 the large letter "C" should be eliminated or reduced in size. It was also suggested that if design #1 were chosen, "The Centennial State" should be substituted for "Colorful Colorado."

On March 17, the Commission of Fine Arts met to consider the Colorado design. The consensus was that there were too many small images that tended to get lost at quarter size. Designs #1 and #5 would best lend themselves to simplification. In either case, the depiction of the mountains should be brought down so that it filled the whole coin, and the other tiny details eliminated. "Colorful Colorado," about which "America the Beautiful" was written, was selected with the governor's (and treasury secretary's) blessing. The Colorado state quarter became the last design produced in 2006.

Mintage Figures

PROOF "S": 2.8 million
PROOF SILVER "S": 1.5 million
UNCIRCULATED "P": 274.8 million
UNCIRCULATED "D": 294.2 million

Price Record

PRICE: $42
DATE OF ISSUE: 2006 Mintmark P
GRADING SERVICE: PCGS MS-69
DATE OF SALE: 9/2006
AUCTIONEER: Teletrade

PRICE: $42
DATE OF ISSUE: 2006 Mintmark D
GRADING SERVICE: PCGS MS-69
DATE OF SALE: 12/2006
AUCTIONEER: Heritage

Common Errors and Values

NOT STRUCK ON QUARTER
PLANCHET: N/A

DOUBLE STRUCK: $1,500

STRUCK 3–4 TIMES $2,500

OBVERSE CLAD MISSING: $400

REVERSE CLAD MISSING: $800

OFF CENTER MINOR: $120

OFF CENTER MAJOR: N/A

ROTATED REVERSE: N/A

BROCKAGE: $400

BROADSIDE: $75

STRUCK-THROUGH: $20

PARTIAL COLLAR: $35

CLIPPED "MINOR": $75

CLIPPED "MAJOR": $125

Grading Hints

OBVERSE: The high points of the coin's obverse are prone to wear; the field off Washington's nose, and the area behind the head curls, are prone to contact marks. Wear is most likely to be evident on the hair above Washington's ear and on the cheekbones. High-grade (MS-67 and above) coins will have no contact marks in the field.

REVERSE: This is the more important side for grade. High grade (above MS-67) has minimal (few if any) contact marks in the field. The high points of the coin—mountains at center of planchet—show wear first.

Investment Potential

Most "slabbed" state quarters are in MS-66 or better condition. Those that have gone up most in value and which have the greatest potential are MS-68 and better.

Past performance is no guarantee of the future, but from circulation the average (out of 56 states and territories) for P and D ranks 36. In 2008, based on auction sales records covering from the commencement of the State Quarters program to date, of more than 90 issues (P and D) taken from circulation, these coins ranked as follows: (P) 62, (D) 63.

NORTH DAKOTA

STATE, YEAR OF ISSUE: North Dakota, 2006

State Information

YEAR OF STATEHOOD: 1889
ORDER IN UNION: 39
SIZE: 70,704 sq. mi.
POPULATION: 640,000
STATE MOTTO: "Liberty and Union, now and forever, one and inseparable"
STATE FLOWER: wild prairie rose
STATE BIRD: western meadowlark
STATE TREE: American elm

Coin Specifications

MINTMARKS: P, D, S
OBVERSE DESIGNER: John Flanagan, modified by William Cousins (1997)
REVERSE DESIGNER: Donna Weaver
REVERSE DESIGN: At top: state name above date entered Union. At bottom: date of issue above motto "E Pluribus Unum," describing how the divided colonies became the United States of America. State design: a pair of grazing American bison in the foreground; sunset view of the rugged buttes that define the Badlands region in the background. Initials DW in sod at right.

Design History

The North Dakota Quarter Design Selection Process was launched by Governor John Hoeven in April 2004, when the state's seven-member commission was announced. After reviewing thousands of suggestions, the commission recommended three designs for development:

- aerial portrait of a farm

- two geese (the state bird) flying over a typical North Dakota landscape

- scene in the Badlands showing two buffalo

ALTERNATE DESIGN NOT
CHOSEN FOR ND QUARTER.

On January 25, 2005, the Commission of Fine Arts met to discuss the results. The minutes tell the story: "The members at first seemed to favor the bird design, but then switched to the buffaloes; they did not think the farm scene would be effective at coin size. Their recommendations were that the two buffaloes be separated in some way, possibly by a change in position, so that when reduced to coin size, it would be clear that there were two animals. It was also requested that the sun be omitted, and that the topographical features of the Badlands receive more emphasis." CCCAC on the other hand recommended design #1. The agriculture theme was praised by members as an excellent representation of the state. Members felt that the design could be improved by omitting the farmhouse on the left side of the coin, enhancing the definition of the crop fields to clarify that they represent wheat, and increasing the size of the trees. Regarding design #3, members expressed concern that buffalo had already appeared on many recent American coins, and further that the relief of the background would render the overall design unclear."

The state agreed with the Fine Arts Commission, and design #3 was the winner. The Department of the Treasury approved the design on July 20, 2005.

Mintage Figures

PROOF "S": 2.8 million
PROOF SILVER "S":1.5 million
UNCIRCULATED "P": 305.8 million
UNCIRCULATED "D": 359.0 million

Price Record

PRICE: $170
DATE OF ISSUE: 2006 Mintmark P
GRADING SERVICE: PCGS MS-69
DATE OF SALE: 2/2007
AUCTIONEER: Teletrade

PRICE: $140
DATE OF ISSUE: 2006 Mintmark D
GRADING SERVICE: PCGS MS-69
DATE OF SALE: 10/2006
AUCTIONEER: Teletrade

Common Errors and Values

NOT STRUCK ON QUARTER
PLANCHET: N/A

DOUBLE STRUCK: $1,500

STRUCK 3–4 TIMES: $2,500

OBVERSE CLAD MISSING: $400

REVERSE CLAD MISSING: $800

OFF CENTER MINOR: $120

OFF CENTER MAJOR: N/A

ROTATED REVERSE: N/A

BROCKAGE: $400

BROADSIDE: $75

STRUCK-THROUGH: $20

PARTIAL COLLAR: $35

CLIPPED "MINOR": $75

CLIPPED "MAJOR": $125

Grading Hints

OBVERSE: The high points of the coin's obverse are prone to wear; the field off Washington's nose, and the area behind the head curls, are prone to contact marks. Wear is most likely to be evident on the hair above Washington's ear and on the cheekbones. High-grade (MS-67 and above) coins will have no contact marks in the field.

REVERSE: This is the more important side for grade. High grade (above MS-67) has minimal (few if any) contact marks in the field. The high points of the coin show wear first: bison hindquarter at right.

Investment Potential

Most "slabbed" state quarters are in MS-66 or better condition. Those that have gone up most in value and which have the greatest potential are MS-68 and better.

Past performance is no guarantee for the future, but from circulation the average (out of 56 states and territories) for P and D ranks 22. In 2008, based on auction sales records covering from the commencement of the State Quarters program to date, of more than 90 issues (P and D) taken from circulation, these coins ranked as follows: (P) 23, (D) 49.

SOUTH DAKOTA

STATE, YEAR OF ISSUE: South Dakota, 2006

State Information

YEAR OF STATEHOOD: 1889
ORDER IN UNION: 40
SIZE: 77,121 sq. mi.
POPULATION: 796,000
STATE MOTTO: "Under God the people rule"
STATE FLOWER: pasqueflower
STATE BIRD: Chinese ring-necked pheasant
STATE TREE: Black Hills spruce

Coin Specifications

MINTMARKS: P, D, S
OBVERSE DESIGNER: John Flanagan, modified by William Cousins (1997)
REVERSE DESIGNER: John Mercanti
REVERSE DESIGN: At top: state name above date entered Union. At bottom: date of issue above motto "E Pluribus Unum," describing how the divided colonies became the United States of America. State design: Mount Rushmore National Monument, featuring the faces of four American Presidents: George Washington, Thomas Jefferson, Theodore Roosevelt, and Abraham Lincoln. State bird, a Chinese ring-necked pheasant, in flight above. The design is bordered by heads of wheat. Initials JM in rock below Lincoln.

Design History

In October 2003, Governor Mike Rounds appointed a five-member South Dakota Quarter Advisory Committee made up of individuals in the tourism, banking, and economic development industries that were responsible for submitting narratives to the Mint. The South Dakota Quarter Advisory Committee began accepting ideas from the citizens of South Dakota via telephone, letters, and e-mail. More than 30,000 responses were had in the first week, but in the end, the committee boiled it down to five designs:

ALTERNATE DESIGN NOT CHOSEN FOR SD QUARTER.

- Mount Rushmore National Memorial

- American bison (buffalo)

- ring-necked pheasant

- Mount Rushmore and a buffalo

- Mount Rushmore and a ring-necked pheasant.

At its meeting on September 21, 2004, the Commission of Fine Arts reviewed candidate designs for the 2006 South Dakota state quarter. There was unanimous approval for the bison, with some discussion as to whether the grass shown underneath the animal's feet would be intelligible at coin size. The commission's unanimous choice was also for Design #2.

On April 27, 2005, South Dakota Governor M. Michael Rounds announced his recommendation of the "Mount Rushmore and pheasant" design, echoing the choice of those who participated in the statewide vote.

The Department of the Treasury approved the design on May 28, 2005. On November 13, 2006, at Mount Rushmore, Edmund Moy, director of the U.S. Mint, members of the Black Hills Coin and Stamp Club, the Mount Rushmore National Memorial Society, and more than 3,200 attendees helped the governor officially launch the quarter to the world.

Mintage Figures

PROOF "S": 2.8 million
PROOF SILVER "S": 1.5 million
UNCIRCULATED "P": 245.0 million
UNCIRCULATED "D": 265.8 million

Price Record

PRICE: $90
DATE OF ISSUE: 2006 Mintmark P
GRADING SERVICE: PCGS MS-69
DATE OF SALE: 10/2006
AUCTIONEER: Teletrade

PRICE: $60
DATE OF ISSUE: 2006 Mintmark D
GRADING SERVICE: PCGS MS-69
DATE OF SALE: 10/2006
AUCTIONEER: Teletrade

Common Errors and Values

NOT STRUCK ON QUARTER
PLANCHET: N/A
DOUBLE STRUCK: $1,500
STRUCK 3–4 TIMES: $2,500
OBVERSE CLAD MISSING: $400
REVERSE CLAD MISSING: $800
OFF CENTER MINOR: $120
OFF CENTER MAJOR: N/A

ROTATED REVERSE: N/A
BROCKAGE: $400
BROADSIDE: $75
STRUCK-THROUGH: $20
PARTIAL COLLAR: $35
CLIPPED "MINOR": $75
CLIPPED "MAJOR": $125

Grading Hints

OBVERSE: The high points of the coin's obverse are prone to wear; the field off Washington's nose, and the area behind the head curls, are prone to contact marks. Wear is most likely to be evident on the hair above Washington's ear and on the cheekbones. High-grade (MS-67 and above) coins will have no contact marks in the field.

REVERSE: This is the more important side for grade. High grade (above MS-67) has minimal (few if any) contact marks in the field. The high points of the coin show wear first: Theodore Roosevelt and nose of George Washington.

Investment Potential

Most "slabbed" state quarters are in MS-66 or better condition. Those that have gone up most in value and which have the greatest potential are MS-68 and better.

Past performance is no guarantee for the future, but from circulation the average (out of 56 states and territories) for P and D ranks 29. In 2008, based on auction sales records covering from the commencement of the state quarter program to date, of more than 90 issues (P and D) taken from circulation, these coins ranked as follows: (P) 40, (D) 51.

MONTANA

STATE, YEAR OF ISSUE: Montana, 2007

State Information

YEAR OF STATEHOOD: 1889
ORDER IN UNION: 41
SIZE: 147,046 sq. mi.
POPULATION: 957,000
STATE MOTTO: "Oro y plata" (gold and silver)
STATE FLOWER: bitterroot
STATE BIRD: western meadowlark
STATE TREE: ponderosa pine

Coin Specifications

MINTMARKS: P, D, S
OBVERSE DESIGNER: John Flanagan, modified by William Cousins (1997)
REVERSE DESIGNER: Don Everhart II
REVERSE DESIGN: At top: state name above date entered Union. At bottom: date of issue above motto "E Pluribus Unum," describing how the divided colonies became the United States of America. State design: a bison skull is depicted above the Montana landscape with the inscription "Big Sky Country." DE in Mountains at lower left in foreground.

Design History

The Montana Quarter Design Selection Commission was created by Governor Brian Schweitzer in June 2005. In early 2006, he invited residents to vote electronically for their choice. The committee sorted through nearly 400 designs to select the images that they would forward to the U.S. Mint:

- bull elk in open landscape with the rising sun

- bison skull over a landscape, with the inscription "Big Sky Country"

ALTERNATE DESIGN NOT CHOSEN FOR MT QUARTER.

- state outline with landscape and a rising sun

- a landscape with river and mountains; in the sky the inscription "Big Sky Country"

On January 19, 2006, the Commission of Fine Arts met to discuss Montana designs and decided to recommend design #4. The bison skull motif was also considered good, but at quarter size possibly not easy to read; in addition, it was too strongly associated with artist Georgia O'Keeffe, who worked primarily in New Mexico.

The Citizens Coinage Advisory Committee met January 24 to discuss the same designs. The minutes reveal the following thoughts: While design #1 was generally popular, the sun was rising over the western mountains, which was not correct. Committee members felt that the symbol represented in design #2 was a powerful one and that the large image would translate well onto a coin. Design #3 was not well-liked, due to the fact that the CCAC was generally averse to state outlines. Some members thought that design #4 was representative of the Montana landscape; others thought that it was not powerful enough. There were also concerns about how it would translate into the small size of a coin.

Design #2, with the bison skull, was the committee's top recommendation. The Department of the Treasury approved the design on June 22, 2006. A public announcement was made by the governor a week later: "Today's announcement means that my mom might not let me come to Christmas dinner. And, I didn't even get my favorite quarter, the mountain and river scene. But after reviewing the votes and the numerous thoughts and comments that came to my office, Montana's quarter, by popular choice, will be the bison skull." The bison skull design received about 34 percent of the public vote, with the elk design receiving a little more than 30 percent. The other two designs received about 18 percent each.

Mintage Figures

PROOF "S": 1.6 million
PROOF SILVER "S":1.2 million
UNCIRCULATED "P": 257 million
UNCIRCULATED "D": 256.2 million

Price Record

PRICE: $55
DATE OF ISSUE: 2007 Mintmark P
GRADING SERVICE: PCGS MS-67
DATE OF SALE: 5/2007
AUCTIONEER: Teletrade

PRICE: $60
DATE OF ISSUE: 2007 Mintmark P
GRADING SERVICE: PCGS MS-67
DATE OF SALE: 12/2007
AUCTIONEER: Teletrade

Common Errors and Values

NOT STRUCK ON QUARTER PLANCHET: N/A
DOUBLE STRUCK: $1,500
STRUCK 3–4 TIMES: $2,500
OBVERSE CLAD MISSING: $400
REVERSE CLAD MISSING: $800
OFF CENTER MINOR: $120
OFF CENTER MAJOR: N/A

ROTATED REVERSE: N/A
BROCKAGE: $400
BROADSIDE: $75
STRUCK-THROUGH: $20
PARTIAL COLLAR: $35
CLIPPED "MINOR": $75
CLIPPED "MAJOR": $125

Grading Hints

OBVERSE: The high points of the coin's obverse are prone to wear; the field off Washington's nose, and the area behind the head curls, are prone to contact marks. Wear is most likely to be evident on the hair above Washington's ear and on the cheekbones. High-grade (MS-67 and above) coins will have no contact marks in the field.

REVERSE: This is the more important side for grade. High grade (above MS-67) has minimal (few if any) contact marks in the field. The high points of the coin show wear first: bison skull at center, mountain peak at 8 o'clock.

Investment Potential

Most "slabbed" state quarters are in MS-66 or better condition. Those that have gone up most in value and which have the greatest potential are MS-68 and better.

Past performance is no guarantee for the future, but from circulation the average (out of 56 states and territories) for P and D ranks 41. In 2008, based on auction sales records covering from the commencement of the State Quarters program to date, of more than 90 issues (P and D) taken from circulation, these coins ranked as follows: (P)56, (D) 11.

WASHINGTON

STATE, YEAR OF ISSUE: Washington, 2007

State Information

YEAR OF STATEHOOD: 1889
ORDER IN UNION: 42
SIZE: 70,637 sq. mi.
POPULATION: 6.4 million
STATE MOTTO: "Alki" (by and by)
STATE FLOWER: western rhododendron
STATE BIRD: willow goldfinch
STATE TREE: western hemlock

Coin Specifications

MINTMARKS: P, D, S
OBVERSE DESIGNER: John Flanagan, modified by William Cousins (1997)
REVERSE DESIGNER: Charles L. Vickers
REVERSE DESIGN: At top: state name above date entered Union. At bottom: date of issue above motto "E Pluribus Unum," describing how the divided colonies became the United States of America. State design: king salmon breaching the water in front of majestic Mt. Rainier. The coin bears the inscriptions "The Evergreen State." Initials CLV at Rainier's base, lower right.

Design History

In April 2005, Governor Christine Gregorian established the Washington State Quarter Advisory Commission to help guide the quarter selection process. The commission requested that residents submit design narratives representing various Washington themes. The commission received more than 1,500 suggestions and chose three narratives to pass on to the U.S. Mint:

- a salmon, Mt. Rainier, and apples within an outline of the state, with the inscription "The Evergreen State" in the center

- a salmon leaping from the water with Mt. Rainier in the background and "The Evergreen State" under the forest.

ALTERNATE DESIGN NOT CHOSEN FOR WA QUARTER.

- a northwest Native American West Coast style version of an orca, with some elements from the South Coast style, so that all tribes within the state would be represented.

On January 19, 2006, the Commission of Fine Arts met in Washington, D.C., and discussed Washington state designs. They felt that design #3 was the strongest. There was agreement that the orca would make an attractive coin and a welcome relief from so many landscape designs.

The Citizens Coinage Advisory Committee met January 24, 2006, in Washington, D.C., and offered its take: They considered design #1 to be too cluttered and busy. Committee members generally agreed that designs featuring a collage of various elements are not successful. The members strongly endorsed design #2, which was seen as attractive and significant for the state. It was suggested to remove the drops of splashing water, and perhaps to replace the small waves with a few simple lines to indicate the water's surface. Some members expressed concern about the accuracy of the salmon's appearance. Most

MILT PRIGGEE'S VIEW. USED BY PERMISSION.

members thought that design #3 was fundamentally flawed—resembling a cartoonish airplane—and was far too simplistic.

The residents of Washington participated in a statewide vote, in which more than 130,000 votes were cast. Gregorian announced Washington's recommendation at Centennial Elementary School in Olympia, Washington. The governor's recommendation, a king salmon breaching the water in front of Mt. Rainier, received the majority of votes cast in the statewide poll. The Department of the Treasury approved the design on June 22, 2006.

Mintage Figures

PROOF "S": 1.6 million
PROOF SILVER "S":1.2 million
UNCIRCULATED "P": 265.2 million
UNCIRCULATED "D": 280 million

Price Record

PRICE: $39
DATE OF ISSUE: 2007 Mintmark P
GRADING SERVICE: PCGS MS-67
DATE OF SALE: 3/2008
AUCTIONEER: Teletrade

PRICE: $6
DATE OF ISSUE: 2007 Mintmark D
GRADING SERVICE: PCGS MS-68
DATE OF SALE: 2/2008
AUCTIONEER: Teletrade

Common Errors and Values

NOT STRUCK ON QUARTER PLANCHET: N/A
DOUBLE STRUCK: $1,500
STRUCK 3–4 TIMES: $2,500
OBVERSE CLAD MISSING: $400
REVERSE CLAD MISSING: $800
OFF CENTER MINOR: $120
OFF CENTER MAJOR: N/A

ROTATED REVERSE: N/A
BROCKAGE: $400
BROADSIDE: $75
STRUCK-THROUGH: $20
PARTIAL COLLAR: $35
CLIPPED "MINOR": $75
CLIPPED "MAJOR": $125

Grading Hints

OBVERSE: The high points of the coin's obverse are prone to wear; the field off Washington's nose, and the area behind the head curls, are prone to contact marks. Wear is most likely to be evident on the hair above Washington's ear and on the cheekbones. High-grade (MS-67 and above) coins will have no contact marks in the field.

REVERSE: This is the more important side for grade. High grade (above MS-67) has minimal (few if any) contact marks in the field. The high points of the coin show wear first: fish head, top of Mt. Ranier.

Investment Potential

Most slabbed state quarters are in MS-66 or better condition. Those that have gone up most in value and which have the greatest potential are graded MS-68 and better.

Past performance is no guarantee for the future, but among coins taken from circulation, the average (out of 56 states and territories) for P and D mint coins ranks as follows: (P) 85, (D) 97.

IDAHO

STATE, YEAR OF ISSUE: Idaho, 2007

State Information

YEAR OF STATEHOOD: 1890
ORDER IN UNION: 43
SIZE: 83,574 sq. mi.
POPULATION: 1.5 million
STATE MOTTO: "Esto perpetua" (Let it be perpetual)
STATE FLOWER: syringa
STATE BIRD: mountain bluebird
STATE TREE: white pine

Coin Specifications

MINTMARKS: P, D, S
OBVERSE DESIGNER: John Flanagan, modified by William Cousins (1997)
REVERSE DESIGNER: Don Everhart II
REVERSE DESIGN: At top: state name above date entered Union. At bottom: date of issue above motto "E Pluribus Unum," describing how the divided colonies became the United States of America. State design: map of Idaho in outline form with star at Boise, peregrine falcon, and state motto "Esto Perpetua." Initials DE in lower left falcon feathers.

Design History

In August 2005, the Idaho Commission on the Arts announced it would be accepting ideas for the new Idaho quarter. Four designs were forwarded to the U.S. Mint:

- a peregrine falcon as main subject, in profile with head and shoulders on the left side; state outline in the lower right quadrant with a star to indicate the capital and state motto "Esto perpetua" in the open space to the right

ALTERNATE DESIGN NOT CHOSEN FOR ID QUARTER.

- Sawtooth Mountains with a river cutting through them (as the river widens it creates an outline of the state); tall ponderosa pines frame the view on each side

- aerial view of planted and fallow strips of land

- state outline centered on the coin, with first two lines of the state song written on either side

On January 19, 2006, the Commission of Fine Arts met in Washington to choose Idaho designs. There was consensus that design #2 would make the best coin.

On January 24, the Citizens Coinage Advisory Committee met to offer its opinion: "Regarding design #1, members liked the strong design of the falcon head, but felt strongly that the state outline detracted from the overall design. Most members felt that the state outline should be removed, and two members felt that it should at least be reduced in size. It was also noted that the star indicating the location of the capital Boise was unnecessary and probably unrecognizable in reduced size on the quarter. It was requested that the design of bird and outline, if chosen, should be more balanced and leave less space on the right side of the field."

For design #2, it was questioned whether the mountainous landscape was representative of the agricultural state of Idaho. However, most members expressed admiration for a clever incorporation of the state outline. Design #3 was considered appropriate for Idaho's vast fields but the execution of lines with mountains was viewed as far too cluttered and difficult to render in relief on a small coin. Design #4 was seen as too busy. The committee recommended #1 and #2 equally.

Governor Dick Kempthorne announced that the recommended design by the state and the governor was the peregrine falcon. The Department of the Treasury approved the design on June 26, 2006.

Mintage Figures

proof "S": 1.6 million
proof silver "S": 1.2 million
uncirculated "P": 294.6 million
uncirculated "D": 286.8 million

Price Record

PRICE: $79
DATE OF ISSUE: 2007 Mintmark P
GRADING SERVICE: PCGS MS-66
DATE OF SALE: 3/2008
AUCTIONEER: eBay

PRICE: $368
DATE OF ISSUE: 2006 Mintmark D
GRADING SERVICE: PCGS MS-68
DATE OF SALE: 12/2007
AUCTIONEER: Teletrade

Common Errors and Values

NOT STRUCK ON QUARTER PLANCHET: N/A
DOUBLE STRUCK: $1,500
STRUCK 3–4 TIMES: $2,500
OBVERSE CLAD MISSING: $400
REVERSE CLAD MISSING: $800
OFF CENTER MINOR: $120
OFF CENTER MAJOR: N/A

ROTATED REVERSE: N/A
BROCKAGE: $400
BROADSIDE: $75
STRUCK-THROUGH: $20
PARTIAL COLLAR: $35
CLIPPED "MINOR": $75
CLIPPED "MAJOR": $125

Grading Hints

OBVERSE: The high points of the coin's obverse are prone to wear; the field off Washington's nose, and the area behind the head curls, are prone to contact marks. Wear is most likely to be evident on the hair above Washington's ear and on the cheekbones. High-grade (MS-67 and above) coins will have no contact marks in the field.

REVERSE: This is the more important side for grade. High grade (above MS-67) has minimal (few if any) contact marks in the field. The high points of the coin show wear first: falcon head and beak

Investment Potential

Most "slabbed" state quarters are in MS-66 or better condition. Those that have gone up most in value and which have the greatest potential are graded MS-68 and better.

Past performance is no guarantee for the future, but among coins taken from circulation, the average (out of 56 states and territories) for P and D mint coins ranks as follows: (P) 86, (D) 92.

WYOMING

STATE, YEAR OF ISSUE: Wyoming, 2007

State Information

YEAR OF STATEHOOD: 1890
ORDER IN UNION: 44
SIZE: 97,818 sq. mi.
POPULATION: 523,000
STATE MOTTO: "Equal rights"
STATE FLOWER: Indian paintbrush
STATE BIRD: western meadowlark
STATE TREE: plains cottonwood

Coin Specifications

MINTMARKS: P, D, S
OBVERSE DESIGNER: John Flanagan, modified by William Cousins (1997)
REVERSE DESIGNER: Norman E. Nemeth
REVERSE DESIGN: At top: state name above date entered Union. At bottom: date of issue above motto "E Pluribus Unum," describing how the divided colonies became the United States of America. State design: uses Wyoming's trademark symbol, bucking horse and rider, with inscription "The Equality State." Initials NEM above "m" in "Unum."

Design History

On December 28, 2004, Governor Dave Freudenthal formed the Wyoming Coinage Advisory Committee, including 13 Wyoming historians and other experts. The state invited citizens to submit design ideas, and approximately 3,200 were accepted over a three-month period.

Freudenthal then recommended five concepts that were developed into design candidates by the U.S. Mint:

- bucking horse and rider in silhouette style with state motto "The Equality State"

ALTERNATE DESIGN NOT CHOSEN FOR WY QUARTER.

- bucking horse and rider in relief with state motto in a state outline

- bucking horse and rider with Teton mountain range in the background

- bucking horse and rider in typical Wyoming setting

- Old Faithful geyser from Yellowstone National Park, a design adopted from a very popular 1934 postage stamp.

On January 19, 2006, the Commission of Fine Arts met in Washington and discussed coinage from Wyoming. The minutes reveal: "The members all thought that Old Faithful could be a strong image for Wyoming, but not as it had been rendered. The horse and rider was an equally powerful theme, and the consensus was that of the four designs, they would prefer #1, the silhouette version."

The Citizens Coinage Advisory Committee views were expressed at its Washington meeting of January 24: There was much discussion about the unusual silhouette design of #1, which would be new to the state quarter program if chosen. Members were keen to know from the U.S. Mint employees how the difference between the rider and the remaining surface would differ to achieve a silhouette effect. Members agreed that this could be an innovative quarter if such a difference in texture could be created. The smooth surface turned out to be the one for high speed production.

Design #5 was seen as successful, although some members thought that it would be hard to render the steam properly, which presently resembled dust or an explosion. It was also mentioned that the design was based on the stamp, whereas the actual appearance did not take into account movement because of the wind and other present-day localities. Design #4, though conventional, was seen as the most authentic and successful and was the recommendation of the Committee.

On May 12, 2006, Governor Freudenthal announced his recommendation of the silhouette bucking horse and rider design. The Department of the Treasury approved the design on June 22, 2006.

Mintage Figures

PROOF "S": 1.6 million
PROOF SILVER "S":1.2 million
UNCIRCULATED "P": 243.6 million
UNCIRCULATED "D": 320.8 million

Price Record

PRICE: $65	PRICE: $65
DATE OF ISSUE: 2008 Mintmark P	DATE OF ISSUE: 2008 Mintmark P
GRADING SERVICE: PCGS MS-67	GRADING SERVICE: PCGS MS-67
DATE OF SALE: 3/2008	DATE OF SALE: 3/2008
AUCTIONEER: eBay*	AUCTIONEER: eBay*

*Combined as one lot; evenly divided.

Common Errors and Values

NOT STRUCK ON QUARTER PLANCHET: N/A	ROTATED REVERSE: N/A
DOUBLE STRUCK: $1,500	BROCKAGE: $400
STRUCK 3–4 TIMES: $2,500	BROADSIDE: $75
OBVERSE CLAD MISSING: $400	STRUCK-THROUGH: $20
REVERSE CLAD MISSING: $800	PARTIAL COLLAR: $35
OFF CENTER MINOR: $120	CLIPPED "MINOR": $75
OFF CENTER MAJOR: N/A	CLIPPED "MAJOR": $125

Grading Hints

OBVERSE: The high points of the coin's obverse are prone to wear; the field off Washington's nose, and the area behind the head curls, are prone to contact marks. Wear is most likely to be evident on the hair above Washington's ear and on the cheekbones. High-grade (MS-67 and above) coins will have no contact marks in the field.

REVERSE: This is the more important side for grade. High grade (above MS-67) has minimal (few if any) contact marks in the field. The high points of the coin show wear first: horse and rider (flat).

Investment Potential

Most "slabbed" state quarters are in MS-66 or better condition. Those that have gone up most in value and which have the greatest potential are graded MS-68 and better.

Past performance is no guarantee for the future, but among coins taken from circulation, the average (out of 56 states and territories) for P and D mint coins ranks as follows: (P) 84, (D) 100.

UTAH

STATE, YEAR OF ISSUE: Utah, 2007

State Information

YEAR OF STATEHOOD: 1896
ORDER IN UNION: 45
SIZE: 84,904 sq. mi.
POPULATION: 2.6 million
STATE MOTTO: "Industry"
STATE FLOWER: sego lily
STATE BIRD: seagull
STATE TREE: blue spruce

Coin Specifications

MINTMARKS: P, D, S
OBVERSE DESIGNER: John Flanagan, modified by William Cousins (1997)
REVERSE DESIGNER: Joseph Menna
REVERSE DESIGN: At top: state name above date entered Union. At bottom: date of issue above motto "E Pluribus Unum," describing how the divided colonies became the United States of America. State design: golden spike union of the transcontinental railroad at Promontory Summit in 1869.

Design History

Utah's governor appointed the Utah Commemorative Quarter Commission, which invited narrative submissions from the citizens of Utah. The commission received more than 5,000 submissions and recommended three concepts to the U.S. Mint.

- two locomotives facing each other, with the golden spike between them, mountains in the background, with "Crossroads of the West" above; this design represents one of the most significant events in American history: the completion of the transcontinental railway in 1869 brought east and west together

- a beehive and the phrase "The Beehive State"

ALTERNATE DESIGN NOT CHOSEN FOR UT QUARTER.

- an airborne snowboarder participating in the 2002 Winter Olympic Games, as Salt Lake City was the first U.S. city to host the games with snowboarding as an official sport

The Fine Arts Commission met in Washington on January 19, 2006, to examine Utah and several other state coins due out in 2006. The last state examined that day by the CFA was Utah. Minutes note that "Because of its simplicity, the members preferred the beehive, design #2. [One member] suggested removing the table beneath the beehive, as it did not contribute to the design, and [another member] thought the state flower should be taken out also as it interfered with the symmetry. She thought just the beehive and a bee—the state insect—would be enough and would make the design more comprehensible. If 'The Beehive State' had to be used, the phrase could be placed under the beehive."

Next, The CCAC met in Washington to examine three design concepts forwarded by the governor for elaboration by Mint artists. The three design proposals for Utah were generally seen as successful. There was some discussion about which design was most representative for modern-day Utah.

Some members thought that the depiction of the historical event in design #1 deserved support. However, others thought that the depiction of the event was perhaps not clear enough and that the subject was too complex for a depiction on the quarter. There was some criticism of the details of the locomotives, which were not viewed as historically accurate. It was suggested that if this design were adopted, the words "Transcontinental Railroad" should appear beneath the scene, and the date and location of the event should also be indicated in the coin. In design #3, the depiction of a young woman in a thoroughly modern sport was seen as a depiction of modern-day Utah. But members were concerned that the design did not translate well onto a coin. Design #1 was the preferred choice.

The official bodies spoke, but in the end the people decided. More than 150,000 citizens voted in a 25-day statewide vote in April 2006. "Crossroads of the West" prevailed as the favorite design among voters. Governor Jon M. Huntsman Jr. announced the state's recommendation at the Golden Spike National Historic Site in Promontory on May 10, 2006, the 137th anniversary of the joining of the rails. The Department of the Treasury approved the design on June 22, 2006.

Mintage Figures

PROOF "S": 1.6 million
PROOF SILVER "S": 1.2 million
UNCIRCULATED "P": 255 million
UNCIRCULATED "D": 253.2 million

Price Record

PRICE: $13

DATE OF ISSUE: 2007 Mintmark P

GRADING SERVICE: PCGS MS-68

DATE OF SALE: 7/2008

AUCTIONEER: eBay

PRICE: $19

DATE OF ISSUE: 2008 Mintmark D

GRADING SERVICE: NGC MS-67

DATE OF SALE: 3/2008

AUCTIONEER: eBay

Common Errors and Values

NOT STRUCK ON QUARTER PLANCHET: N/A

DOUBLE STRUCK: $1,500

STRUCK 3–4 TIMES: $2,500

OBVERSE CLAD MISSING: $400

REVERSE CLAD MISSING: $800

OFF CENTER MINOR: $120

OFF CENTER MAJOR: N/A

ROTATED REVERSE: N/A

BROCKAGE: $400

BROADSIDE: $75

STRUCK-THROUGH: $20

PARTIAL COLLAR: $35

CLIPPED "MINOR": $75

CLIPPED "MAJOR": $125

Grading Hints

OBVERSE: The high points of the coin's obverse are prone to wear; the field off Washington's nose, and the area behind the head curls, are prone to contact marks. Wear is most likely to be evident on the hair above Washington's ear and on the cheekbones. High-grade (MS-67 and above) coins will have no contact marks in the field.

REVERSE: This is the more important side for grade. High grade (above MS-67) has minimal (few if any) contact marks in the field. The high points of the coin show wear first: golden spike, two mountain peaks.

Investment Potential

Most "slabbed" state quarters are in MS-66 or better condition. Those that have gone up most in value and which have the greatest potential are graded MS-68 and better.

Past performance is no guarantee for the future, but among coins taken from circulation, the average (out of 56 states and territories) for P and D mint coins ranks as follows: (P) 83, (D) 94.

OKLAHOMA

STATE, YEAR OF ISSUE: Oklahoma, 2008

State Information

YEAR OF STATEHOOD: 1907
ORDER IN UNION: 46
SIZE: 69,903 sq. mi.
POPULATION: 3.6 million
STATE MOTTO: "Labor omnia vincit" (labor conquers all things)
STATE FLOWER: Indian blanket
STATE BIRD: scissor-tailed flycatcher
STATE TREE: redbud

Coin Specifications

MINTMARKS: P, D, S
OBVERSE DESIGNER: John Flanagan, modified by William Cousins (1997)
REVERSE DESIGNER: Susan Gamble, designer; Phebe Hemphill, sculptor
REVERSE DESIGN: At top: state name above date entered Union. At bottom: date of issue above motto "E Pluribus Unum," describing how the divided colonies became the United States of America. State design: scissor-tailed flycatcher (the state bird) in flight with its tail feathers spread. The bird is soaring over the state wildflower, the Indian blanket, backed by a field of flowers. Depiction of the Indian blanket (or Gaillardia) symbolizes the state's rich Native American heritage and native long grass prairies that are abundant in wildlife. Oklahoma was formed by the combination of the Oklahoma Territory and the Indian Territory of the "Five Civilized Tribes"—Choctaw, Chickasaw, Creek, Seminole, and Cherokee. The state's name is derived from the Choctaw words "kola" and "home," meaning "red" and "people."

Design History

Oklahoma celebrated its centennial in 2007, and a year earlier, on February 16, 2006, Governor Brad Henry and the Oklahoma Centennial Commission asked Oklahomans to provide input on the design of the state's commemorative quarter. "On the eve of the Oklahoma Centennial, it is only appropriate that we go to the people to help us create a lasting tribute

ALTERNATE DESIGN NOT CHOSEN FOR OK QUARTER.

to our great state," said Henry. "We're seeking as many ideas as possible so that we will have a good range of proposals to submit to federal authorities." The Internet was the primary contact point. Five finalist concepts were chosen and sent to the Mint:

- a three-dimensional outline of the state, with rays radiating behind it; a Native American calumet (ceremonial peace pipe); shocks of wheat, symbolizing the importance of agricultural in the state; and an image inspired by a pioneer woman, celebrating the Ponca City statue that honors the courage, tenacity, and ingenuity of those who endured hardship to achieve their dreams

- state wildflower, the Indian blanket, saluting the state's Native American heritage and native long-grass prairies; above a field of flowers is the scissor-tailed flycatcher in flight, with tailfeathers spread

- old-fashioned windmill and gushing oil derrick; taken together, they represent agriculture and oil and gas innovations. In the middle of the coin is waving wheat, along with a figure inspired by the pioneer woman statue

- tilted three-dimensional shape of the state of Oklahoma in the background, with oil derrick and rendering inspired by the pioneer woman statue

- three-dimensional shape of the state in the background, calumet, and rendering inspired by the pioneer woman statue; the calumet is bisecting the state to distinguish the original Oklahoma Territory and the Indian Territory

At its meeting of January 18, 2007, the Commission of Fine Arts reviewed the five designs and recommended design #2.

On January 23, 2007, the Citizens Coinage Advisory Committee met to discuss the designs. Many members considered several of the Oklahoma designs to be rather cluttered. Many members appreciated the artistry of #2, but felt that the design did not sufficiently show the state's history. Their recommended design for Oklahoma was #5.

In the end, the governor agreed with the CFA and chose design #2 as the final design.

Mintage Figures

PROOF "S": 1.6 million
PROOF SILVER "S": 1.2 million
UNCIRCULATED "P": 194.6 million
UNCIRCULATED "D": 222.0 million

Price Record

PRICE: $66
DATE OF ISSUE: 2008 Mintmark P
GRADING SERVICE: PCGS MS-67
DATE OF SALE: 3/2008
AUCTIONEER: eBay

PRICE: $56
DATE OF ISSUE: 2008 Mintmark D
GRADING SERVICE: PCGS MS-67
DATE OF SALE: 3/2008
AUCTIONEER: eBay

Common Errors and Values

NOT STRUCK ON QUARTER PLANCHET: N/A
DOUBLE STRUCK: $1,500
STRUCK 3–4 TIMES: $2,500
OBVERSE CLAD MISSING: $400
REVERSE CLAD MISSING: $800
OFF CENTER MINOR: $120
OFF CENTER MAJOR: N/A

ROTATED REVERSE: N/A
BROCKAGE: $400
BROADSIDE: $75
STRUCK-THROUGH: $20
PARTIAL COLLAR: $35
CLIPPED "MINOR": $75
CLIPPED "MAJOR": $125

Grading Hints

OBVERSE: The high points of the coin's obverse are prone to wear; the field off Washington's nose, and the area behind the head curls, are prone to contact marks. Wear is most likely to be evident on the hair above Washington's ear and on the cheekbones. High-grade (MS-67 and above) coins will have no contact marks in the field.

REVERSE: This is the more important side for grade. High grade (above MS-67) has minimal (few if any) contact marks in the field. The high points of the coin show wear first: bird's back and top of head, tips of flowers.

Investment Potential

Most "slabbed" state quarters are in MS-66 or better condition. Those that have gone up most in value and which have the greatest potential are graded MS-68 and better.

Past performance is no guarantee for the future, but among coins taken from circulation, the average (out of 56 states and territories) for P and D mint coins ranks as follows: (P) 89, (D) 96.

NEW MEXICO

STATE, YEAR OF ISSUE: New Mexico, 2008

State Information

YEAR OF STATEHOOD: 1912
ORDER IN UNION: 47
SIZE: 121,598 sq. mi.
POPULATION: 1.969 million
STATE MOTTO: "Crescit Eundo" (it grows as it goes)
STATE FLOWER: yucca
STATE BIRD: roadrunner
STATE TREE: piñon

Coin Specifications

MINTMARKS: P, D, S
OBVERSE DESIGNER: John Flanagan, modified by William Cousins (1997)
REVERSE DESIGNER: Don Everhart II
REVERSE DESIGN: At top: state name above date entered Union. At bottom: date of issue above motto "E Pluribus Unum," describing how the divided colonies became the United States of America. State design: Zia sun symbol over a topographical outline of the state with inscription "Land of Enchantment."

Design History

New Mexico's distinctive insignia is the Zia sun symbol, which originated with the Indians of Zia Pueblo. Four is the sacred number of Zia, and the figure is composed of a circle from which four points radiate. These points are made up of four straight lines of varying lengths personified. To the Zia Indian, this sacred number is embodied in the earth, with four directions: in the year, with four seasons; in the day, with the sunrise, moon, evening, and night; in life, with its four divisions—childhood, youth, manhood, and old age.

When asked their thoughts on potential designs for the New Mexico state quarter, the state's citizens were most enthusiastic about including the Zia symbol on the quarter. The following four designs were forwarded to the U.S. Mint:

ALTERNATE DESIGN NOT
CHOSEN FOR NM QUARTER.

- Zia symbol centered over a textured outline of the state

- textured Zia symbol over outline of the state, with the inscription "Land of Enchantment"

- a topographical view of New Mexico, with the Zia symbol marking the location of the capital, Santa Fe, and the inscription, "Land of Enchantment"

- a textured outline of the state, with the Zia symbol marking the location of the capital, Santa Fe, and the inscription, "Land of Enchantment"

At its meeting of January 18, 2007, the Commission of Fine Arts reviewed these designs. The commission recommended design #1, since it features the largest rendition of the Zia symbol in the center of the coin.

The Citizens Coinage Advisory Committee held a public meeting on January 23, 2007, at the United States Mint headquarters to discuss the New Mexico designs. Some members noted the fact that all four of New Mexico's designs were reflective of the same theme, which revealed a clear preference by the state. Several members expressed appreciation for the incorporation of topography into the state outline on design #3. The CCAC's recommendation for New Mexico's quarter was design #3.

Ultimately, design #3 was chosen. "New Mexico's quarter design is simple, artistic and intriguing," said Governor Bill Richardson. "It would be difficult to incorporate all the facets of our history and culture through any one image or a collage of images. The design is a creative, alluring symbol and a distinct representation of New Mexico."

Mintage Figures

PROOF "S": *
PROOF SILVER "S": *
UNCIRCULATED "P": 241.4 million
UNCIRCULATED "D": 241.2 million

*Figures not available at press time. Visit www.americasstatequarters.com for updated figures.

Price Record

PRICE: $8
DATE OF ISSUE: 2008 Mintmark P
GRADING SERVICE: NGC MS-66
DATE OF SALE: 6/2008
AUCTIONEER: eBay

PRICE: $33
DATE OF ISSUE: 2008 Mintmark P
GRADING SERVICE: NGC MS-67
DATE OF SALE: 6/2008
AUCTIONEER: eBay

Common Errors and Values

NOT STRUCK ON QUARTER PLANCHET: N/A	**OFF CENTER MINOR:** $120
DOUBLE STRUCK: $1500	**OFF CENTER MAJOR:** N/A
STRUCK 3–4 TIMES $2500	**ROTATED REVERSE:** N/A
OBVERSE CLAD MISSING: $400	**BROCKAGE:** $400
REVERSE CLAD MISSING: $800	**BROADSIDE:** $75
	STRUCK-THROUGH: $20

Grading Hints

OBVERSE: The high points of the coin's obverse are prone to wear; the field off Washington's nose, and the area behind the head curls, are prone to contact marks. Wear is most likely to be evident on the hair above Washington's ear and on the cheekbones. High-grade (MS-67 and above) coins will have no contact marks in the field.

REVERSE: This is the more important side for grade. High grade (above MS-67) has minimal (few if any) contact marks in the field. The high points of the coin show wear first: Zia symbol may pick up nicks and scratches evenly. This coin may prove to be elusive in higher grades, except as a special mint set or as a proof—but not from genuine circulated coins.

Investment Potential

Most "slabbed" state quarters are in MS-66 or better condition. Those that have gone up most in value and which have the greatest potential are graded MS-68 and better.*

---

*Investment potential not available at press time. Visit www.americasstatequarters.com for updated figures.

ARIZONA

STATE, YEAR OF ISSUE: Arizona, 2008

State Information

YEAR OF STATEHOOD: 1912
ORDER IN UNION: 48
SIZE: 114,006 sq. mi.
POPULATION: 6.3 million
STATE MOTTO: "Ditat deus" (God enriches)
STATE FLOWER: giant cactus
STATE BIRD: cactus wren
STATE TREE: paloverde

Coin Specifications

MINTMARKS: P, D, S
OBVERSE DESIGNER: John Flanagan, modified by William Cousins (1997)
REVERSE DESIGNER: Joel Iskowitz, designer; Joseph Menna, sculptor
REVERSE DESIGN: At top: state name above date entered Union. At bottom: date of issue above motto "E Pluribus Unum," describing how the divided colonies became the United States of America. State design: the Grand Canyon with a saguaro cactus in the foreground. A banner reading "Grand Canyon State" separates the two images. The Grand Canyon covers more than 1.2 million acres in northwestern Arizona. Naturally sculpted by the mighty Colorado River, the canyon is 6,000 feet deep at its deepest point and 18 miles at its widest. It is home to numerous rare and threatened plant and animal species, though the saguaro cactus is not one of them. The Grand Canyon joined the National Park system in 1919 and is visited by more than four million tourists a year.

Design History

In November 2005, Governor Janet Napolitano created the 24-member Arizona Quarter Commission to develop narrative design concepts to present to the U.S. Mint and make recommendations to the governor for the final design of the Arizona state quarter. Arizonans with backgrounds in the arts, humanities, history, education, finance, and business, as well as the general public, representing the geographic and demographic

ALTERNATE DESIGN NOT CHOSEN FOR AZ QUARTER.

diversity of the state, were selected to serve on the commission. Napolitano appointed a fourth-grade student to ensure that students were involved in the process.

More than 4,200 suggestions for the design were whittled down to five finalists:

- overview of the Grand Canyon, with enough detail to suggest the immensity of its natural wonder, and with the sun in the background; inscription reads, "Grand Canyon State"

- view of the Grand Canyon in the upper background, with the sun rising or setting; in the foreground, a saguaro cactus; to the left, a banner establishing a clear separation between the design elements, since the saguaro cactus does not actually grow in the Grand Canyon

- saguaro cactus as the central design element, supported by a simple background of a mountain, with desert vegetation and additional proportional saguaros in the distant background, as well as the sun; inscription reads, "Grand Canyon State"

- view of the Grand Canyon and the Colorado River, showing a wooden boat going through the rapids, with members of the John Wesley Powell expedition; inscription reads, "Powell's Grand Canyon Expedition"

- two Navajo code talkers in Marine combat uniform, using World War II field communication equipment; with inscription "Navajo Code Talkers"

At its meeting of January 18, 2007, the Commission of Fine Arts reviewed alternatives for the last five reverse designs. Several members said the design should relate to the Grand Canyon and supported #1 or #3. The commission ultimately voted to recommend design #1.

The Citizens Coinage Advisory Committee held a public meeting on January 23 at the U.S. Mint headquarters to discuss the designs. Members generally felt that the more historically oriented designs, #4 and #5, were unsuitable because they depicted events that were relatively little known. Discussion focused on the relative merits of the two images featuring the Grand Canyon, #1 and #2. They recommended design #1.

On April 10, 2007, Napolitano asked Arizonans for their input. They responded overwhelmingly, and on May 1, Arizonans choose design #2 as their favorite. Napolitano sent the people's decision to the U.S. Mint.

Mintage Figures

PROOF "S": *
PROOF SILVER "S": *
UNCIRCULATED "P": 238 million
UNCIRCULATED "D": 238 million

Price Record

PRICE: $64**
DATE OF ISSUE: 2008 Mintmark P
GRADING SERVICE: PCGS MS-67
DATE OF SALE: 7/2008
AUCTIONEER: eBay

PRICE: $64**
DATE OF ISSUE: 2008 Mintmark D
GRADING SERVICE: PCGS MS-67
DATE OF SALE: 7/2008
AUCTIONEER: eBay

Common Errors and Values

NOT STRUCK ON QUARTER
  PLANCHET: N/A
DOUBLE STRUCK: $1,500
STRUCK 3–4 TIMES: $2,500
OBVERSE CLAD MISSING: $400
REVERSE CLAD MISSING: $800
OFF CENTER MINOR: $120
OFF CENTER MAJOR: N/A

ROTATED REVERSE: N/A
BROCKAGE: $400
BROADSIDE: $75
STRUCK-THROUGH: $20
PARTIAL COLLAR: $35
CLIPPED "MINOR": $75
CLIPPED "MAJOR": $125

Grading Hints

OBVERSE: The high points of the coin's obverse are prone to wear; the field off Washington's nose, and the area behind the head curls, are prone to contact marks. Wear is most likely to be evident on the hair above Washington's ear and on the cheekbones. High-grade (MS-67 and above) coins will have no contact marks in the field.

REVERSE: This is the more important side for grade. High grade (above MS-67) has minimal (few if any) contact marks in the field. The high points of the coin show wear first: horizontal cactus (body) and "Grand Canyon" banner. Mountain peaks may take some scratches.

*Figures not available at press time. Visit www.americasstatequarters.com for updated figures.
**Combined as one lot; evenly divided.

Investment Potential

Most "slabbed" state quarters are in MS-66 or better condition. Those that have gone up most in value and which have the greatest potential are graded MS-68 and better.*

*Investment potential not available at press time. Visit www.americasstatequarters.com for updated figures.

ALASKA

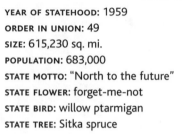

State Information

YEAR OF STATEHOOD: 1959
ORDER IN UNION: 49
SIZE: 615,230 sq. mi.
POPULATION: 683,000
STATE MOTTO: "North to the future"
STATE FLOWER: forget-me-not
STATE BIRD: willow ptarmigan
STATE TREE: Sitka spruce

Coin Specifications

MINTMARKS: P, D, S
OBVERSE DESIGNER: John Flanagan, modified by William Cousins (1997)
REVERSE DESIGNER: Susan Gamble, designer; Charles Vickers, engraver
REVERSE DESIGN: At top: state name above date entered Union. At bottom: date of issue above motto "E Pluribus Unum," describing how the divided colonies became the United States of America. State design: a grizzly bear emerging from the waters with a salmon in its jaws. Also shown is the North Star displayed above the inscription "The Great Land." The wildlife symbolizes Alaska's natural beauty. The grizzly flourishes in Alaska and can be observed in places such as Denali and Katmai National Parks.

Design History

The Alaska Commemorative Coin Commission was established by Governor Sarah Palin in April 2005. It consisted of 11 members who submitted four narrative designs to the U.S. Mint. Final designs were selected based on aesthetic beauty, historical accuracy, appropriateness, and coin-ability, and consisted of:

- a polar bear with the midnight sun and the text "Land of the Midnight Sun"

- Denali National Park with a dogsled musher, the Big Dipper with the North Star, and the text "North to the Future"

ALTERNATE DESIGN NOT CHOSEN FOR AK QUARTER.

- a brown bear with salmon, the Big Dipper with the North Star, and the text "The Great Land"

- Denali National Park with a gold panner and the text "Denali, the Great One"

At its meeting of January 18, 2007, the Commission of Fine Arts reviewed the design options. Members supported #1 and #3 due to the power and grace of the bear images, but questioned the phrase "Land of the Midnight Sun" because it is not unique to Alaska. The Commission ultimately suggested that Design #1 be used but with the phrase "The Last Frontier," the official phrase for the state.

The Citizens Coinage Advisory Committee held a public meeting on January 23, 2007, at U.S. Mint headquarters to discuss the designs. Members were generally impressed by all four designs, considering all of them to be representative of the state, and well-executed. However, the CCAC's recommendation for Alaska's quarter was also design #1.

Palin unveiled the final design for the Alaska commemorative quarter in April 2007. The governor selected the bear with salmon and the North Star. Mark Vinsel, chair of the Alaska Commemorative Coin Commission, joined Palin for the unveiling ceremony at the Alaska Mint in Anchorage.

"This was a hard decision," Palin said. "All of these designs are very fitting for Alaska. I heard from many Alaskans across our state who helped me decide which design best represents Alaska. I would like to extend a special thank-you to all of the students and teachers who took part in this process, too. Their input was especially helpful."

Mintage Figures*

PROOF "S":
PROOF SILVER "S":
UNCIRCULATED "P":
UNCIRCULATED "D":

*Figures not available at press time. Visit www.americasstatequarters.com for updated figures.

Price Record*

Common Errors and Values

NOT STRUCK ON QUARTER PLANCHET: N/A

DOUBLE STRUCK: $1,500

STRUCK 3–4 TIMES: $2,500

OBVERSE CLAD MISSING: $400

REVERSE CLAD MISSING: $800

OFF CENTER MINOR: $120

OFF CENTER MAJOR: N/A

ROTATED REVERSE: N/A

BROCKAGE: $400

BROADSIDE: $75

STRUCK-THROUGH: $20

PARTIAL COLLAR: $35

CLIPPED "MINOR": $75

CLIPPED "MAJOR": $125

Grading Hints

OBVERSE: The high points of the coin's obverse are prone to wear; the field off Washington's nose, and the area behind the head curls, are prone to contact marks. Wear is most likely to be evident on the hair above Washington's ear and on the cheekbones. High-grade (MS-67 and above) coins will have no contact marks in the field.

REVERSE: This is the more important side for grade. High grade (above MS-67) has minimal (few if any) contact marks in the field. The high points of the coin show wear first: bear's snout, shoulder, and left front claw.

Investment Potential

Most "slabbed" state quarters are in MS-66 or better condition. Those that have gone up most in value and which have the greatest potential are graded MS-68 and better.*

*Price record and investment potential not available at press time. Visit www.americasstatequarters.com for updated figures.

HAWAII

STATE, YEAR OF ISSUE: Hawaii, 2008

State Information

YEAR OF STATEHOOD: 1959
ORDER IN UNION: 50
SIZE: 6,459 sq. mi.
POPULATION: 1.28 million
STATE MOTTO: "The life of the land is perpetuated in righteousness"
STATE FLOWER: yellow hibiscus
STATE BIRD: Hawaiian goose
STATE TREE: kukui (candlenut)

Coin Specifications

MINTMARKS: P, D, S
OBVERSE DESIGNER: John Flanagan, modified by William Cousins (1997)
REVERSE DESIGNER: Don Everhart II
REVERSE DESIGN: At top: state name above date entered Union. At bottom: date of issue above motto "E Pluribus Unum," describing how the divided colonies became the United States of America. State design: Hawaiian monarch King Kamehameha I dominates the reverse, stretching his hand toward the eight major Hawaiian Islands. Inscriptions are the state motto "Ua mau ke ea o ka 'aina i ka pono" (the life of the land is perpetuated in righteousness).

Design History

Governor Linda Lingle established the Hawaii Commemorative Quarter Advisory Commission in February 2006. The last of the advisory committees forwarded five design suggestions to the U.S. Mint:

- surfer with Diamond Head in the background and the text "Aloha"

- hula dancer and a map of the Hawaiian islands with the text "Aloha"

- Diamond Head and a well-known statue of King Kamehameha I with the text "Aloha"

ALTERNATE DESIGN NOT CHOSEN FOR HI QUARTER

- King Kamehameha I and a map of the islands with the Hawaiian-language phrase that is the state motto

- Another version of design #4

At its meeting of January 18, 2007, the Commission of Fine Arts reviewed the potential designs. Although the commission members did not support any design as presented, they recommended a simplified version of design #3, with only the image of Diamond Head and omitting the rendition of King Kamehameha. The minutes reflect that members felt that the map of the islands resulted in weak compositions, and several members commented that the figures of the surfer and hula dancer were not well executed.

The Citizens Coinage Advisory Committee met on January 23. Members expressed general appreciation for the inclusion of the Kamehameha statue on the proposed designs for Hawaii, due to its historical importance and its role as an important symbol of the state. The CCAC recommended design #3.

In late April 2007, Lingle announced that she had selected "Hawaii, the Island State" design which shows Kamehameha and the main islands (design #4) as the design for Hawaii's commemorative quarter. "I feel this design best represents the host culture of Hawaii and its people," she said. The governor made her selection based on recommendations from the Hawaii Commemorative Quarter Advisory Commission, which met to review the results of a public online poll conducted earlier that month. The final design depicts the King Kamehameha I statue on the right side of the coin, with his hand stretching toward the eight main Hawaiian islands.

Mintage Figures*

PROOF "S":
PROOF SILVER "S":
UNCIRCULATED "P":
UNCIRCULATED "D":

*Figures not available at press time. Visit www.americasstatequarters.com for updated figures.

Price Record*

PRICE:

DATE OF ISSUE:

GRADING SERVICE:

DATE OF SALE:

AUCTIONEER:

PRICE:

DATE OF ISSUE:

GRADING SERVICE:

DATE OF SALE:

AUCTIONEER:

Common Errors and Values

NOT STRUCK ON QUARTER PLANCHET: N/A

DOUBLE STRUCK: $1,500

STRUCK 3–4 TIMES: $2,500

OBVERSE CLAD MISSING: $400

REVERSE CLAD MISSING: $800

OFF CENTER MINOR: $120

OFF CENTER MAJOR: N/A

ROTATED REVERSE: N/A

BROCKAGE: $400

BROADSIDE: $75

STRUCK-THROUGH: $20

PARTIAL COLLAR: $35

CLIPPED "MINOR": $75

CLIPPED "MAJOR": $125

Grading Hints

OBVERSE: The high points of the coin's obverse are prone to wear; the field off Washington's nose, and the area behind the head curls, are prone to contact marks. Wear is most likely to be evident on the hair above Washington's ear and on the cheekbones. High-grade (MS-67 and above) coins will have no contact marks in the field.

REVERSE: This is the more important side for grade. High grade (above MS-67) has minimal (few if any) contact marks in the field. The high points of the coin show wear first: king's outstretched arm and staff, outermost (9 o'clock) island.

Investment Potential

Most "slabbed" state quarters are in MS-66 or better condition. Those that have gone up most in value and which have the greatest potential are graded MS-68 and better.*

*Price record and investment potential not available at press time. Visit www.americasstatequarters.com for updated figures.

7

EXPANDING THE STATE QUARTERS PROGRAM: WASHINGTON, D.C., PUERTO RICO, GUAM, AMERICAN SAMOA, U.S. VIRGIN ISLANDS, AND NORTHERN MARIANA ISLANDS

In 2009, the State Quarters program will be expanded to include the District of Columbia (Washington, D.C.) and the five insular territories: Commonwealth of Puerto Rico, Guam, American Samoa, the U.S. Virgin Islands, and the Commonwealth of Northern Mariana Islands. Signed into law by President George W. Bush on December 26, 2007, aboard Air Force One, the expansion on what was a 10-year program (2008 would have been its 10th and final year) now has a new lease on life.

The road to expanding the State Quarters program beyond the 50 states was a long one. Several times in the past 10 years, the House of Representatives voted to issue these six additional coins, but the Senate took no action and the measure died. The elected representatives of the five insular territories—Guam, American Samoa, the U.S. Virgin Islands, Commonwealth of Puerto Rico, and Commonwealth of Northern Mariana Islands—plus reps for Washington, D.C., and others fought to get the bill passed.

It began when H.R. 5010 was introduced in the 106th Congress to fulfill the same goal of equalizing the territories and the District of Columbia with the states whose coins were to be issued. Rep. Eleanor

Holmes Norton (D-D.C.), participated in the debate, making sure to lobby for Washington, D.C., as a coin component.

"We are very pleased that the first ten states are already online, some of them joyously touting their coin," she said. "We know that the differences between the states, the District, and the territories were never meant to be invidious and never has been in this body; and we have never been so treated in this body. We are all Americans, and we appreciate that this body has, for the most part, included all of us whenever possible. That was always the intent on both sides of the aisle here."

Congressman Mike Castle, who played a large role in legislating the original 50 State Quarters program had this to say: "The State Quarters program has dramatically increased general knowledge of the historical contributions of our 50 states. [This legislation] would do the same for the District and the territories. These areas have some of the highest enlistment rates in our armed forces; have made many historical, cultural and athletic contributions to our nation, and this bill is a great opportunity to recognize them, in artwork on the reverse of the quarters."

He also expressed that "As an education tool, recognizing D.C. and territories is imperative. Students are learning about the 50 states with this program; unfortunately they may know even less to begin with about the history and role of D.C. and the territories. This legislation will serve as a great tool to rectify that problem."

Former Mint director Henrietta Holsman Fore, now an assistant secretary of state, added, "The United States Mint recognizes the continuing enthusiasm for the 50 State Quarters program with more than 130 million Americans collecting. If the District of Columbia and United States Territories Circulating Quarter Dollar Program Act is approved, the United States Mint will ensure that the mandate is carried out with beautiful and evocative designs that befit them all."

Finally, in December 2007 (the sixth time the measure had reached the Senate), it finally passed and was sent to the president to be signed.

WASHINGTON D.C.

DISTRICT OR TERRITORY, YEAR OF ISSUE: Washington D.C., 2009

General Information

YEAR OF U.S. ESTABLISHMENT: 1800
SIZE: 68 square miles
POPULATION: 588,000
MOTTO: "Justitia omnibus" (Justice for all)
FLOWER: American beauty rose
BIRD: wood thrush
TREE: scarlet oak

Coin Specifications

MINTMARKS: P, D, S
OBVERSE DESIGNER: John Flanagan, modified by William Cousins (1997)
REVERSE DESIGNER: William Cousins
REVERSE DESIGN: At top: District name above date it became part of U.S. At bottom: date of issue (2009) above motto "E Pluribus Unum," describing how the divided colonies became the United States of America. District design: N/A.

Design History*

The Washington, D.C. coin is the first due under the new law. The office of the secretary of the District of Columbia, headed by Stephanie D. Scott, coordinated the campaign to collect potential designs from the public. From more than 350 entries, four were forwarded to the U.S. Mint, each of which contained the phrase "Taxation without Representation," a reference to the fact that the District of Columbia residents, alone among American citizens, have no United States Senator or voting congressional representative.

They do, however, have a mayor elected by the people, Adrian Fenty, and a nonvoting congressional delegate, Rep. Eleanor Holmes Norton, who in 2008 was in her ninth two-year term. "The new quarter will teach people across the country about our city and its history," said Mayor Fenty. "It's my hope that those who don't know about our disenfranchisement will soon learn about it when they're paying a toll or buying a soda."

The four designs forwarded by the mayor were as follows:

- the "Stars and Bars" of the District flag, which originated from the Washington family crest some 600 years ago

- a standing figure of Benjamin Banneker, astronomer and mathematician dressed in the style of an 18th-century gentleman, as depicted on the USPS 1980 stamp (tricornered hat, coat with tails, ascot, leather boots or buckled shoes), and the caption "Benjamin Banneker," with or without surveyor's instruments (e.g., tripod and looking glass). It would also contain a diamond shape representing the original outline of the District of Columbia—a square standing up on one corner—with or without the Potomac and Anacostia rivers indicated.

- world-renowned musician Edward Kennedy "Duke" Ellington, seated at or standing next to a whole or partial image of a grand piano, with the caption "Duke Ellington"; the outline of the current boundaries of the District of Columbia, with or without one or both of the rivers

- abolitionist Frederick Douglas

The Mint rejected the first choice because its guidelines preclude the use of flags. Modified versions of Douglas, Ellington, and Banneker went to the Citizens Coinage Advisory Committee and the Commission of Fine Arts in May 2008. The CCAC said that "the complexity of all three alternatives would be difficult to appreciate at the scale of a quarter." The commission further said, in letter to the U.S. Mint, that the quarters were too small for an elaborate design, and "requested that the design alternatives be reworked."

Mayor Fenty announced on May 23 that D.C. residents could vote for their favorite design, three days after the Citizens Coinage Advisory Committee criticized the designs and a week after the Commission of Fine Arts told the Mint that it could truly do better. At the time this book went to press, the final quarter design had not yet been selected.

Potential Designs

*For updates, visit www.americasstatequarters.com.

PUERTO RICO

DISTRICT OR TERRITORY, YEAR OF ISSUE: Commonwealth of Puerto Rico, 2009

General Information

YEAR BECAME U.S. TERRITORY/COMMONWEALTH: 1898
SIZE: 3,508 sq. mi
POPULATION: 3.9 million
MOTTO: "Joannes est nomen eius" (John is his name)
FLOWER: maga
BIRD: reinita
TREE: ceiba

Coin Specifications

MINTMARKS: P, D, S
OBVERSE DESIGNER: John Flanagan, modified by William Cousins (1997)
REVERSE DESIGNER: N/A
REVERSE DESIGN: At top: commonwealth name above date it became a U.S. pos-
session. At bottom: date of issue (2009) above motto "E Pluribus Unum,"
describing how the divided colonies became the United States of America.
COMMONWEALTH DESIGN: N/A.

Design History*

Governor Anibal Acevedo Vilá of Puerto Rico decided that the state quarter
design process would not be open to the public. With the help of a few advi-
sors, he chose two different concepts that were sent to the United States Mint.
Based on the concepts, the Mint produced two attractive designs focusing on
aesthetic beauty, historical accuracy, appropriateness, and coinability:

- the Spanish Phrase "Palacio de Santa Catalina," with a drawing of the
  fortress that serves as the Governor's residence. Dating to 1533, it is
  Puerto Rico's most important building and is the oldest government
  building in continued use in the Americas.

- the Spanish phrase "Isla del Encanto" ("The Enchanted Island"), with a
  drawing of the fortress parapet and Puerto Rico's national flower, the
  flor de maga. The maga is closely related to the hibiscus, but unlike the
  common hibiscus, the maga is a tree.

The U.S. Commission of Fine Arts and the Citizens Coinage Advisory Committee reviewed the designs in May 2008. The Commission recommended alternative #2, commenting that "the sentry box from the fortifications of old San Juan provides the more simple and legible composition for a coin design and as a representation of the island's history." The minutes of the Fine Arts unit show that the commissioners still asked for designs to be "simplified" and stripped of multiple design element. At the time this book went to press, the final quarter design had not yet been selected.

Potential Designs

GUAM

DISTRICT OR TERRITORY, YEAR OF ISSUE: Guam, 2009

General Information

YEAR BECAME U.S. TERRITORY/COMMONWEALTH: 1898
SIZE: 217 sq. mi.
POPULATION: 173,000
MOTTO: "Where America's day begins" (unofficial)
FLOWER: puti tai nobio (*Bougainvillea spectabilis*)
BIRD: Guam rail
TREE: Ifit

Coin Specifications

MINTMARKS: P, D, S
OBVERSE DESIGNER: John Flanagan, modified by William Cousins (1997)
REVERSE DESIGNER: N/A
REVERSE DESIGN: At top: territorial name above date it became a U.S. possession.
At bottom: date of issue (2009) above motto "E Pluribus Unum," describing
how the divided colonies became the United States of America.
TERRITORIAL DESIGN: N/A.

Design History*

Guam has been an American possession since 1898. A part of Oceania, this
island in the North Pacific Ocean is about three-quarters of the way from
Hawaii to the Philippines. Chamorro men prior to the 1700s were mariners and
star navigators who voyaged the Pacific utilizing the "flying proa" canoes which
were hydrodynamically swifter than the Spanish galleons. They were also
ocean divers whose catches were large fish from the deep. The Spanish, in order
to control the population of warriors called "Magas I Tasi" whom they had bat-
tled in the 1600s, forbade seafaring and destroyed the canoes. Hence, the art
of ocean navigation and deep-sea spearing was lost, but young Chamorros are
making the effort to revive the culture today.

"We are one step closer to circulating an image of our island throughout our
country that will make us all very proud and showcase the beauty and distinc-
tiveness of our culture," said Governor Felix Perez Camacho. A total of 59 state
quarter design entries were received by Camacho on February 25, 2008. On

March 3 the governor's office released the two final design choices to the U.S. Mint:

- outline of Guam in the center of the coin, with the phrase "Guåyhan Tåynå I Man Chamorro" inscribed on the left side. The phrase, also on Guam license plates, means "Land of the Chamorro," the precolonial inhabitants of the island. The right side shows images of the latte and the Flying Proa, one sitting on top of the other. (The latte is not a brand of coffee, but rather the foundation remains of stone pillars noted for their two-piece construction. The supporting column, halagi, is topped with a capstone, tasa.)

- a collage of Guam's most familiar cultural and tropical images, featuring East Hagatna Bay with the Two Lovers Point in the background. In the foreground is a coconut tree bending toward the left. To the right of the coconut tree is the phrase, "Tåynå I Man Chamorro." To the left of the coconut tree is a flying proa, distant from the shore and sailing within the reef. To the right of the base of the coconut tree is a latte. To the left of the base of the coconut tree is a break in the sandbar depicting the Hagatna River Channel.

The Fine Arts Commission "recommended alternative #2 as the simplest and most successful composition. Noting that the multitude of design features would be difficult to understand at the scale of a quarter, the Commission requested that this alternative be simplified further to eliminate some of the background elements and to emphasize the image of the boat, which could then be enlarged to improve its legibility." The Citizens Coinage Advisory Committee approved the submissions with minor modifications. At the time this book went to press, the final quarter design had not yet been selected.

Potential Designs

*For updates, visit www.americasstatequarters.com.

AMERICAN SAMOA

DISTRICT OR TERRITORY, YEAR OF ISSUE: American Samoa, 2009

General Information

YEAR BECAME U.S. TERRITORY/COMMONWEALTH: 1899 (by treaty with Germany)
SIZE: 77 sq. mi.
POPULATION: 57,600
MOTTO: "Samoa muamua le Atua" (In Samoa, God is first)
FLOWER: Paogo (Ula-faka)
BIRD: none designated
TREE: none designated

Coin Specifications

MINTMARKS: P, D, S
OBVERSE DESIGNER: John Flanagan, modified by William Cousins (1997)
REVERSE DESIGNER: N/A
REVERSE DESIGN: At top: territorial name above date it became a U.S. possession. At bottom: date of issue (2009) above motto "E Pluribus Unum," describing how the divided colonies became the United States of America.
TERRITORIAL DESIGN: N/A.

Design History*

Governor Togiola Tulafono announced on May 20, 2008 that the United States Mint had created three candidate designs for the American Samoa Quarter:

- a man with traditional Samoan tattoo (*soga'imiti*) standing tall, and holding a dried coconut cup, which is used during the *ava* ceremony, symbolizing the importance of servitude in Samoan culture; coconut leaves (fronds), leaves of a breadfruit tree (with two breadfruits), and taro leaves signifying the three staples of Samoa.

- symbols of Samoan life: *fale* (guest house); *tuiga* (ceremonial head-dress); *tanoa* (ava [kava] bowl); *fue* (orator's fly whisk); *to'oto'o* (orator's staff); and the inscription "Samoa muamua le Atua" (the Territory's motto, which means, "In Samoa, God is first").

- the *tanoa* (ava [kava] bowl) which is used to make Samoa's special ceremonial drink for chiefs and guests; the *fue* (fly whisk), which symbolizes wisdom of the orator; and the *to'oto'o* (staff), which signifies authority. The inscription "Samoa muamua le Atua" (the Territory's motto, which means, "In Samoa, God is first").

"As you can see in the three candidate designs, each design attempts to best capture what totally makes us unique as a proud people with a proud culture and traditions, and a beautiful island home that is part of America," the Governor said.

The Fine Arts Commission members "recommended alternative #1 for its image of a Samoan in traditional dress"; they also commented that "the elements depicting vegetation arranged around the central figure would be difficult to understand at the scale of a quarter and should be eliminated." The Citizens Coinage Advisory Committee approved the submissions with minor modifications.

"I am sure that all our wonderful school children, their teachers and parents, local artists and aspiring artists, and concerned individuals are speculating about what the final design selection would look like and what best represents the spirit of American Samoa," said Governor Togiola. At the time this book went to press, the final quarter design had not yet been selected.

Potential Designs

U.S. VIRGIN ISLANDS

DISTRICT OR TERRITORY, YEAR OF ISSUE: U.S. Virgin Islands, 2009

General Information

YEAR BECAME U.S. TERRITORY/COMMONWEALTH: 1917
SIZE: 171 sq. mi.
POPULATION: 108,000
MOTTO: none designated
FLOWER: yellow elder or yellow rumpet
BIRD: yellow breast
TREE: none designated

Coin Specifications

MINTMARKS: P, D, S
OBVERSE DESIGNER: John Flanagan, modified by William Cousins (1997)
REVERSE DESIGNER: N/A
REVERSE DESIGN: At top: territorial name above date it became a U.S. possession. At bottom: date of issue (2009) above motto "E Pluribus Unum," describing how the divided colonies became the United States of America.
TERRITORIAL DESIGN: N/A

Design History*

Governor John deJongh, Jr. appointed community members and historians to the Virgin Islands coin selection committee. The committee ultimately forwarded three design concepts to the Mint:

- the symbol of the July 3, 1848, Emancipation Day—a bare-chested former slave with a cane bill used for harvesting sugar cane in one hand, blowing a conch shell to proclaim the freedom granted to all slaves in the Danish West Indies. The coin design features the words "First in Freedom."

- three slave women wearing traditional coal carriers' clothing, loosely representing the "Three Queens" of Virgin Islands history, as well as the three main islands of the territory. One woman is holding a cane bill to symbolize agriculture on St. Croix. The second woman is holding a sickle, which is an emblem of the St. John slave revolt of 1733. The third woman is holding an oar to represent the maritime trade that flowed through St. Thomas. Two of the women clutch some cedar flowers—the territorial flower.

- items representative of the natural beauty of the Virgin Islands. The left side of the coin features a bananaquit—the territorial bird—perched on a branch with cedar blossoms. Tyre palms, which are native to the territory, grow behind the bird and flowers, and a sandy beach stretches out beneath the scene. A small map of St. Thomas, St. John St. Croix, and Water Island is in the upper right portion of the coin, and it features the territory's motto: "United in Pride and Hope."

"The Mint said we had some of the most interesting and different designs," said Government House special assistant Lesley Comissiong, liaison to Gov. John deJongh, Jr.

The Fine Arts Commission recommended alternative #2, showing the three women representing the islands. However, the Commission members suggested that the island maps be eliminated and the depiction of the women be enlarged as the primary design feature. The Citizens Coin advisory Committee approved the submissions with minor modifications. At the time this book went to press, the final quarter design had not yet been selected.

Potential Designs

*For updates, visit www.americasstatequarters.com.

Northern Mariana Islands

DISTRICT OR TERRITORY, YEAR OF ISSUE: Commonwealth Northern Mariana Islands, 2009

General Information

YEAR BECAME U.S. TERRITORY/COMMONWEALTH: 1947 (U.N. trusteeship)
SIZE: 189 sq. mi.
POPULATION: 84,000
MOTTO: none designated
FLOWER: none designated
BIRD: none designated
TREE: none designated

Coin Specifications

MINTMARKS: P, D, S
OBVERSE DESIGNER: John Flanagan, modified by William Cousins (1997)
REVERSE DESIGNER: N/A
REVERSE DESIGN: At top: commonwealth name above date it became a U.S. possession. At bottom: date of issue (2009) above motto "E Pluribus Unum," describing how the divided colonies became the United States of America.
COMMONWEALTH DESIGN: N/A.

Design History*

The acquisition of the Marianas occurred following the naval Battle of Saipan during World War II. The battle killed nearly 3,000 American servicemen (including four Congressional Medal of Honor winners) and wounded over 10,000 more.

Ether Fleming, the governor's special assistant for administration, chose the coin selection committee for the Northern Mariana coin. Three design choices were forwarded to the U.S. Mint:

- latte stones, birds, boats, and fauna. Latte stones are stone pillars used as the foundation for ancient houses notable for their two-piece construction; the supporting column (halagi) topped with a capstone (tasa).

- A second rendition of the same elements.

- An image of Marine infantrymen storming ashore. This design focuses on the islands' role in World War II, showing armed soldiers and featuring the date "June 15, 1944," when the historic Battle of Saipan began.

Neither the Citizens Coinage Advisory Committee nor the Commission of Fine Arts particularly liked the Northern Marianas designs. The Fine Arts Commission members were brutal, saying that they "did not support any design as presented," commenting that all were too visually complicated for the scale of a quarter. They requested the submission of new design alternatives, suggesting that design #1, featuring a latte stone, could be used as a starting point in developing a simplified proposal.

The designs were reworked, and on June 16, 2008 Governor Benigno R. Fitial unveiled the design of the Northern Marianas commemorative quarter. The design features a latte stone sitting on the shoreline, an outrigger canoe, a pair of white fairy terns, and a mwar. "This represents everybody in, and everything about, the CNMI," said the governor.

Potential Designs

*For updates, visit www.americasstatequarters.com.

APPENDIX:
ADDITIONAL RESOURCES

The prices chosen in this book represent high auction prices that are likely to be sustained over time. Those that were records in 2003 are only being surpassed in late 2007 and early 2008. When this book was in its early phases, a set of top-notch (MS-68 and MS-69, mostly) state quarters would have cost more than $13,000 to put together. By early 2008, it exceeded $31,000. It is unlikely, in that sense, that quoted prices will "soon" become outdated. Nonetheless, for readers who wish to find up-to-the-moment prices, there are some online Web sites that provide current pricing.

The recommended Web sites are:

www.pcgs.com/prices/PriceGuideDetail.aspx?c=112 (Professional Coin Grading Service price guide)

www.numismedia.com/fmv/prices/wshqtr/pricesgd.shtml (Numis-Media pricing guide; grades up to MS-60 are free. MS/Proof-61 though MS/Proof-70 by subscription)

www.coinvaluesonline.com (Coin World Trends Online, subscription-based) numismaster.com (Krause Publications, online pricing guide available by subscription)

In addition, the newly published *Numismedia Wholesale Market Dealer Price Guide* for modern coins now prices state quarters on a wholesale basis from about uncirculated (AU-50) to MS-70 (though there are not many MS-70 prices for uncirculated coins).

Professional Grading Services

There are many independent grading services, but the two largest are the Professional Coin Grading Service and Numismatic Guaranty Corporation; they have processed the most state quarters according to published data. Readers may wish to consult the Web sites of other services to find out additional information.

Acronym Name Web Site Location

ACCGS American Coin Club Grading Service www.accgs.org Beverly Hills, CA

ACG ASA Accugrade, Inc. www.asa-accugrade.com Melbourne, FL

ANACS ANACS Certification Service, Inc. www.anacs.com, Englewood, CO

ICG Independent Coin Grading Company www.icgcoin.com Englewood, CO

NGC Numismatic Guaranty Corporation www.ngccoin.com Sarasota, FL

PCGS Professional Coin Grading Service www.pcgs.com Newport Beach, CA

PCI PCI Inc. www.pcicoins.com Rossville, GA

SEGS Sovereign Entities Grading Service www.segscoins.com Chattanooga, TN

SGS Star Grading Services www.stargrading.org Bellville, OH

SELECTED BIBLIOGRAPHY

The bibliography is selected and not complete because so much of the data came from a rich mine of original sources, secondary sources such as numismatic periodicals, and the Internet.

Official Documents

Annual Report of the Citizens Commemorative Coin Advisory Committee to the Congress of the United States, 1994, 1995, 1996, 1997, 1998

Department of the Treasury, U.S. Mint, 50 State Quarters Information Kit, 1998, www.usmint.gov

Hearing on the U.S. Mint's Commemorative Coin Program before the Subcomm. On Domestic & International Monetary Policy of the House Committee on Banking & Financial Services, 104th Cong., 1st sess., Serial 104–25, July 12, 1995

Minutes of the Citizens Commemorative Coin Advisory Committee and its successor, the Citizens Coin Advisory Committee, 1993–present

Minutes, Calendars, and Hearings (transcripts) before the Commission of Fine Arts, 1910–present

Statistical Abstract of the United States 1996–1997, 116th ed. 1996–2007, online edition.

United States Mint Annual Report, 1993–2006

Public Laws

Pub. L. 104–329, 110 Stat. 3514, Oct. 24, 1996 (U.S. Commemorative Coin Act of 1996)

Pub. L. 105–124, 111 Stat. 2534, Dec. 1, 1997, (50 State Commemorative Coin, 1999)

Pub. L. 105–176, 112 Stat. 104, May 29, 1998 (50 State Commemorative Coin, official Web sites)

Official Web site of each of the 50 states, Washington, D.C., and each of America's five insular territories and commonwealths

Governors' Web sites of each state (relative to State Quarters program)

Web site of the U.S. Mint, www.usmint.gov

The *CIA World Fact Book 2008* (government online edition) was used for information on America's territories, www.cia.gov/library/publications/the-world-factbook/index.html

Pricing and Grading Guides and other Coin Books

NumisMedia Fair Market Value Price Guide, various issues, 1999–2007

The Teletrade Real Price Guide, 12th ed. 1998–1999, Teletrade, 2000, www.teletrade.com

The PCGS Population Report, Collector's Universe, 2000 (various), www.pcgs.com

United States Coins Census Report, Numismatic Guaranty Corp., 2000 (various), www.ngccoin.com

Travers, ed., *Official Guide to Coin Grading and Counterfeit Detection*, House of Collectibles, 1997

Yeoman, *A Guide Book of U.S. Coins* (Bressett, ed.), various editions

Bowers, *A Guide Book of Washington and State Quarter Dollars*, Whitman, 2006

Harper, ed. *2008 U.S. Coin Digest*, Krause Publications, 2007

Correspondence
E-mails and letters from governors of the 50 states

Correspondence from the Commission of Fine Arts

E-mail correspondence with selected artists and engravers

Almanacs
New York Times Almanac, 1999

The World Almanac, 2000

Auction Catalogues
Heritage Numismatic Auctions (various) and Web site www.ha.com

Bowers & Merena Galleries (various)

Price Lists and Pricing Information
Fred Weinberg, Inc. www.FredWeinberg.com

Works of the Author Utilized
Ganz, "Toward a Revision of the Minting and Coinage Law of the United States," 26 Cleveland State Law Review, pp. 175–257 (1977)

Ganz, "Valuation of Coin Collection," 5 Proof of Facts 3rd 577 (Lawyer's Coop., 1989)

Ganz, "Proof of Value of Coin Collection," vol. 95 Proof of Facts 3d pp 155–465 (Thompson-West, 2007)

Ganz, *The Official Guide to U.S. Commemorative Coins* (Bonus Books, 1999)

Ganz, *The World of Coins and Coin Collecting* (3rd ed., Bonus Books, 1998)

Ganz, *Planning Your Rare Coin Retirement* (Bonus Books, 1999)

Periodicals Consulted

Coinage Magazine (various issues)

Coin World (various issues)

The Congressional Record (various issues)

Numismatic News (various issues)

The Numismatist (various issues)

CREDITS

Photo credits for state quarter coins: U.S. Mint. Credit for state quarter drawings: U.S. Commission of Fine Arts. Error coins from Fred Weinberg, Inc., and Colony Coin and author's collection, except $1.25 Sacagawea coin from Heritage Auctions. Editorial cartoons credited to cartoonists and their syndicates, used by permission. Photos of the 1995 Congressional hearing by the author. Photos of Citizens Commemorative coin Advisory Committee by the author. Photos of Mint Director Mary Brooks and Treasury Secretary Simon (1974) and Rep. Wright Patman, Leonor K. Sullivan, and John Jay Pittman, courtesy of the author. Some error coinage was photographed by the author. All other U.S. coins courtesy of Heritage Auctions (www.ha.com). Engravers and sculptors photos from U.S. Mint. Supplies from Littleton and Whitman. Color photos of Washington Mint product by Washington Mint, used by permission. Photo composition and editing by Kathy Ganz.

ABOUT THE AUTHOR

DAVID L. GANZ is a lawyer, author, and speaker. He is the youngest person ever appointed by the president of the United States (Nixon) to the annual Assay Commission (1974) and also hold a Clinton Administration appointment (1993–1996) to the Citizens Commemorative Coin Advisory Committee. He has lectured on topics that range from Z to A—zoning law to African literature—and many in between.

DAVID L. GANZ, 2007

Ganz is the managing partner and principal litigator in the law firm of Ganz & Sivin, LLP, of Fair Lawn, N.J., and Ganz & Hollinger, P.C. (www.ganzhollinger.com) in New York City.

His books include *14 Bits: A Legal & Legislative History of America's Bicentennial Coinage, 31 USC §§324d-i* (1976), *The World of Coins & Coin Collecting* (first published in 1980, 3rd revised edition, 1998), *Planning Your Rare Coin Retirement* (Bonus Books, 1998), *The Official Guide to Commemorative Coins* (Bonus, 1999), *The Smithsonian Guide to Coin Collecting* (HarperCollins, 2008), *Profitable Coin Collecting* (Krause, 2008) and the predecessor to this book, *The Official Guidebook to America's State Quarters* . He is also the author of a number of law review articles and a 1973 graduate of the School of Foreign Service at Georgetown University where he followed Bill Clinton by five years.

Ganz served from 1985–1995 as an elected member of the board of governors of the American Numismatic Association, the largest educational nonprofit organization of collectors in the world, and the only hobby organization chartered by the U.S. Congress. He became the organization's 48th president in July 1993, serving until August 1995.

In December 1993, Treasury Secretary Lloyd Bentsen appointed Ganz a charter member of the Citizens Commemorative Coin Advisory Committee. He was reappointed in 1995 for a second one-year term, leaving office in February 1996. As a CCCAC member, he was the initial advocate for circulating commemorative coinage and fought to include such a plea in the CCCAC's first two reports to Congress. He chaired the World Mint Council in 1994 and 1995 at its meetings held in conjunction with the American Numismatic Association annual convention.

He is also a 20-year board member of the Token & Medal Society (TAMS) and served as the organization's President (2004–2006). He previously received TAMS Medal of Merit, its highest award for service, in 1997. In August 2006, he was named a *Numismatic News* "Ambassador" in recognition of his achievements in the field.